Jerry. Birthday
from
Dad + Mom

J. GOLDEN KIMBALL

JONATHAN GOLDEN KIMBALL

J. GOLDEN KIMBALL

The Story of a
Unique Personality

CLAUDE RICHARDS

BOOKCRAFT
Salt Lake City, Utah

ISBN 0-88494-144-2

Ninth Printing, 1985

Printed in the United States of America

INTRODUCTION

When this book was first published over thirty years ago its colorful subject was still with us. With a Church membership increase of two million since that time, a new generation has arisen to whom the name of J. Golden Kimball is either a vague legend or completely unknown. This reprint of the 1934 edition offers to both old and new friends the account of its uniquely interesting personality, the son of the outstanding leader and prophet, Heber C. Kimball.

The brief biographical material included effectively portrays the circumstances and decisions which formed the mold for the mature J. Golden. Left fatherless at fifteen, living thereafter virtually without external restraint, early proficient in the hard life and the racy language of the teamster, the rancher and the logger, he might easily have taken the wrong road and been lost. But opportunity and motivation converged on his life in the form of the great Latter-day Saint educator and inspirer Karl G. Maeser, and from then on J. Golden Kimball was a man with a purpose. Two missions for the Church focussed that purpose and made it an integral part of his being.

That purpose illuminates the talks by Elder Kimball which form the major part of this book. His speaking style was not a studied, scholarly eloquence but rather that of a plain man speaking of what he knew in simple terms that the common man understood. His natural gift for humor, his "unorthodoxy" of expression, his directness of approach, his genuine humility — such attributes made him a loved figure and a never-failing focus of attention on the public platform.

But content counts more than style in speech as in life, and here too J. Golden Kimball was not lacking. Taken from those given over most of the 46 years of his membership of the First Council of the Seventy, the talks reproduced here reveal him as a stalwart in the faith. They embrace practical religious concepts of

Church membership and are punctuated with homely stories, recollections of the speaker's illustrious father, and faith promoting or otherwise illustrative personal experiences. Even his counsel on many of the day-to-day matters has a timely and relevant ring today: Get out of debt; don't speculate; ease, luxury and idleness threaten the youth of Zion; and so on.

While noted for novelty of character and independence of thought and will, J. Golden Kimball found his true joys in the group activity of service under the restored Gospel. In a sense then, this book by Claude Richards portrays not only an individual man but also the genius of the Church of Jesus Christ of Latter-day Saints which gently but firmly attracts, holds and builds the most diverse characters. Bookcraft takes pleasure in making such a book available to the modern reader.

The Publisher

July 1966

Preface

About a year and a half ago I suggested to a friend who was writing sketches of certain of the leaders of the Mormon Church that he include two other men. These were Elders Brigham H. Roberts and J. Golden Kimball; for I considered these two men, both presidents in the First Council of the Seventy, to be outstanding.

Nothing came of this suggestion. My friend explained to me later that he had prepared his sketches on order of a certain magazine and that the commission did not include the two men named.

Since that suggestion was made, President Roberts has passed away and I have learned with deep satisfaction that the account of his life and labors were written by himself and that his family intends to publish his autobiography.

Also since that suggestion one of my friends came to me and urged that I write up President Kimball. "His sayings and talks and the story of his life," said he, "should be put on paper so that they will be preserved and be made available to the people." The result is the present work.

The task was a hard one. Not only is J. Golden Kimball an exceedingly difficult person to put on paper, but, except for his Tabernacle talks,

I could find nothing recorded about this man save only a short writing of probably a dozen pages made by him in 1912. Part of this was helpful. To Elias S. Kimball, a brother, I am indebted for some of the biographical material. Naturally, many interviews were held with President Kimball, from whom most of the information for the biography was obtained.

CLAUDE RICHARDS

Salt Lake City
March, 1934

Contents

List of Illustrations

The Next Speaker

CHAPTER I

AT THE RADIO

On a Sunday afternoon, not long ago, a small group sat in the living room of a suburban home near Salt Lake City, listening to Aunt Rebecca and relishing her latest comments on current events, personal affairs, and things in general. In one end of the room, near the radio, a lone member of the family reclined on the davenport, dividing his attention alternately—sometimes simultaneously—between Aunt Rebecca and the radio speaker.

"What's the laughing for?" inquired Aunt Rebecca.

"The speaker has forgotten something. He wants to start reading his speech."

"Just like you men. You're always forgetting something." The words rolled freely as Aunt Rebecca spoke. Although past seventy, she exhibited the vivacity and vigor of a high-school girl. "I wish you men would forget to write speeches and books and everything else and let the people stay awake at meeting and around the fireside in the evening. Who's speaking?"

"Brother X."

"He's one of the best. I like to hear him." And without further thought or comment regarding this favorite speaker, Aunt Rebecca continued to dispense her philosophy, setting everybody right in her terse, interesting, humorous style and adjusting all matters, at least the major ones, in the family, the state, and the nation.

The competition against Brother X was proving too great. Aunt Rebecca was winning out better than seven to one. And why shouldn't she? The odds were against the radio speaker. Aunt Rebecca was right there on the job. Her comments were timely, her personality commanding, her manner pleasing, and her wit rare, and as a member of the family remarked later, "There is a lot of good sense in what Aunt Rebecca says." Moreover, she was covering a wide range, selecting her subjects here and there, while her opponent was confining himself to one thing—the field of religion.

"Elder J. Golden Kimball will be the next speaker," came from the radio.

"Did he say Kimball?"

"Yes, Aunt Rebecca, J. Golden."

"Bob and Joe!" her voice rang clearly to the up-stairs rooms, "come down here. Brother Kimball is going to speak."

A brief silence ensued; then quietly our ten-year-old daughter whispered as she edged over to the davenport, "Papa, why does Aunt Rebecca stop talking?"

"J. Golden Kimball is going to speak over the radio," replied her daddy.

[4]

"Who is J. Golden Kimball and why should Aunt Rebecca stop talking, even if he is going to speak?" questioned the little girl.

"Because she wants to hear what he has to say."

"Where is he?"

"At the Tabernacle."

"What does he look like?" asked the daughter.

"Oh, he is a tall, slim man. I'll tell you later. He is getting ready to talk," answered her daddy.

"Has he a tall, slim voice?" inquired the little girl.

"Yes, he has. Be quiet, dear, so we can hear him," insisted the father.

"Let's have the radio loud enough so we can all hear," came from Aunt Rebecca. "Guess I hear enough things; but you know these old ears of mine are not quite what they used to be."

There was a moment's silence. Then the high, shrill voice from the radio began:

I take it that we will all be relieved when I get through. I certainly got the surprise of my life being called on this morning. I anticipated being in agony most of the conference. I desire you to know and feel that I am trying to tell the truth, which I find is a very difficult thing to do. It is not my intention to skate around on thin ice and keep you people in anxiety. I know as well as I know anything that a man cannot speak to the Latter-day Saints—in fact, he should not, if he can only determine the matter—except when he is un-

[5]

der the influence of the Holy Ghost. I have never been able to determine when I am going to speak by the direction of the Holy Ghost, and sometimes when I thought I had it, some of the brethren did not think so. So it leaves me in doubt and uncertainty.

I do not know why we should be fearful among our people, or anywhere else, as long as we make efforts to serve God and keep His commandments.

I have been thinking about something for some time. I haven't got it in the form of a speech. Men come to me occasionally, not very often, and shake me by the hand and say, "I am glad to shake hands with a good man." I never feel so "cheap" as when that happens, and I have always been thankful that they did not know me so well as I know myself. It is along that line that I would like to talk to you for a few minutes.

What is a good man? That has been a big problem with me. I have had a good many business dealings with men who claimed to be good men. They said they were good, and they told me how good they were, and when they got through with me I did not have anything left. [Laughter] Whenever a man comes to me now and tells me how honest he is, how good he is, I am not going to do business with that man.

I am going to read to you a little from the *Book of Mormon*. I remember an apostle on one occasion said to me—I had been interviewed regarding something I had preached—"Golden, why don't you read the *Book of Mormon?*" I said, "I do as much as you do." And that was true at that time.

I have read the *Book of Mormon*. I have tried to understand it; I have tried to appreciate it; I have tried to believe it as my father believed it. There was no book that Heber C. Kimball read, and believed in, more than he did the *Book of Mormon*.

I find that a man can act good and talk good and look good and not do any good. That which I am going

[6]

to read to you is from Moroni's writings in which he tells something about a good man, which his father, Mormon, had told him. I haven't the time to tell you about the goodness and greatness of Mormon and Moroni, but I have great love for those characters. I quote the following:

"For I remember the word of God, which saith by their works ye shall know them; for if their works be good, then they are good also. * * * Wherefore, a man being evil cannot do that which is good."

I am glad he bears down on that.

"For behold, a bitter fountain cannot bring forth good water; neither can a good fountain bring forth bitter water; wherefore, a man being a servant of the devil cannot follow Christ; and if he follow Christ he cannot be a servant of the devil."

Now, there is another part I want to read, and I believe this. I may be of the old school, but I have heard it all my life. I believe it in my heart and with my whole soul. If it is not true, "then there is no truth, but we have been mistaken from our youth." We as a Church know this to be true: "And again, I exhort you, my brethren," [says Moroni, and this was about the last that he wrote] "that ye deny not the gifts of God, for they are many; and they come from the same God. And there are different ways that these gifts are administered; but it is the same God who worketh all in all; and they are given by the manifestations of the Spirit of God unto men to profit them.

"For behold, to one is given the Spirit of God that he may teach the word of wisdom."

What a wonderful gift!

"And to another, that he may teach the word of knowledge by the same Spirit;

"And to another, exceeding great faith; and to another, the gifts of healing by the same Spirit;

[7]

"And again, to another, that he may work mighty miracles;" * * *

"And again, to another, the beholding of angels and ministering spirits." * * *

"And all these gifts come by the spirit of Christ; and they come unto every man severally, according as he will.

"And I would exhort you, my beloved brethren, that ye remember that every good gift cometh of Christ."

Patriarchs tell me that prophecy is one of my gifts. It is only my gift through faith and through living up to the precepts of the Gospel of Christ.

I have been told that I should prophesy. I want to say to you Latter-day Saints that to be a prophet of God all fear and all doubt have to leave your mind, and you then open your mouth and God gives you words. But I have become so fearful about things I would be afraid to let loose. I want to tell you there are a lot of us in the same fix. We are afraid of what people will think and are doubtful about the fulfilment.

When Heber C. Kimball prophesied that goods would be sold as cheap on the streets of Salt Lake as in New York, he himself turned to President Young and said: "Brother Young, I think I have made a mistake."

Brother Young said: "Never mind, Heber. Let it go."

Charles C. Rich, after the meeting, said: "Heber, I don't believe a word you said."

Heber said: "Neither do I." [Laughter] But he said: "God has spoken." And God had spoken.

No wonder he was frightened, for the people were in the depths of poverty, a thousand miles from nowhere.

My testimony to you is that those gifts and promises are the heritage of God's children. I am not a visionary man; I am not a dreamer. I sometimes wonder what my gift is. I have never seen an angel, but I have the assurance that comes to me and is burned in my heart, like a living fire by the power of the Holy Ghost, that God is the Father, that Jesus is the Christ. I believe with all my soul that Joseph Smith was a prophet and is a prophet of God, and God knows there is ample proof to substantiate it. I also believe that Heber J. Grant is a Prophet of God, and, whenever God gets ready to give him something to tell you, I promise you in the name of the Lord you will get it, and you will get it straight, too.

The Lord bless you. Amen.

"Some talk!" said Bob. "He sure sized up the good people about right—the kind that brag about themselves."

"He always could size people up and situations, too," spoke Aunt Rebecca. "He is a keen observer and has the power of discernment, as well. His father had it before him."

"What about the gifts he spoke of?" inquired Joe.

"Oh, that's straight goods," replied Bob; "that comes from the *Doctrine and Covenants*."

"He certainly is a unique character," said Joe.

"I think he is the Mark Twain of Mormonism or the Will Rogers of the Church. I don't know which," returned Bob.

"He is neither." Aunt Rebecca settled the question decisively. "He is J. Golden Kimball and when he is gone, there will never be another. He was the original product and when Providence had finished him, the pattern was lost and never found again."

[9]

It is fair to assume that many people were enlightened and cheered along life's way by this brief talk, and that the audience was refreshed and put in good humor for the succeeding speaker, whom Aunt Rebecca declared to be one of the best in the Church. But, for some reason difficult to explain, she paid no further attention to the radio, but again assumed the stage in that suburban living room with her spontaneous and entertaining comments and philosophy, this time based upon that Tabernacle talk just concluded. And again our little daughter put the question: "Who is J. Golden Kimball and what does he look like?"

CHAPTER II

A UNIQUE PERSONALITY

For the benefit of those who are not familiar with J. Golden Kimball and the church to which he belongs, some explanations are perhaps necessary. The occasion of the radio address of the last chapter was the general conference of the Mormon Church held at the great Mormon Tabernacle in Salt Lake City. Let us shift the scene from that suburban living room to the Tabernacle. Ten thousand people are present at this gathering—probably many times that number are listening over the radio.

J. Golden Kimball is one of the general authorities of the Church, being a member of the First Council of the Seventy, the quorum next in rank to the apostles. As such, he is called upon to speak at these conferences and at many other meetings.

In his unique and interesting way he instructs and counsels the people. He tells them stories, often humorous, each one with a point; recalls faith-promoting incidents; quotes scripture and interprets it; makes his observations; and presents his views and philosophy. Someone has remarked, "He drives his points home with humor, teaches in his own original way; and the people remember what he says." From the talk over the radio, it may already be apparent that he is a man who does his own

[11]

thinking. That he is fundamentally sound and full of faith, no one who knows him will question. Few there are who want to miss him. Even Aunt Rebecca, as we have seen, with her inherent propensity for expressing herself, was willing to yield the floor to J. Golden Kimball—an undeniable tribute to him.

Let us picture him as he appears in the Tabernacle when his name is called as "the next speaker" at the conference.

A tall figure, "six-foot-three," so exceedingly thin that he seems almost transparent, responds to the announcement of the presiding officer. All eyes are upon him as he slowly arises from his seat and makes his way to the speaker's stand. He is within a few weeks of his eightieth birthday; his step therefore is rather cautious and deliberate, as he climbs the flight of steps leading from the second row, where the First Quorum of the Seventy are assigned to sit, up to the fourth row, occupied by the First Presidency of the Church. Presently he reaches the upper pulpit and the microphone.

It would be difficult to visualize such a unique and picturesque figure as is presented by "the next speaker." Let us get a close-up of him as he stands there in the pulpit: Seventy-five inches in height; very slender; somewhat bent by the heavy physical work done in his teens and the burden of his four score years; a head unusually large and unlike any other, with a sizeable bump at the back; his complexion sandy; a few lonesome hairs on top that have triumphantly weathered the storm; keen and penetrating eyes, black and beautiful, expressive of humor and sympathy; a very long, narrow, perpendicular face, intensely interesting, with features regular; withal, a serious countenance, expressive of sadness rather than of the humor for which he is noted. He seldom laughs, but is often seen to smile dryly as he speaks.

Let us think of him, not too much as a humorist, but rather as a man with a message, a minister of the Gospel, who just naturally uses a bit of his humor and originality to put the message over.

You will be convinced that the message is the thing uppermost in his mind. The message is the medicine, the humor is his way of getting the medicine down. He learned the lesson early. "When as children we needed a dose of something," he says, "my Aunt Ruth used to hold us down while mother poured the medicine into our mouths. Not so with my father; he used to say, 'If you have to give a baby medicine, tickle it under the chin and when it starts to laugh, down goes the medicine.'" It must be admitted that J. Golden Kimball is an adept in administering spiritual and moral dosages as his father prescribed.

His language is just as natural and spontaneous as the things he says. It is, of course, the vehicle of his thought. "Seldom, if ever, do I study my words," he remarked recently. "Usually I have something in mind to say, but more often do I depend upon the inspiration of the occasion for the message, and always for the language to put it over."

As a heritage from cow-boy days, he uses some of the Western phraseology. " 'Hell' and 'damn' seem to stick with me," says he; "just can't get rid of them. I have a moving-picture mind, and when I get in conversation or before an audience, usually the pictures and ideas come thick and fast. Unpremeditated, the language comes with them and I pass it on, those two words included—I suppose for emphasis."

His first talk may have revealed that this man does not really preach. It is seldom, as you will notice from that radio talk, that he has a well-defined theme carefully and logically developed. Usually, he talks frankly and freely, making one point after another—in that motion-picture style. Often the points are unrelated, but seldom are they without value and "punch."

Now and again it will be observed that things irrelevant and in lighter vein and even without any point proceed from his mouth. "I mix the wheat with the chaff," he has said in his public addresses, "and it's up to you to take your choice. In my talks you will find foolishness, maybe some wisdom, and I hope a lot of truth." One thing is certain: these talks are never tiresome.

[14]

The Biographical Road

CHAPTER III

FIRST YEARS

Pioneer life was but six years old in "Great Salt Lake City" when a baby came to the old "Kimball mansion" on North Main Street, built in 1849. Not only was this infant sent to a residence which was, for those days, "a palace fit for a king," but it was to be a member of one of the most prominent families, a family of first importance in the church and the state.

His father was no less a person than Heber C. Kimball, apostle, prophet and First Counselor to Brigham Young in the First Presidency of the Mormon Church. Heber C. Kimball, as is well known, was outstanding for his faith and spiritual strength, for his prophetic gift and vision, and for his undying loyalty to his associates. He was a giant in physical strength. His chest measured the same from front to back as from side to side. It is related that one day when a favorite mule got stuck in a ditch, Heber C. Kimball took hold of the mule's harness with one hand while several men pulled on a rope held in his other hand, and in this way the animal was extricated. You may have read that he used to wrestle with Joseph Smith. Wrestling was an occasional pastime of the Prophet. "But

I never threw him," said he; and then added, with characteristic Kimball humor and good fellowship, "You see, he was the Prophet of God."

Heber C. Kimball possessed marked business ability. Through keen understanding and foresight, coupled with industry and good management, he was able to build for himself homes, grist mills and other mills, and school houses, and also to raise crops sufficiently great to feed his large family and many others as well, when they needed food.

He served as first Chief Justice, also as Lieutenant Governor of the Provincial Government of the State of Deseret. He was a member of the first legislative assembly of the Territory of Deseret, and in the March session, 1851, he was President of the Council Branch of the Assembly. He was a useful citizen until his death in 1868.

We shall let his son tell more of this illustrious parent. Were it not for J. Golden's frequent references to his father and the eloquent picture he has drawn of him, as presented later in this book, chiefly in one of his talks, we should feel it necessary to speak at greater length here of this outstanding and remarkable man: prophet, church leader, counselor, pioneer, educator, business man, citizen, husband, father and friend.

Turning from his father, we now present J. Golden Kimball's own brief but expressive account of his mother, which is taken from a writing by him in 1912:

My mother, God bless her memory, was the youngest daughter of her parents and the only one of that family who joined the Church of Jesus Christ of Latter-day Saints. Her name was Christeen Golden. She was born of honest, moral parents, who were farmers in Hopewell, Mercer County, New Jersey. Mother's grandfather was the famous John Goldy, whose farm at Hopewell joined the farm of John Hart, a signer of the Declaration of Independence.

It is related, by a member of the family, that in the battle of Trenton, New Jersey [Revolutionary War] five of the sons of John Goldy left the farm one day, all of them barefooted, to circle around and join Washington's troops. They had but one gun. It is now on exhibition at the Capitol Building at Trenton, New Jersey, and is said to be the longest barrel shot-gun in America. As they walked along they came within firing distance of the enemy. One of the Goldy boys quickly fired and "killed several British officers. * * * The guns were then turned on our boys. Three of them disappeared and were never heard of again.

Mother married Heber C. Kimball at Nauvoo, Illinois, and she knew not her number as one of his polygamous wives. I don't know either. Mother didn't have any idea, as father never told her. My mother was no concubine, but an acknowledged wife. She was a wife and mother. And not many lived who, to my mind, were quite so good.

Mother was simple, plain, and cheery in her living and manners and most generous, hospitable, and kind in her nature—a true and devoted wife and Latter-day Saint. She taught us by example rather than by precept, and her example was fine, noble, and elevating. She never nagged us, and I don't believe there ever was a mother who was more anxious than she was that her sons should live good lives, go on missions, and be honest, honorable, and upright.

[19]

Her life was one continual devotion and sacrifice. She was falsely accused, and suffered just as I suffer, only she kept still about it. I love her memory more than I do anything else at this date.

From that same writing we quote a paragraph or two regarding his early schooling:

Yes, I was educated, as hard as it is to believe, in many, many schools of the kind. But, for some reason I never advanced very fast, as the schools, each succeeding year, changed teachers, changed methods, and continued reviewing. However, I gained something, learning line upon line, and stood among the best educated of that pioneer age. My life scholarship was paid in the University of Utah at that date—1867. The University of Deseret, it was then called, was established in the old Council House, which stood where the Deseret News Building now stands. But my father died in 1868, which ended my schooling for many years.

Speaking of early Utah schools, let me say that my father built at Salt Lake City, just west of our present Lafayette School building, the first school house west of the Missouri River. For many years, he maintained a private school for his family and the neighbors. All the children in the neighborhood were invited to attend the Kimball School, and without any cost whatever to them. Father hired first one teacher and then another to run the school. It was in his school that I and many others made a start.

Seemingly it was Heber C. Kimball's intention to supplement this training. Golden was a favorite son. His father began training him to become his private secretary when Golden was only well into his teens. His father had great confidence in him and spoke of him as a boy of unusual promise. For

GOLDEN AND ELIAS   GOLDEN AT TWELVE
HEBER C. KIMBALL, CHRISTEEN GOLDEN KIMBALL (1853)
and Their First Daughter, Cornelia, who Died at Four Years of Age

the sake of discipline he was very strict with Golden. Along with bookkeeping, penmanship, etc., he would test him as to character, often setting a trap for him by leaving coins or candy in tempting places. But Golden never touched them. This pleased the father greatly. The father's influence on the son was potent in the years to come. The son's profound admiration for his father lives to this very day, as is evidenced by the high tributes which this son so often has been pleased to pay to his illustrious and noble parent.

Listen to one of these tributes: "You Latter-day Saints know well how proud I am of my parentage. When I stop believing in my father and mother I will stop believing in the human race; for where they go, I want to go."

In that same talk he tells something of his early training:

I will tell you how I was brought up and then you can make some excuse for my general makeup. A lot of us boys used to meet up in the Eighteenth ward, right where now stands the Lafayette School, that beautiful building which cost over $170,000. I was educated in a very small building on the same block. We had a brother who was somewhat of a general, and he trained us boys—that is, when father was away. He would get us behind the barn, where no one could see us; then he would put a chip upon one of our shoulders and tell one of the other boys to knock it off. Then we would fight. That was part of the training he gave us, and when we asked why he did it, he said, "It makes you tough."

My father had a great garden, and it was fenced in by a six or eight foot stone wall. He told us we couldn't have any of the fruit; but we got it anyhow, and I will tell you how we got it. This same brother of ours took one of the boys and dangled him over the wall with a rope, and he loaded his shirt bosom and pockets with apples. One time, Father Tucker, the gardener, got after him with a willow, and lambasted him. Brother said that would make him tough.

For fifteen years of my life I was disciplined and instructed by my father, which has been an anchor to my soul. The things I was taught in my childhood (father died when I was fifteen years old) have been the savor of my soul; and the Holy Ghost has brought them to my remembrance.

CHAPTER IV

THE BOY BECOMES A MAN OVERNIGHT

Upon the death of his father in 1868, J. Golden Kimball became a man. He was the eldest of three children. Besides him were Elias and Mary Margaret. How true it is that responsibility develops character. Here is an instance of a man being born almost overnight. By a single event, the son of a prominent man was brought face to face with a compelling situation. A challenge was before him; a mother and three children needed support. His dear mother, ever sacrificing as she was, wanted him to continue his education at this time. But, he would not. Under the circumstances it was not fair to her. So he set out to become a specialist in driving mules, for he considered that would be "a profession of some immediate value." Thus, as one man put it, "J. Golden Kimball became one of the early M. D.'s of the West, for he was as good a mule driver as could be found in these parts."

Unhesitatingly, he assumed a man's responsibility and worked with the vigor and determination of a man. "I was a worker," he says, "and had enough ambition to have made me President of the United States of America."

About four o'clock every morning found him tending the horses for the man who employed him, and from then on till after dark he was busy driving or caring for the teams.

Several years later, having served a practical apprenticeship, he went into the contracting business for himself: freighting, digging cellars, hauling rock, and doing all kinds of teaming work. As time went on, he completed many contracts and dealt with many people. It is reported that he always saw to it that the work was done right and that the price paid for it was reasonable. He never took advantage of people, but was honest in his dealings with every one under all circumstances.

Convincing evidence of his consideration of others lies in a statement given by his brother, Elias: "Golden always went over the situation, figured the job, took the full responsibility of the contract himself, and then, when the work was completed, he shared equally with his brothers who helped him. If five of us worked on the job, he would split the returns five ways. He would never take a cent more for himself than he gave to us. One time when Golden was figuring the rock-hauling for a large mill near Tooele, Utah, for Elias Morris, some of his brothers objected to hauling the big stones. He decided, however, to take the contract and hauled the large rock himself. When settling time came, he divided the proceeds from the contract equally among us."

Needless to say, these admirable qualities won for him the universal respect and esteem of his brothers and of all those with whom he dealt. His contracting business increased until, as he reached his twentieth year, he found himself doing some of the larger contracting jobs in the community.

All in all, however, the contracting business proved unprofitable for J. Golden. "Between stations" he and his immediate family nearly starved. "Finally," he says, "we starved out. Just couldn't make it. Mother sewed for Z. C. M. I. at those early starvation prices, kept boarders, with poor surroundings and accommodations, as by this time we had been boosted out of father's mansion and lived in a two-room house. Mother went to Brother Brigham repeatedly to secure a position for me, but of no avail. I suppose there were too many others who wanted work. So we were left to hustle for ourselves, and that's how I became a hustler."

CHAPTER V

PIONEERING IN BEAR LAKE VALLEY

In 1876, the family decided to leave their home and try their fortune elsewhere. His mother had emigrated to Utah as a pioneer in 1848, his father being one of the original pioneers of 1847. In 1876, after eight years of hard struggle since the father's death, the mother joined her children and left Salt Lake City. They located in Meadowville, Rich County, four miles from Bear Lake and about a hundred miles northeast, as the crow flies, from Salt Lake City. There they bought squatter's claims from Isaac and Solomon Kimball, who had been called there by Brigham Young to help settle that country. In all there were eleven sons of Heber C. Kimball in that territory. Golden and his brother, Elias, assumed the obligation to pay Isaac and Solomon one thousand dollars for their claims. It was the first time they had gone in debt, and to them at that time it seemed a tremendous undertaking.

"There was no house or improvements," says J. Golden Kimball, "no title, and the land not yet surveyed by the United States, and we commenced a fight for life. God knows it was a hard fight with poverty and terrible blizzards in winter. We felt

[26]

some years that we had nine months winter and three months late fall. We worked, we toiled early and late, and the strange part of it was we never got discouraged. We hadn't sense enough to know when we had failed. Fifteen long years of hard work and sacrifice, but final success. Mother remained with us until we sold out in 1892—or about that time."

Those were pioneer days with all the work, hardships, privations, successes and failures incident to life in a new and forbidding country. To begin with, one log room, sixteen by twenty, housed the family. Later a kitchen lean-to was added.

There were the usual long, strenuous hours extending from before daylight till after dark; mother, daughter, and sons all cooperating and exerting every effort to make things go. The wolf came pretty close many and many a time. Once he hung around for three whole days. The family had no bread, not an ounce of flour in the house and, of course, not a cent of money. Finally Golden saddled his horse, went to the store keeper at Lake Town and asked for a sack of flour on credit, offering to leave his horse, bridle, and saddle until the flour was paid for.

"Not much," replied the staunch old Englishman. "I want the money. One of your brothers owes me now for some goods I sold him."

Later, it was learned that the amount of this bill was twenty-five cents, which, being so small a sum, had been overlooked. But, the merchant obstinately insisted that he was right; someone in the family had neglected to pay him, and Golden failed to get the flour.

In dire necessity, he turned his horse towards the bishop's house, where he offered the horse and saddle as security for a sack of flour. "That isn't necessary," quickly responded Bishop Ira Nebeker; "I'll let you have the flour and want you to come back any time you are in need." As soon as possible the flour was paid for.

As the years passed, the worldly circumstances of the family improved. By sheer hard work and good management, the struggle was crowned with victory, and these two brothers, Golden and Elias, became the proud owners of one of the finest and most successfully operated cattle and horse ranches in the Bear Lake district.

Even during the poverty and desperate struggle of those first years, they were happy in that little one-room log cabin. Some of their evenings were devoted to reading. Many of Elias's were spent that way; he was a little more studious than his brother. Golden read a little, but was more socially inclined and liked to go to all the parties and dances.

Looking back on those days, J. Golden has this to say in one of his Conference talks:

For twelve years of my life, after my father's death, I was as free as the birds that fly in the air! there was no restraint further than the counsel from my mother. I took no active part in the Church. I was just as free as non-members of the Church feel that they are free. That is a part of my history I am not making much noise about; I am trying to forget some things that I did. However, I don't want you to be impressed with the idea that I committed anything criminal, anything that would deprive me of the Spirit of God. But I am sorry, oh how sorry! that there was no restraint or responsibility placed upon me, that I was not actively engaged in church work during those twelve years.

CHAPTER VI

LOGGING DAYS

When the call came to Bear Lake for volunteers to go to the canyon during winter months and cut logs for the construction of the temple at Logan, J. Golden Kimball responded. Joining others from the entire section, he worked in Logan canyon in temperatures ranging from "ten to forty below zero in snow to the waist."

Strange as it may seem, there were no immediate bad results so far as their health was concerned. Each night they would return to camp with their clothes "frozen as stiff as a board from the waist down." After supper, they would lie around in front of the fire until they were thawed out, and then go to bed. No one caught cold or got sick during those winters as a result of exposure to the weather. There was no money paid or expected for this service. It was a voluntary contribution to the Church.

Over a hundred men worked at this camp, felling the logs, bringing them to the mill, sawing them into lumber, and hauling the lumber to Logan. While the men were decent and wholesome, they were rough and careless in some ways. Golden was one of the ring leaders when fun was brewing. One evening when their spirits ran high, he and his brother led the crowd in a spontaneous demonstration against the cook, "a large Danish woman who would take the prize anywhere for being the dirtiest and most careless cook in the country."

No inconsiderable fun was had at the expense of this defenseless, yet careless, woman. Biscuits were suspended by threads of hair found in them, dirty dishes were exhibited, songs were sung, stories were told, and thoughtless comments made, half in jest, half in seriousness, but greatly to the embarrassment of the woman who presided in the kitchen.

During the next visit to the sawmill of Brother C. O. Card, then in general charge of the camp, the matter was reported, and a trial was arranged for J. Golden Kimball and the other ringleader in the affair. Attorneys were selected, the jury was chosen, and the case tried. "We were guilty as could be," says J. Golden, "but the jury let us off. It was made up of men who were on our side."

Following the trial, Brother Card called J. Golden to him and said, "I want you to take charge of this camp."

"Why so, when I've been causing all this trouble?"

"I can see you were guilty this time, although you were acquitted," responded Brother Card. "But I can see, also, that you have got the right stuff in you."

Included in the directions to the new superintendent were the instructions to have the men stop their swearing, to hold meetings, and to have prayers in camp morning and evening. "Everyone is to pray," said Brother Card; "call on a different man each time."

"That's a pretty big order, either one of them," replied J. Golden. "There are men in this camp, I reckon, (I being one of them) who never have prayed in public but have been in this business of swearing all their lives."

But the new man showed that he merited the confidence placed in him. Difficult as the task was, he had the courage to tackle it. Moreover, he was frank and honest and "had a way with him" and the men liked him. He was one with them, and, though it may sound incredible, the meetings were held, and he induced every man in that camp to pray. Some of the prayers were funny, but they were all sincere.

To quit swearing was the hardest part. A habit, deep-rooted in youth and followed persistently thereafter, is not so easily broken. These were cowboy days, and most of the men came from ranching districts. The whole country was new. The men were genuine, as evinced by their whole-hearted support of the Church in this strenuous undertaking to build a temple. This response and many other big, fine things about them would have convinced one of their sterling worth. But, at the same time, they were rough.

The superintendent recalls that he worked his way up a little side canyon to the spot where George X, the champion swearer of them all, was wielding his ax to fell a tree. "He was an excellent woodsman," J. Golden says, "and as we stood there in the snow four feet deep and way below zero, I said, 'George, you must stop this damn swearing; those are the orders.' "

"But, damn it, Golden, I just can't do it. I was raised on it. That's my native language, and its pretty hard to ask a fellow to start learning new speech this late in life."

"But, George, we've got to do it; that's my orders. I've quit already, and if I can do it, you can."

"All right, Golden, if you've quit, I'll quit too, if you say I have to."

The man liked J. Golden Kimball. With strenuous effort that man stopped his swearing, excepting "hell" and "damn it," and in those days, in a rough country, that wasn't considered swearing. "The whole camp fell into line," relates Elias S. Kimball, "and many times since as I have thought about that thing it has appealed to me as a most outstanding example of leadership resulting in part at least from the high esteem of the men for their leader. Of course, the Lord may have helped out, too."

The logging-days over, J. Golden accepted a position as superintendent of a private lumber mill,

5

owned by Hyrum Woolley, where he remained for some time and then returned to the ranch.

Following is one of his own stories of those logging days:

Joe Morris was the best man with oxen I ever saw. One time when we were hauling some of those temple logs to the sawmill, he turned the whip over to me. There were six yoke. I had never tackled half so many. "You can't learn younger, go ahead," Joe said to me. So I took the whip and started in. The oxen, dumb as they were, knew a change had been made. Immediately they lagged and some of them turned around to look at me. I fancied they were all laughing at my shrill voice. Joe stood by and laughed; he wouldn't help a bit. I spoke quite respectable for a time to those oxen, but what good did it do? Then I started to cuss. (It was after the manifesto on swearing, too, but I was mad and had to turn loose. I never did it again; that was the last time.) And, boy, how I did cuss! Did I wax eloquent! I'm afraid I did. But, did those oxen sit up and take notice? They sure did; every one of them got down to business. You see, they were Church oxen, and when you talked that language to them, they understood it.

CHAPTER VII

THE ROAD TURNS

For twelve years after his father's death J. Golden Kimball felt no restraint of any kind except to be good to his mother. No man's hand was stretched out to guide him in the footsteps of his father. He was living the out-of-door, carefree, rancher's life, and, except for his mother's gentle example, he was thinking of cattle and horses and good times, rather than of anything else. But soon he was to stand at the bend of the road and to feel the influence of a good man once more.

In the summer of 1881 something happened to change once again the destiny of this unique character. It was a thing less tragic than the death of his pioneer father, but one doubtless just as effective in turning this young man, now twenty-eight, in another direction.

A rather stout man of German accent came one day to that little town of Meadowville to hold a meeting. In his outward appearance he was not specially attractive. Certainly there was nothing pleasing in his deep, gutteral, broken accent. However, one could not be long in his presence without feeling that that sturdy body was the tabernacle of a great, inspiring soul. That person was Dr. Karl G. Maeser.

[35]

The meeting was called. The people responded well; yet the number was not great. Under the inspiration of the Holy Spirit, for one hour and a half Karl G. Maeser testified of God, made a plea for education, and spoke in the interest of the Brigham Young Academy (now the Brigham Young University). Golden and Elias were thrilled. His words electrified their souls. From that night their ambition was kindled not only for education but for a greater knowledge of God as well. The very next day they commenced laying their plans for an education. They began to see that there was something more in life than caring for horses and cattle. In one single hour, speaking under the influence of the Holy Spirit, Dr. Maeser had enlarged their vision and set their ambition on fire. From then on they wanted to do something and to be somebody.

They sold some things off the ranch at considerable sacrifice and decided to peddle washing machines to get the balance of the necessary money to go to school. They worked as hard as two men could, soliciting and selling the machines for miles around. Finally they got enough money to buy fifty more machines, which, when sold, would yield them the coveted sum to send them for one winter to the Brigham Young Academy. They paid the agent the cash for these washing machines, but never saw the machines or the agent again. He had skipped with the money. You can imagine

what a blow this was to them. Their disappointment was terrible; the way seemed black in every
drection. But they kept on plugging and finally
came out triumphant. More washers were sold,
and, "after sweating blood to get it," the money
was secured (at least part of it) and they set out one
cold winter's night for the Academy at Provo,
Utah, the first young men to leave this section for
an education.

Golden and Elias had engaged transporta-
tion on the stage but, to accommodate a friend, they
cancelled the order and went with him in a wagon,
leaving Meadowville about 8 p. m. It was forty degrees below zero. One of them would drive for a
while and the other two would run behind the
wagon to keep from freezing to death. It was a trip
long to be remembered. Upon arriving at Evanston next morning at four a. m., they were more
dead than alive, and it took the warm room of the
hotel and hot drinks to revive them.

Their mother, also, moved to Provo for the
school term and boarded, besides her own sons, five
young men to help pay expenses. In addition, it
became necessary for them to haul coal from Coal-
ville, and vegetables on return trips to earn addi-
tional money.

Two school years were thus spent by J. Golden
Kimball at the B. Y. A. Here, he secured a fairly
good education for that day. He excelled in some

of his subjects and won recognition in several of the speaking contests.

But of greater value even than the technical training was the inspiration of that great educator, Karl G. Maeser. From him the students learned of the real purpose of life, the value of achievement, the meaning of service. From him they learned that great man's interpretation of life, of character, of success. From him they received many valuable suggestions as to the place they might fill in the great drama of life. "Whatever you are, don't be a scrub," he would say in his characteristic, earnest style. And he used often to say, "Let me tell you what I mean by giving my word of honor. If I were to be locked in a prison with walls twenty feet thick, there would be a chance that I might escape. But should you place me in the center of this room and draw a circle around me with a piece of chalk, and I should give you my word of honor that I would stay inside that circle, do you think I would step over that line? No! Never! I would die first."

Of those who were under the inspiration of this great teacher, one man became a judge in the Supreme Court of the United States and others became apostles, college presidents, and national and local senators and representatives. Scores of his graduates worked their way to the front ranks of education. Many others became prominent in the law and divers other professions. These and hundreds of others became conspicuous for distinctive service in the various walks of life, to say nothing of the excellent contribution of the rank and file of his students (men and women alike) to the building up of the home, the church, and the state. J. Golden Kimball received his share of that inspiration.

Many years later, the Maeser incident at Meadowville and the days at the Brigham Young Academy were recalled by Brother Kimball:

President Grant told us last evening of a spot of ground he will never forget. And it impressed me with a feeling which never can be blotted out—my experience as a pioneer in Bear Lake when I went into that log meeting-house and heard Brother Maeser talk. He was talking about the Gospel. I shall never forget it. Although I have never remembered what he said, I know how I felt, and my brother Elias and I, and our mother with us, made as great a sacrifice as I have ever seen made to go to school, and later to go on a mission, when we moved from Bear Lake down through Evanston and through the deep snow by team, and not by railroad or auto. It took us three or four days to reach Provo. We went to school. I attended two years and my brother Elias three.

That is my testimony. I do not think I have to get myself all exercised and all wrought up and tear my lungs all to pieces to impress you, after forty years of labor in the ministry. Notwithstanding all my mistakes and blunders I have had a testimony of the Gospel from the beginning, and the beginning was in the Brigham Young Academy under the teaching and instruction of Brother Karl G. Maeser.

CHAPTER VIII

"WAY DOWN SOUTH"

April 6, 1883, immediately following his second year at the Brigham Young Academy, J. Golden Kimball received a call from President John Taylor to go on a mission to the Southern States. Eight days later, he was set apart by Elder Moses Thatcher, and soon thereafter he arrived at Chattanooga, Tennessee, where he was appointed by the Mission President, Brigham H. Roberts, to labor in Virginia "without purse or scrip." One year later, he was made secretary of the mission with headquarters at Chattanooga. He was familiar with the martyrdom of Elders Gibbs and Berry and the shooting of the two Condor boys in 1884, which occurred near his field of labor.

B. H. Roberts, just before his death, related to the author that J. Golden Kimball, a missionary at that time in the vicinity of the Gibbs-Berry killing, exhibited a courageous and valiant attitude. "Brother Kimball not only volunteered, but was insistent that he should go to recover the bodies of these two elders and thus spare me the danger," said President Roberts. "His offer was as generous as it was sincere. But, finally, I prevailed upon Brother Kimball that I should take the risk, pointing out that with that long, lean, greyhound figure of his, effective disguise would be impossible and that the danger from our enemies, bitter and enraged as they were, would be too great if he were to go."

During the last year of his mission, Golden's health and constitution were broken. He contracted malaria fever, which left with him its effects for the years to come.

In 1885 after two years of service he received an honorable release and returned home by way of Hopewell, New Jersey, where he visited with his mother's relatives, the Goldens. Here he was well received and, before leaving, was invited to preach in the local church. His own account of this visit will appear in another place.

Six years later, in 1891, he was called by President Wilford Woodruff to succeed William Spry as president of the Southern States Mission. After serving three years in this capacity he was again honorably released and returned home in 1894.

No attempt is made here to tell of his excellent service and the many faith-promoting incidents of those years in the missionary field, since frequent references to his missionary experiences are made in his talks. Some of these experiences, taken from his Tabernacle talks, are quoted later in this chapter; others appear in Section IV. It is enough to say that those same qualities of leadership and character that attracted men to him in the contracting and logging days made friends for him and the cause he espoused as a missionary. His exceptional faith, loyalty and humility, his splendid humor, originality, frankness and honesty, his interesting manner and dependable nature, all combined to win the hearts of the missionaries and the people. During this period while in the service of his church he had a rich and wonderful experience. We shall now let him tell some of his missionary experiences.

MISSIONARY EXPERIENCES AS TOLD BY HIMSELF

Brethren, what I want to talk to you about for a few minutes is my own experience. I know more about myself than any man living in the flesh. I am getting pretty well acquainted with myself. I am surprised sometimes at the things I do and say, more than you are. I remember after I went to school I came home and went to Bear Lake. I came down to Salt Lake on a little business which I happened to have with William C. Spence, of the President's office. He said, "Brother Kimball, President Taylor sent you a letter calling you on a mission, and he is disturbed because you have not answered." I said, "How could I answer it, when I never got it?" "Well, you'd better go in and see him."

I went to the President's office, the first time since I was a young boy with my father, and I met that great and wonderful prophet. I said, "President Taylor, I never received your letter."

"Well, Brother Kimball," (he was so kind; he thought so much of Heber C. Kimball and that made him think a lot of me) "you cannot go now."

I had been praying for it, I had been asking the Lord why I could not go. My mother had been praying that God would send me out. I said, "President Taylor, give me one hour and I will give you my answer." I went out on the street and the first man I met was Bishop Thomas Jenkins of the Seventh ward, who had been to Bear Lake, and I knew him. I said, "Brother Jenkins, will you sign my note for a hundred dollars?" "You bet, I will," he answered. So we went down to the Deseret National Bank, and he endorsed my note.

I came back to the office with one hundred dollars in my pocket, and I said, "President Taylor, I am ready." I went on that mission. No greater blessing has ever come into my life.

GUIDED BY HOLY SPIRIT

Now, brethren, I confess to you that I have been among this people for a considerable length of time, and have tried to fill my appointments as best I could. I have traveled among the people from Canada to Mexico, but I have never in all my labors felt the thrill and the flame of the Holy Spirit as I did when I was on my mission. It has been

[43]

strange to me that I have not been able to reach the hearts, to attain the humility, the childlike simplicity, the perfect faith in God that I enjoyed in the Southern States, as an ignorant elder, perhaps, and with very little information. I traveled without purse or scrip absolutely, and I had such perfect confidence that I never doubted but that I would be cared for.

When I was an elder in the missionary field, I was sent out into the woods—for that is about where we went in the years 1883-4. We did not go in cities; they were not safe places to go. So we went to the woods, among the poor people, and preached the Gospel. And we were sent forth without purse and without scrip—all it cost me to fill a mission was to get to my field of labor. I paid for that myself, and it was up to me to get back home as best I could. That is about all the money I had, with enough to buy a few clothes, and I remember they were rather poor. At one time I was up in the Blue Ridge mountains of Virginia, in the winter, with a straw hat and a duster on. It was not very suitable; it was not very warm. We could not wear overcoats—could not carry them in that country. All we carried was an umbrella.

We never were at a loss to know what to do, my companion and I, when we had the spirit of our calling. We heard that voice—not very often, not as often as we should have done, but we heard it behind us saying, "This is the way, walk ye

in it, when ye turn to the right and when ye turn
to the left."

I stand before you as a witness for God that
he never forsook us. I walked—and I am a very
poor walker; I am not built for it—hundreds and
hundreds of miles, and I never lay outdoors but
twice, though I want to confess to you I hustled.
There is nothing I dreaded worse than lying outside on the ground. I prayed, and my companion
prayed, and then we got up and moved on. I guess
we would have starved to death if we had kept
praying and had not hustled; the Lord doesn't help
people who do not hustle and move, after they pray,
and do their duty.

I remember thirty-seven years ago I was secretary for Brother Roberts, who presided over the
Southern States Mission. After I had traveled for
a year without purse or scrip and had tested God
thoroughly, I found the Lord's word good. He
never failed me. I traveled in the state of Virginia.
I went on one trip with a young elder—and I say
it with a good deal of pride—six hundred miles
without purse and without scrip and without
friends. No man had ever heard the voice of a
Mormon elder where we traveled. We left a trail
behind us, a trail that other elders have traveled.
At no time during that three months did I sleep
outdoors, but I came mighty near it a lot of times.
I thought the Lord surely had forsaken us, at times,
but when it came to the last test, some one's heart

was softened, and they fed us, and they gave us a bed; so we had no use for money.

MALARIA

During my labors in Chattanooga with Brother Roberts, as it was in the early history of that city, I was thoroughly poisoned with malaria. I was drunken, not with strong drink, but with malaria. I was as yellow as a parchment. As I went along the streets one day in Chattanooga, a stranger met me. He happened to be a physician. He said, "Young man, I don't know who you are, but if you don't do something for yourself, you will die."

"Well," I said, "I won't die, as I'm a Mormon —you can't kill them."

When Brother Morgan came down and relieved Brother Roberts, I was still in the office, looking worse than ever. Brother Morgan looked me over carefully. He said, "Brother Kimball, you better go home. The mission is very hard-run for money. It will cost twenty-four dollars to send you home alive, but it will cost three hundred to send you home dead." It was a matter of business in that office; they had no money. I think maybe that was all I was worth.

"No," I said, "Brother Morgan, I don't want to go home. I believe I was called on this mission by revelation; at least they told me so in my blessing. Now God has been good to me and He has been faithful and true; I have tested Him out and if

[46]

He can't take care of me, when I have been as faithful as I have, and made the sacrifices I have, then He is not the God of my fathers."

VISITS MOTHER'S FOLK

So Brother Morgan let me stay, and I filled my mission. I have my release. It is the only release I have ever had, and I prize it very much. When I was released President Morgan said, "Brother Kimball, now you'd better go right straight home." I said, "Brother Morgan, I can't. My mother suffered the pain of death to give me life. She watched over me from my childhood to manhood, and she loved her people. She heard Brother Jedediah M. Grant, President Grant's father, preach in Philadelphia, when she was a girl twenty years old. She heard only the one discourse and she embraced the Gospel. Then she took the Church works and went to her people, a good people, an honest people, a wonderful people, but they all rejected it, and she had to leave. And it broke her mother's heart. She went back to Philadelphia, and in company with President Jedediah M. Grant and his wife traveled by team to Nauvoo and married my father. And that is how I happen to be here today. My mother watched me grow to maturity. You know the one great vision and dream she had: It was that her son, her eldest son, should grow to manhood and go back to her people and let them see what Mormonism had done."

And I went, and God kept me alive and I visited them for five weeks and I preached in their church. My mother's relatives told their old minister, who had preached there for thirty years, that unless he let Christeen Golden's son preach, they would leave his church. So I got to preach. He was a clever old fellow, too. I thought I would ease up on him a little and get another chance. So I preached in his splendid church building and when I got through he said to his people, "This man has told the truth. I have preached it to you for thirty years." "Well," I said, "I'll fix you the next time," but I never got another chance. At any rate, while I was there I secured the names of over 150 of my mother's people and I brought them back to her, and her dream was fulfilled. For in the winter of 1884 my brother Elias and I accompanied our mother, and we did the temple work for the Golden family—and I am still alive.

PREACHES TO TREES

I remember when we arrived at Chattanooga, Brother Roberts sent me and a son of an apostle into Virginia. When we reached our field of labor, we lay around there for three weeks. I said to my companion, who was from the Brigham Young Academy, "Let us go up into the woods and see if we can sing." (I couldn't carry a tune; I never tried to sing in the Academy.) "And let us go up and learn to pray." We did not have any audience, only those great big trees. And I said, "Let us learn to preach." I would advise young elders to do that before they start out and not practice so much on the people—we practiced on the trees. So I prepared myself and occupied the time. My companion was prepared, and we sang. We made an awful mess of it, but after a while—and that is another testimony—God brought the tunes to us, and we could sing the songs that we had listened to in the Academy. Then we preached. God was kind to us and he loosed our tongues and we found we were able to express the things we had studied. I remember my companion was dismissing. We had our eyes shut and our hands up. I thought he would never get through. And when he said, "Amen," we looked back, and there were four men standing behind us with guns on their shoulders. I said to my companion, "That is another lesson; from this time on in the South I shall pray with one eye open."

So I will conclude my remarks by saying that I filled that mission. Brother Roberts and Brother John Morgan are my witnesses that I completed it, although I was broken down with malaria. But I came home with an honorable release; it was in 1884 that I came home. I worked in the Mutuals in Bear Lake and with the elders. I wound up as Superintendent of the Mutuals. I traveled from Evanston to Soda Springs in snow and cold weather, and suffered. By the way, when I went on my first mission I told President Taylor, "If you let my brother Elias stay at home, I can fill my mission." That put the idea in his head, and Elias was called right after I was, and we both went. We left our cattle and our horses and everything we had.

ORDAINED A PRESIDING SEVENTY

Then came my second mission. There was no noise about it; word just came, "You are called to preside over the Southern States Mission, and Brother Spry will take you down and turn the mission over to you." He did, and he did it mighty hurriedly, too, and left me to preside. During my first year I came home with an emigration. And while I was trying to comfort my wife, who was sick, Brother Roberts telephoned me to come down and be ordained as one of the First Council of the Seventy. They never asked me, they never consulted with me, they just sent for me, and I have been in this council thirty-three years [1922]. I filled my mission. One day, Brother Reynolds and I came out of the council meeting, and when we got to the gate, he said, "Brother Kimball, you are released, and your brother, Elias, is appointed." The two of us spent ten years in the South and when we came back we didn't have a thing but our families and our lives.

The Lord has been good to me. No man in the Church has been favored more or treated more kindly than I have been. I have got all that I have deserved and a good deal more.

J. GOLDEN KIMBALL, BEN E. RICH, AND ELIAS S. KIMBALL
Three Presidents of the Southern States Mission
(Taken at Chattanooga, Tenn., about 1889)

PERSECUTIONS

I want to ask in all soberness, if you think this Gospel, that has been revealed by the Lord through the Prophet Joseph Smith, can be advocated and preached among the children of men without serious consequences. I tell you, if our elders go out and advocate the truth of this work, it will bring upon them persecution and whippings. It may not be the better element will do that; they never have whipped our elders; it has generally been the same class as those who are killing the negroes in the South, but the people winked at it. I was almost a witness to the killing of our elders in Tennessee, on Cane Creek, and I know something about the spirit of mobocracy.

REMARKABLE HEALINGS

Let me call your attention to an incident. It happened away down in Alabama. That was at a time in the nineties when I presided over the Southern States Mission. The elders had been asked to assemble. They were laboring in that low, marshy, malarial district that was scarcely safe for a human being to live in. And they came straggling in, suffering with malaria, rather low-spirited, because they had been traveling without purse or scrip through that section of the country. We met and held a conference. After the two-day conference was over, we were to hold a priesthood meeting. In those days we had no place to meet in except the woods, but I had instructed the elders to clean some place off in the woods—a circle, where we could meet and hold our priesthood meeting.

On that occasion there was a young man, whose mother was a remarkable woman, a Latter-day Saint. The father had left the Church years and years before. He opposed the boy, he stood out against him, he refused to assist him. But the mother's faith and the faith of the young man, who was in that conference, did not fail. I don't know what his trouble was, but one of his legs was as large as my body, and it looked like a great piece of raw meat. It looked as if it would burst. The people there did the best they could for him. He had no physician. We did not know what a physician was in the South in my day. So on this occasion I said to this elder: "Well, you will have to stay here with the people. You can't go up there."

"Why," he said, "Brother Kimball, I have been dreaming about this, and I have been talking about it. It would ruin my whole mission unless I can be at that priesthood meeting."

"Well," I said, "if you feel that way, two of the elders will carry you up there, one mile."

We went there in order to get away to a place where we would be secluded. When we got into the woods in that little circle and sat down, as best we could, I looked those elders over. I was not very well myself, but I said: "Brethren, what are you preaching?"

"We are preaching the Gospel of Jesus Christ."

"Are you telling these people that you have the power and authority, through faith, to heal the sick?"

"Yes," they said.

"Well, then, why don't you believe it?"

This young man spoke up and said: "I believe it!"

He sat down on a stump and the elders gathered around him. He was anointed and I administered to him, and he was healed right in their presence. It was quite a shock. And every other elder that was sick was administered to, and they were all healed. We went out of that priesthood meeting and the elders received their appointments, and there was a joy and a happiness that cannot be described. The people gathered around. And the elders, before their departure, got down and they cried. Those elders, many of them, had never seen one another until they assembled in that conference, and "Such love," those people said, "we have never known."

CHAPTER IX

HOME AGAIN

Following the first mission, J. Golden Kimball returned to the ranching business in Bear Lake Valley. While here he served as stake president of the Young Men's Mutual Improvement Association, as home missionary, and as president of an elder's quorum.

In 1887 he married Jennie Knowlton, a daughter of John Q. and Ellen Smith Knowlton. For several months the couple lived at Meadowville and then moved to Logan, Utah, where three of their six children were born. Further reference to his wife and children will be found in later chapters.

Golden and his brother, Elias, bought property in Logan City and close proximity, and accumulated real estate in and near that city. Hoping to gain honor and renown by becoming rich, the Kimball brothers went into the implement business at Logan, Utah, and Montpelier, Idaho. For the first time, except for that thousand dollars paid to Isaac and Solomon Kimball in those ranching days, they went into debt, signing notes for the significant sum of thirty thousand dollars.

After four years of hard work in this business, they came out with "experience plus experience,"

MRS. KIMBALL AT THE TIME OF HER MARRIAGE
MRS. KIMBALL ABOUT TEN YEARS LATER
J. GOLDEN KIMBALL AS A STUDENT AT B. Y. ACADEMY
J. GOLDEN KIMBALL AT THE TIME OF HIS MARRIAGE

having lost their capital. They did, however, save their good name by paying off their debts.

The Bear Lake ranch was exchanged for Cache Valley property and their horses and cattle and other chattels were sold and the money invested in real estate. Not yet convinced of the dangers of speculation and financial overreaching, they bought almost everything for sale. Finally, they joined others and purchased nineteen thousand acres of land in Canada. This time, these brothers paid seven thousand dollars and signed notes for seven thousand dollars. The venture was a total failure. "And thus," writes J. Golden, "we were prevented from chasing the golden calf. Moral: Don't set your heart upon riches, don't speculate, and don't go in debt. After this, again the Lord came to my rescue and called me to succeed Elder William Spry as president of the Southern States Mission." This event has already been briefly chronicled.

It is only fair to say that J. Golden was unduly influenced by others in this speculation. According to his own statement and the testimony of others who know him well, his disposition is rather to be saving, conservative, and careful. "I believe in living within my income and in building up a reserve," he says. "I don't like speculation and never did like it but was induced to speculate by others. Not that I would shift the blame for my own acts, but it is against my nature to speculate and to go in debt. Those who do it nearly always pay the price, just as I have done."

In 1895 he came to Salt Lake City to reside, after having lost all his earthly possessions.

CHAPTER X

IN THE FIRST COUNCIL OF THE SEVENTY

April 6, 1892, while serving as president of the Southern States Mission, J. Golden Kimball was chosen a member of the First Council of the Seventy, one of the high positions in the Church. In 1896, following his return from the mission field, he was selected one of the aids of the Young Men's Mutual Improvement Associations. His devoted service, these many years, to these two organizations and to the church is generally known. For approximately forty years, he has attended the executive meetings of these organizations and traveled throughout Zion, speaking words of encouragement and inspiration to the people. It may be safely said that, without exception, his labors have been unusually effective for good in the many thousands of meetings in which he has participated among the priesthood, the young people, and the people generally. Scores and even hundreds of his listeners, upon literally hundreds of occasions, have accepted and retained the spiritual medicine he has offered them. Abundant evidence lies in the innumerable quotations from his sayings and talks everywhere quoted among the people.

It is in this work, seeking the advancement of

God's program, that President Kimball, as one of the general authorities of the Church, has spent the last half of his years. This work has become his life, as his talks will reveal. His ambitions, his thoughts, his fondest hopes are linked with the Church. To a friend, he recently wrote, "I would rather be tied to a whipping post and have my flesh stripped from my bones than to lose my faith in this Church and have my spirit killed."

For twenty-two years, from 1900 to 1922, in addition to acting as one of the First Presidents, he was office secretary to the First Council of the Seventy.

For nearly fifty years, in all, he has served his people in the capacity, first, as missionary, second, as mission president and, third, as one of the general authorities of the Church. No wonder he loves the faith and the people. And no wonder the thousands of seventies and the people generally, whom he has counseled and inspired for nearly half a century, love and admire him.

Following are some items and incidents related to the seventies:

LINE OF ORDINATION OF J. GOLDEN KIMBALL TO THE
OFFICE OF SEVENTY AND AS A PRESIDENT
THE FIRST COUNCIL OF THE SEVENTY

The Prophet Joseph Smith ordained Levi W. Hancock a seventy on Feb. 28, 1835.

Levi W. Hancock ordained William M. Allred a seventy on May 20, 1845.

J. GOLDEN KIMBALL
When he was made a Member of the First Council of the Seventy

William M. Allred ordained J. Golden Kimball a seventy on July 21, 1886.

J. Golden Kimball was ordained one of the First Seven Presidents of the Seventy on April 8, 1892, by Apostle Francis M. Lyman.

Francis M. Lyman was ordained an apostle on October 27, 1880, by President John Taylor.

John Taylor was ordained an apostle on December 19, 1838, by Brigham Young and Heber C. Kimball.

Brigham Young was ordained an apostle by David Whitmer, one of the Three Witnesses of the *Book of Mormon*, on February 14, 1835, and the ordination was confirmed at the same time by the First Presidency of the Church, then Joseph Smith, Jr., Sidney Rigdon and Frederick G. Williams.

Heber C. Kimball was ordained an apostle by Martin Harris, one of the Three Witnesses of the *Book of Mormon*, on February 14, 1835, and the ordination confirmed as above stated.

Joseph Smith was ordained an apostle under the hands of Peter, James and John, some time in June, 1829.

Peter, James and John were ordained apostles by the Lord Jesus Christ—*St. John XV.*

WILLING TO SERVE

I am acquainted with the seventies. If you want seventies to go on missions I can speak for them. If you call them they will go, but if you want them to stay home they will do so, and so will I. I will go on a mission if called. I am not just talking either, God knows it, and I know it. I would go if I were brought back in a casket, and I do not know but I would be tickled to death to have it come that way.

I have never been more greatly impressed than by Colonel William J. Bryan, an admirable man who died fighting for God and testifying as far as his knowledge went. What more can any man do? That is the way I feel. I shall stay in this work.—*J. G. K.*

NO RESIGNING FROM PRIESTHOOD QUORUMS

It must be understood by the Priesthood of God in this Church, that there can be no such thing as resigning from a quorum of priesthood in the Church. When you have made covenant with God and the Church and received the priesthood, you cannot resign. The only way to get out of a quorum of priesthood is to commit sin and get disfellowshipped from the Church. As long as you hold that priesthood we have the right to receive you into the quorums, and it is the duty of those who preside to labor with those who are careless and indifferent.—*J. G. K.*

CARELESS SEVENTIES

I want to ask the Latter-day Saints if they have ever heard of a seventy being handled that is slothful and careless regarding his duties. I have heard of men being handled who waded out into the mysteries of the Kingdom and commenced advocating false doctrine. One brother asked me the other day if I had ever heard of a man being handled for not knowing anything, and I could not remember a single case of that kind in the history of the Church.—*J. G. K.*

BRIEFLY PUT

J. Golden was addressing the Seventies Convention at the Granite Stake Tabernacle. A large crowd had gathered to hear him. He had been asked to talk on "the fund", as the treasurer needed support.

"Brethren," the shrill voice began, "how many of you would give your lives for this Church?" Every hand went up.

"How many of you would give fifty cents to the seventies' fund?"

He said nothing more about the fund. But the men saw the point and responded.—*From a Seventy.*

SEVENTIES AROUSED

Golden Kimball said this over twenty years ago, but it has stuck with me ever since. He had been asked to come down and stimulate us seventies. "Brethren, we have got to work together and fellowship together. There is no other way to get along. Let's all pull together. If we don't, what will happen? Suppose, for example, I do everything the Lord asks of me and by and by He says to me, 'Good boy, Golden, go on up there.' And I am exalted to the highest pinnacle and you people lag behind and fail to do your duty. What fun can I have up there all alone playing the jews-harp and talking to myself and knowing you fellows are stuck in the mud somewhere. Now, you fellows have got to get busy. What do you say?" And they did get busy. The speech was retold many times and had its effect upon the men.—*From one who was present.*

Chapter XI

J. GOLDEN KIMBALL AT EIGHTY

On June 9th, 1933, J. Golden Kimball reached his eightieth milestone. The glorious hope of eighty springtimes has cheered his heart and pointed the way of life and achievement. The sunshine of fourscore summers has warmed his path and kept alive within him the torch of that faith and love. The soothing charm of twice forty autumns has wrapped him in the haze of the Indian twilight to muse and ponder the things of life. The cold of eighty winters has pressed against those cheeks and slender frame as it thrust its chill and cleansing power into his soul. And eighty times have these eternal rounds brought faith and cheer, meditation and chill, and the many and varied experiences of life to this tall, slender man.

What kind of man have these seasons made of him? Under the joys and sorrows of these eighty years, what marks have been left upon his brow? What manner of man do we now find living within that huge head and slender frame? Would you like to know some of his innermost thoughts and feelings and something more of his views of life?

Let us go to his home that we might talk with him and view him at his leisure. Scarcely more than a block from the Salt Lake Temple, resting complacently on the southern slope of the North bench and overlooking a most beautiful valley, is his modest home. It stands on the old Heber C. Kimball homestead, within a few feet of the final resting place of that illustrious man. A generous showing of flowers and shrubs lends its springtime beauty to the place and speaks of the artistic temperament of Mrs. Kimball, who loves to be among them and watch them and help them grow. Entering the home, we are aware that the same artistic hand has been at work there.

Rising from his easy chair in the living room, Brother Kimball greets us with his accustomed smile and bids us welcome. Can you not feel the warmth of that smile and the glow of his genial nature?

There is a fine fellowship about this man. Never is he too much in a hurry, even on the street, for a handshake and a visit. He is sociable, frank, and unusually democratic. If ever there were any pride or feeling in his heart that, by reason of his birth or position, he was better than the other fellow, he lost that feeling long ago. He is a people's man. Why shouldn't we feel at home? You will soon notice that his talk reveals the fact that he lives on the same level as you and I, and that he seems to understand us and our problems. For he, too, meets the average vicissitudes of life and knows, also, something of its trials and tribulations. Probably he has had more than his share of life's burdens. At any rate, something has made him intensely human, and inspired in his heart an unusual love and understanding of others.

"Brother Kimball, how are you feeling on your birthday?"

"Well, the old bones and what's on them are telling me that the race is more than half run—some aches and pains, but then, I wouldn't know what to do without them."

"Any trace of the old malaria from the mission days?"

"Oh, a bit when it's damp and stormy."

"How about the moral feeling at eighty?"

"Oh, I guess I'm about as good and about as bad as you fellows. I never did have a very good opinion of myself."

"Well, but do you think that by and by when you go up there, he will pass you right off or stop you and ask a few questions?"

"Being skinny, I may squeeze by. I think, however, he may want me to clear up a few things. Maybe I can explain them and maybe I can't. Wouldn't be surprised if all three of us just get in by the skin of our teeth and, assuming we do get by, what worries me most is location." There was a twinkle in his eye as he went on. "I'm afraid they'll stick me off in some corner or down in the swamps where this old malaria will come back on me."

"Then, you think there will be locations in the next world?"

[64]

"Yes, a lot of them and some of those fellows with a case on themselves, the self-righteous kind, are going to land down in the swamps, too. That will be a sort of catch-all for a lot of us."

"What about this average fellow—the one that's not very good and not very bad?"

"Chances are he will be better off than a lot of people who think they are all right. He may light on high ground. If the average fellow is not pretty well taken care of, you can see that heaven will be rather disappointing and the Lord will prove a poor manager, after running us through this mill to have too many of us land in the swamps."

"Evidently, you don't think much of the old mill?"

"Oh, yes I do, and much as I like that average fellow we have been talking about, I would not want to pass these same eighty mileposts again. Neither am I anxious to kick off right away. So there you are."

"Then you must like something about the good old footstool?"

"I sure do, I love the people, and I hope they like me a little." He was very earnest. "I am a people's man, democratic in my views and always sympathetic with the people in general. I believe in the old Jeffersonian principles of Democracy on which the Constitution was formed. A people's government. That's the thing—not too strong a centralized power that portends to czarism and

[65]

7

king-craft and encourages trusts and multimillion-aires who bear down on the people. Better have poverty and equality than a favored few with slav-ery and bondage."

"Then, you believe the government should be democratic in principle?"

"Yes, and in practice as well, and the church, too."

"You would give everybody an even break, everywhere?"

"Yes, and so would the Lord, I believe, to that average fellow and the poor devil, too."

"Don't you think the average man gets a square deal in this country?"

"The squarest in the world, and yet America is still in the making. Another decade may do a lot more for the masses; let us hope so."

"What about the Church?"

"The most democratic organization on earth —the fairest and squarest to everyone concerned. It belongs to the Lord, and while its affairs are ad-ministered by men, yet the Lord has given them the outline and His spirit to guide them."

"Do you love those men, Brother Kimball?"

"Yes, with all my heart, and while I do not worship at the shrine of men—the Lord does not expect us to do that—yet I believe they are the finest men in the world. I know they are."

"Brother Kimball, for half a century you have

been working for the Church. Have you grown to love that, too?"

"Again, with all my heart. What would any of us do without it? When you have loved a thing for fifty years and kept on loving it, more and more, each winter and summer and spring, I guess it would be pretty hard to live without it." His voice was warm and affectionate as he spoke.

"What about the preaching end of it; do you enjoy that?"

"Well, yes, when I don't have the rheumatism or have to work too hard to get to meeting. I love the people and love to feed them the bread of life when I can get the Spirit. Of course, I know my way is different, but I can't help that. It seems I was made that way."

"Brother Kimball, do you try to make the people laugh?"

"Sometimes, not often. I do think it's best to get the people good-natured and in a mood to take what you give them. You remember what my father used to say about giving the baby medicine; 'Just tickle it under the chin and down goes the medicine.' That's always seemed better to me than the old-fashioned method of using force or too much persuasion."

"Do you figure out what you are going to say beforehand?"

"Yes, sometimes, but I seldom say it. I depend more on the spirit of the occasion, and when

I get up before the audience, my mind seems to work in that motion-picture fashion, and things come before me, one after another, in rather rapid succession."

"Then your language is not usually premeditated?"

"No—very seldom."

"What about those two little words that seem, now and again, to worry the authorities?"

"Oh, I never intend to use them when I get up to speak, but they just come to me as naturally as singing to a bird. I'm not thinking about words; I'm concerned about the ideas and how to put them over. But those words you speak of are what's left over from the cowboy days. They used to be my native language and I don't seem to be able to shake them. Really, they come from a much larger vocabulary, only I've gotten rid of the others. But, let me ask you, do you think you ought to ask a leopard to change his spots this late in life?"

"Brother Kimball, I don't want to tire you out or get too personal."

"Well, I have an easier chair than you have and if you're writing a fellow up, I reckon you have to know something about him—so shoot. If I'm going in print, I'd rather tell how I feel than have some one guessing at it."

"Then, here's hoping you won't object to this one."

"Try it and see. Seems to me you would make

a pretty good district attorney, you and my wife, too. Nothing seems to get by either of you. Go ahead."

"How do you feel when your remarks upset the authorities and there seems to be, temporarily, a slight lack of harmony between you?"

"It hurts me." He was unusually serious. "Some people's skin is as thick as a rhinoceros, but mine is not. I presume that the following description given of me when I was young is pretty true: 'He shall have strong mental powers and be stupid in his own way. None will govern him, for he will possess superior qualities of mind—very lofty and unbending spirit more proper to govern than be governed—a lofty spirit with a kind of noble pride. Generally a smile on his countenance, but when moved he will be bold as a lion.' That was said of me way back in the days of Brigham Young."

He turned in his chair and continued: "Maybe I was born under some such star. I mean well enough, and I regret that my ways don't always please them."

"Possibly, they do not always understand you."

"Often I think people don't understand me any too well and my motives and intentions. My life and words do not always portray my virtues, being made up, as I am, of bone, a little flesh and

[69]

sinew, and largely a bundle of nerves. I am so constituted that I am always keyed up to the highest tension." He paused a moment and then went on. "How can such a person be consistent in public or private, and keep peace with his desires, intentions, position, and religion? Such a person is a continual contradiction to his own true self and, from a superficial standpoint, is condemned or, at least, unjustly censured right from the beginning. All my life, I have been trying to master these nerves of mine and my high-strung disposition."

"Thanks, Brother Kimball. Now, if you don't mind, what does religion mean to you?"

"Well, religion to my mind means more than to be pious and prayerful. That's fine, but that's only part of it. You need these things if you can get them." He seemed sure of his ground. "But, the bigger things are to love your God, your neighbor, to be generous to the poor, to be honest, truthful, moral, etc., to repent, to sell all you have, leave your family, home, country and follow the Master. These things to me are evidence of faith in God. A few of these virtues I boldly claim to possess."

"Amen, Brother Kimball. Now, have you any hobbies in church work?"

"I suppose I have and that they are faith and repentance. Somehow, it seems mighty easy for me, thank heaven, to believe in the Lord, in His goodness, mercy and justice, and in His program of salvation and I love to prᵥ ᵥ these things to the people. So far as repentance is concerned, that appeals to me, too. I know I'm sidestepping right along, although I don't mean to; and if there is one thing in this world I need to do it is to repent and do it often and make a good clean job of it—no reservations."

"Is there anything dearer to your heart than the Church for which you have worked so long?"

"No, only my family. I have worked for them a few years, too. Been married now going on fifty years. Only I don't like to put one of these ahead of the other. Why not let them go along together? You know as well as I do that I would sacrifice anything I have on earth for either of them, except my honor, and neither of them would want me to do that."

"Naturally, your family are most dear to you."

"Yes, my wife is a fine woman. She comes from just as good stock as I do. She has done me good all her days, God bless her. And heaven knows she has had a hard enough row to get along with a fellow like me. If more of us men only realized how stubborn we sometimes are, we might begin to turn over a new leaf. As for our six children, they are, after all, our dividends for our years of family toil and struggle."

"What are the names of your children?"

"Jonathan (we call him Jack), Quince (we

[71]

call her Jane), Elizabeth, Gladys, Richard, and Max."

"Yes, as one advances in life," he continued with an unmistakable show of emotion, "one turns instinctively, more and more, towards home and loved ones, friends and religion, and all the spiritual things that are so satisfying to one's soul."

"That's beautiful, Brother Kimball, and now may I wish you more happy birthdays and ask heaven's peace and blessings upon you?"

"Thanks, I think I'd like to stick around awhile longer if the Lord is willing. Seems like we are never satisfied. And you can say, if you will, that my heart is full of love and sympathy and tolerance for everyone, especially for that average fellow we were speaking of a while ago. Tell them that for half a century I have been trying to understand them and to work for them, and I hope they will try to understand me. I don't know whether I have any weight or not, but tell them that, besides preaching to them, I'm praying for them right along."

The interview over, we leave the home and the presence of this interesting personality. Once having met him or ever having heard him speak, one would not soon forget him. He is so unique in personal appearance and makeup—so humorous and interesting. And, had he been directing the conversation just concluded, it would have sparkled with humor and originality. This man, as we

JONATHAN, QUINCE, ELIZABETH, GLADYS, RICHARD, MAX
"Our Dividends for Our Years of Family Toil and Struggle"

have seen, is truly original. Seldom, does he borrow other people's ideas and speech, the exception being that he does lean on his noted father. The people love him for his humor, his originality, and for his delightful frankness and honesty.

But consciously or unconsciously they love him for his faith. His faith, after all, is his anchor. It furnishes him his footing, his background, and his inspiration for the greater part of what he says and does. Subtract from him this foremost quality and there would be less remaining of J. Golden Kimball than if he were robbed of any other of his virtues.

His faith has led him to a knowledge of God and His program for saving and exalting the race. It has led him to a profound love for his fellows, to a deep concern over their successes and their failures and to a democratic and tolerant attitude toward them. It has led him to an intelligent understanding of life and its values. It has led him to a position of security in the hearts of his people and in the esteem of the Master.

How fortunate there has been this blending of humor, originality, and frankness with the weightier virtues of faith, love, and tolerance! How they have enlivened the interest in the man and his message of truth! How generously have they enriched the makeup of his rare and unique personality!

J. Golden Kimball is prompt, businesslike

[73]

and dependable. His dependability and his sympathetic feeling for others have brought many people to him for counsel. Young men and women and older ones, some of them in serious difficulty, have sought his aid. The sane and kindly help given by him has often contributed to mending their mistakes and troubles and helping them to get back again on the regular highway. "His personal work with such people has been most excellent," declares a life-long acquaintance. "Many people, including some now prominent, have been helped around the bend of the road by Golden." While he is unusually frank, it is said of him that he never betrays a confidence.

One of his special gifts is that of discernment, a gift possessed by his father to an extraordinary degree. J. Golden has inherited a goodly portion of this trait. "Instantly," says a friend, "he can tell whether a man is for or against him. He can discern whether a person is telling the truth. He can size up an audience or a situation more quickly than any one else ever saw. He has the gift of prophecy as well—but is seldom moved upon to use it."

Here is a man who sees straight, one of those rare persons with normal vision. Instinctively his eye travels the direct line through the mist and haze into the center of a problem or a situation. And seeing the truth, he has the courage to express it. Conventionality does not stop him or even swerve

[74]

him from his course. More than form and favorable opinion, he loves truth and is both honest and fearless in telling it.

Clearly, as you will discern, his motive is to help people. It is not his practice to say things that will embarrass or injure others. Rather, he is considerate and kind in his makeup. His love and tolerance have won for him the esteem and friendship of many people in many classes.

One of his lifelong friends, speaking of his honor, cited many convincing incidents pertaining to his conduct. Among them were some actual occurrences of how, on several occasions, he had been known as a young man to protect the honor and virtue of some of his girl friends. Again, his attitude toward certain of his youthful acquaintances, whose conduct was known to him to be questionable, was most generous, tolerant, and conducive to elevating these companions and restoring their self-respect. The golden rule found lodgment in his heart at a very early date.

One cannot be around J. Golden Kimball, even momentarily, without feeling that he is absolutely honest, frank, and genuine. There is no hypocrisy about him, not an ounce. Nor is he superficial in any respect. And while he has regard for the material things, and possesses a financial mind capable of analyzing and appreciating the importance of money and its uses, yet he is not worldly in his desires or ambitions. His mind, rather, runs decidedly towards the spiritual. He is attracted to his family and their spiritual needs, to the church, to friendships (he himself is a true friend and retains his friendships) to the life and work of the Master. "As the years come and go, I find myself and my ambitions," he says, "more and more closely linked to these things. The religion of my father is the religion for me. The same testimony that fired him and spurred him on burns in my soul today."

Like some other servants of the people, and prophets of God, he is rather a sad and lonely man. Much of his time is spent by himself, reading, writing, and meditating. He reads rather extensively. He writes principally for his own use to crystallize and preserve his own thoughts and to record some of the things he reads. Those writings, promiscuous and generally unfinished, often in note form only, he usually files away where, as he remarks, "They can't do any harm." Sometimes, he will carry a few pages in his pocket to a conference but "almost never uses them."

These writings, however, and the hours he spends in meditation are of significant avail. For during those hours he shares the fortunes of his family and his people, their joys and their sorrows; he plans and prays for their welfare and their salvation. During these hours come to him ideas, inspiration, and background for his more active performance in serving those he loves.

Having lived, not the life of the rich man, the

idler, or the aristocrat, but the normal life with most of its ups and downs, he is exceedingly human as his sayings and talks will testify. Especially does he have a warm spot in his heart for the downtrodden and the unfortunate, whom he has befriended all his days. Under the promise of the Master, that the merciful shall obtain mercy, one would say that this man will certainly share in that blessing.

He has had his share of ill health. Contributing have been that malaria germ contracted in the Southern States and doubtless, also, the confinement in his office, especially of those twenty-two long years when, in addition to his other responsibilities, he served as office secretary to the First Council of the Seventy. And inasmuch as our friend has a huge streak of pessimism in his makeup and unhappily learned many, many years ago how to worry, we must list this as one of the contributing factors.

Admirable, indeed, are the modesty and humility of this man. Nothing that is said in his favor ever seems to change his modest opinion of himself. No honor or recognition that has come to him has ever elevated him in his own estimation to a feeling of importance and conceit. In the very midst of his popularity, he has remained modest, humble, and wholly inoffensive from bigotry. These are winning traits. Doubtless, if he had regarded himself more highly, others would have been less attracted to him.

President Kimball has grown to be a familiar and loved figure not only in the pulpit but on the street, in his office and home, and in the homes of his friends as well. Wherever he goes, he is welcome and wanted, both in public and in private life. And when in the course of events, it pleases God to call His servant home, thousands will miss their friend and mourn his passing.

Sayings and Stories
Along the Way

Chapter XII

SAYINGS AND INCIDENTS, HUMOROUS AND OTHERWISE

Introductory

It seems needless to say that the sayings in this and the succeeding chapter suffer from transcription, particularly those that come from the subject of our book. Proceeding from his mouth, his words are enlivened by his unique and interesting personality, by the high, shrill, slender tones of his voice, and by his singular and picturesque appearance. These cannot be transcribed; neither can the soul of this genuine, interesting, humorous character. At best, they can be but feebly imagined or described. All we can suggest is that the reader keep before him as best he can the mental picture of J. Golden Kimball as he reads. Most of the items included in this section that are not otherwise accredited, are by J. Golden Kimball himself. In a few instances, where the source is not given, it will be apparent that someone else is the author.

THE TRUTH STINGS

I want to tell you in a few words that there is nothing in the world that the wicked dislike so much as the truth.

J. GOLDEN KIMBALL

PRESIDENT KIMBALL'S AUTHORSHIP

I write books, but I put them in pigeon holes and lock them up where they cannot do any damage.

SPECULATION—AND AFTER

You see after that speculation, we never got ahead again. Then we went over the hill to the poorhouse, and have been feeding on stubble ever since.

REPENTANCE A SAFE-GUARD

Someone said, "They're liable to cut you off the Church." Guess maybe some of them would like to. But they can't cut me off the Church, I repent too fast.

GOD WILL FORGIVE

I acknowledge that I am imperfect, and no one is more sorry than I am. I have made mistakes, but I have faith in God, and I know God will forgive a man who repents.

TOO MUCH PREACHING

I have heard so much about goodness that sometimes I get unhappy, even at conference, and I feel like a little girl I heard of that did wrong. Her mother importuned her and labored with her, just as we have labored with you people, and she said, "Mother, don't try to make me good; shoot me."

SAYINGS AND INCIDENTS

PURPOSE OF THE MISSIONARY

An elder is sent out, not to represent his personal views or the views of the people, but to proclaim the truth as it is revealed. He is not chosen as a spokesman for the people, not just as a messenger, but as the bearer of a message to the world.

HALF WAY TO THE CELESTIAL GLORY

In one of his recent sermons J. Golden declared, "I would like to preach a man's funeral sermon while he is living; you can't tell the truth about him when he is dead. I have given many a man a ticket to the celestial glory that I knew wouldn't take him half way."

THE LIFE WORTH WHILE

This world was not made just to hold people imbued with selfishness and unhappiness, with no ambition beyond eating, drinking, and begetting. We ought to plan ahead, have some purpose—that is truly living. Life means opportunity. Life means development. Life well spent means knowledge, growth, simplicity of life, and complexity of thought.

TRAINED CITIZENS

Our children need to be taught the great problems of the day. The schools should be ringing with the hammer strokes of the world's workshops. The children will thus become trained citizens of the republic. Then our citizens will hereafter be studying and battling as heroically for their civic and industrial liberties as their forefathers, the war patriots, battled for war ideals.

HOW TO LIVE LONG

Recently someone inquired of Golden as to the state of health of one of his friends. He replied, "Well, he's in a pretty bad fix, but I believe he will live longer than any of us. The only way to live a long time is to get some incurable disease and then take care of yourself. Some people who haven't anything the matter with them don't take care of themselves, and they die."

BANKER'S ADVICE

As is well known, bankers have not been in very good repute during the depression and on one occasion one of them jocularly accosted J. Golden and said, "Brother Kimball, you shouldn't use such language as you employ in our church gatherings."

To which Golden retorted, "I don't think this is a time for bankers to be giving advice to anybody."

FAITH IN PEOPLE

I want to say to you brethren and sisters, if you do not think I am loyal to this Church, and faithful, and keep all the commandments, do not sustain me. I would not have a position in this

Church if I could not have the faith of the people, if I could not reach their confidence and be instrumental in the hands of the Lord in saying something at least that will give them a little courage.

FRANKNESS

Now, if there is any one thing that I am normal in, it is frankness. Whenever the time comes, in my ministerial labors, that I cannot be frank and honest with the people I will feel that my usefulness has come to an end. I cannot talk if I have not freedom, and if I ever feel that I have not the support of the people I will be unable to talk.

THERE'S LIFE IN THE SKELETON

Now there is one other thing before I get started. Everywhere I go among this people they look at me with sympathy and pity, and ask me how my health is. Only a few days ago I walked down Main Street three blocks, and twelve people asked me that question. And I felt like kicking the last one. I want to say to you Latter-day Saints that when I am walking around, I am alive and my head works. That is what keeps my body going. I thank God for that.

MISSIONARY SERVICE

No greater favor ever comes to a man than to be called on a mission. I met a nephew last night, one of Heber C. Kimball's grandchildren. He said,

"Uncle Golden, when I was a young fellow"—he is now a high councilor in one of the stakes—"you came to me and said, 'Are you ready for a mission?' I answered you as I should not have done. The greatest mistake I have ever made in my life was that I did not respond at that time and have you present my name."

MILK-FED GENERATION

This generation has had too much ease, too much money, too much pleasure. They have lived upon milk and honey when they ought to have been fed on bread, cresses, and cold water, and slept in the mountains. I am sorry my children have not lived on the kind of food I was brought up on; then they would have more backbone. We should adopt a policy to stiffen our children's backbones; if necessary, feed them on raw meat, cayenne pepper, and green cactus diet.

GOD SENDS THINGS C. O. D.

About twenty years ago my family went to California, as my wife needed a rest. I remained at home on account of my church duties. Christmas time came and my folks arranged with a mercantile store at Los Angeles for a lovely present for me, to be charged to their account and to be mailed to me in time for Christmas. Through a mistake the store sent it C. O. D. I paid for it without knowing its contents.

A sudden flash came to me. That is exactly how the Lord works. You receive a blessing with promises from a patriarch, or a blessing when set apart for a mission or upon asking the Lord for help; they are all C. O. D. You pay cash and the goods are delivered.

A FAMILY MAN

Some men are cut out especially for family life and get a lot of joy and happiness out of it. Others are fair and square, good husbands, good fathers, kind as a woman but are not what you would call ideal family men. They are not so gifted in this way, yet they are affectionate and loving in their way and are on the dead square fifty-fifty and would do anything on earth they could for them. I suppose Golden belongs to this class—*An intimate friend.*

KIND HUSBANDS

A number of years ago Brother Kimball was appointed to attend a stake conference in the north country. The people were mostly Scandinavian. He said, "You good people build farms and sheds and take wonderful care of your animals, but there isn't one man in a thousand knows how to be good and kind to his wife." A smile of pleasure was visible on the faces of the women. Giving them ample time to enjoy his thrust at the husbands, he shot off the other barrel: "Now, ladies, there isn't

[87]

one woman in 999 that knows when she is well-treated."

Afterwards a little Scandinavian woman shook his hand and said, "Brother Kimball, you say the funniest things, but they stick."

ON THE CARPET

I remember that not so many years ago Francis M. Lyman, a man with whom I traveled a great deal—I don't think he ever worked on a man harder in his life than he did on me to mould me and fashion me like him—said to me, "I am through with you. I don't make any progress." I was on the carpet with him. The next day—you know how he took your hands and rubbed them—he said: "Brother Kimball, do you love your brethren?"

"Well," I said, "I love some of them a damned sight better than I do others."

"That is true," he said, "there is a difference, and the fault isn't all ours."

THE WAY TO KEEP OUT OF DEBT

I can tell you how you can keep out of debt; but I can't tell you how to get out after you get in. I had a man come to me the other day who wanted me to indorse his note. I had sworn, almost on an oath, I would never sign another note, not even for my wife. But he looked at me so pitifully, and was in such dire distress, and I had so much confidence in him, that I told him I would sign it—although

[88]

I was quite sure I could not pay it if he did not. He applied at one of our banks. They did not know me—for which I was thankful. I went to the bank and looked the man in the face. He said, "Mr. Kimball, haven't you got any collaterals?" I said, "Collaterals—I should say not! I haven't got a collateral of any kind." He said, "How do you expect me to take your endorsement?" I replied, "On my looks and general character. That is all I have got." And he turned me down; and I have been tickled to death ever since. That is the way to keep out of debt.

GUNS AND MISSIONARIES

You have listened to three presidents of missions. I know just about as much about missionary work as they do. I spent five years in the Southern States, and filled my first mission in 1883, when they killed elders. I was with Elder Roberts, and I know all about that experience. I never got much notoriety out of it, but I know something about it, just as much as anyone who was there. I know what it means to smell powder, and I am glad of it, and I thank the Lord I did not run. I guess I would have done so, but I had no place to go. These brethren that have been talking to you have been in the Lord's service; they are soldiers of the Cross, and they are too old to go in the army of the United States; and so am I. But I would like to touch off a thirteen-inch gun anyhow. I am a great believer

[89]

in the United States, but my service is first for God, for our Heavenly Father.

COMBS AND HUSBANDS

A well-dressed, fine looking lady entered the ward chapel. It was a rural community. Brother Kimball, the visiting authority, was staying at her home. He knew the family well. "Had to look twice, I hardly knew you Julia." Then he reached down and touched her on the shoulder, "Let me give you some advice; why don't you fix up a little around the house, put on a better dress, slick up your hair a bit, kalsomine your face and wear a big smile like you've got on now? If you don't, you'll be losing your husband one of these days and I wouldn't blame him much, would you?"—*From Julia, herself.*

COLORFUL PREACHING

I will begin by reading a few words from the Prophet Joseph Smith's sayings: "I want the liberty of thinking and believing as I please. It feels so good not to be trammeled." I don't know whether I am able to make myself clear.

Not long ago I met one of my friends—he was a good friend, too, president of a stake. He said, "Brother Kimball, you don't make yourself clear."

Well, I don't know of any man on earth that ever did, so all people could understand all right. The Savior seemed unable, sometimes, to get His children to understand just what He meant, although He was very clear in the doctrine which He preached. I know I have some friends who do not believe in the way I get at it, but I am not trying to please all of them, because that is absolutely an impossibility, so I have given it up. My temperament is such that I cannot say anything inspiring, or bubble with enthusiasm, and be clear, happy, or joyous, if I have to wear a restraining collar and cater to popular sentiment. I would like my preaching to have color, thrill, feel homelike, and revive old memories, and if I can't feel that way among the Latter-day Saints, where on earth can I go that I will feel free?

THE CHURCH MAKES YOU BETTER

Some find a great deal of fault with the Church. I want to tell you there is no fault in the organization of the Church; it is perfect. There is no fault in the Gospel of Christ; if lived up to, it makes you better; it makes you good in your home; it makes you good to your wife, and good to your children. It makes you good on the streets; it makes you honest; it makes you kind and generous. I know that—nobody knows it better than I do. That is what the religion of Christ does.

The Church is all right. I have got no ax to grind; I am not one of those that worship men; I worship God. I do not put my trust in the arm of flesh, but I honor the priesthood of the Church.

[91]

I have this to say concerning the authorities of the Church: I have labored with these men for many years, and the men that work the hardest of any men I have ever lived with in my life are the men who are in authority in the Church of Christ. I know what I am talking about.

Now, where is the fault? I invite every one of you to go home and find it, and I promise that if you find any big fault anywhere it will be right in your own home. If you can handle your own home and mind your own business, you will have no time for fault-finding. I know where my trouble is and I am trying to cure it. I am learning this lesson that there is no use of my trying to govern a family until I govern myself.

GRATITUDE OF CHILDREN

I have learned one lesson with children that I never knew before. There is nothing on this earth that grieves and hurts me worse (outside of sin and wickedness and rebellion) than, when I do everything I can for a child; and there is no evidence given of gratefulness, no gratitude, no thankfulness, but it is regarded as a debt the father owes to the child. Have you ever had a child say to you, "Well, you owe it to me"? I never had any of them do that but once, and it made me feel as if I could have eaten him up.

I don't owe my children anything but love, protection, a home and shelter, and an education.

I owe that to them, and the law requires it. But outside of that, shall they be grateful? Now, wouldn't it make you feel sad when the mother is broken down after she has gone and worked her finger nails off to do something for a child, and, then, he doesn't appreciate it, because he sees something on the outside that is greater, sees someone receive a better present! Did you ever make a Christmas present to a child, and when he got it he was disappointed, and your Christmas was ruined? Were you ever made to feel almost broken-hearted, when you had affectionately expended every dollar you had, because other people's children had presents much better, and the whole day was spoiled for your children and for you, too? Ingratitude is a sin in the sight of God.

Now, then, you children have to learn to love your fathers and mothers and appreciate what they have done for you, and then you will not be ungrateful.

PREJUDICE

I have one more shot at you, and I am going to let you have it right in the neck. I want to say to every bishop, to every president of a stake, to every man who holds authority in this Church: The most dangerous thing that menaces us is to get prejudiced. * * * How I hate it! No man that lives in the flesh can be prejudiced and be just. I remember one of my older brothers who was a kind of reckless, harum-scarum boy. Father worried over

him a good deal, and when father knelt down to
pray with this son he used to pray to God about
him. Before he died my brother said to me: "Gold-
en, father tried to prejudice God against me."

I said: "It isn't true. God cannot be prejudiced. God knows His children; God understands
them."

I pray that we shall not be prejudiced and try
to hurt others. I am going to tell you a truth that
Heber C. Kimball told, and I have it in writing. I
was surprised to learn how early that was in the
history of the Church. He said, "The Lord told me
that there were men that have tried to do me injury
in the eyes of His servant, Brigham Young, and they
shall see sorrow unless they repent, and be removed
from their places."

Brethren, let us be careful. I do not believe
that I am man enough if I am prejudiced against my
wife that I can be just. The Lord knows I owe
her a heap. You cannot be prejudiced against your
own child and be just and charitable and forgiving
and patient and long-suffering. So I would like to
be careful. A lot of things are said to me about
men. When I allow myself to be prejudiced
against a man, no matter how good he is, I don't
like him until I can get rid of that prejudice.

FATE: THE OLD MONKEY

There was a very prominent citizen once that
had an intelligent monkey. He was a mischiev-

ous fellow, and he just went around the house knocking everything down. He knocked over everything that he came to; he discovered that the things he knocked over did not get up again. He was just as mischievous as fate seems to be with us.

Finally, this good citizen took the image of a little man, made of some kind of material, and placed it on a very strong base. It was so arranged that when you knocked it over it would come up again. So he set this little man in the room. The monkey came around, took his right hand and cuffed it over. To his surprise it wobbled a little and staggered, and then rose up and seemingly looked at him. Then he took his other hand and cuffed it again, and it came up again. Then he took the right hind leg and knocked it again, and then with his left hind leg; then he got on it with all four hands and took one hand up at a time. To his surprise the little man rose up.

The intelligent monkey almost became a monkey maniac. He kept at it and kept at it until he hated and despised the little man; and whenever someone would move the little man near the monkey, he would get off in the corner and chatter and become angry. He wouldn't have anything to do with the little man.

The Church of Jesus Christ of Latter-day Saints is similar, or like that little man. You can knock it down one hundred times; you can knock it down one thousand times; it may wobble, but it will rise up again, and it will keep rising up until God has accomplished His work. This is God's work, and I look in sympathy upon men who oppose it. I stood on the street last night—something I hardly ever do—and listened to a man abuse the Church; and I had to laugh. I was a good deal like father was once when he was praying. In the midst of his prayer, he burst out in a loud laugh, and he said, "O Lord, forgive me; it makes me laugh to pray about some men." It always amuses me when I see a man or a coterie of men try to break down this Church. I would say to this kind of men: "You had better let the Church alone; you had better let the people alone, because you can't destroy this Church."

CHAPTER XIII

OTHER SAYINGS AND ADVICE

WHAT MONEY DOES

If I had a million dollars, I'd be the most sought-after man in the Church. But I haven't got it—damn it.

SPEAKING OF SUITS

Walking into a clothing store, J. Golden approached a clerk and said, "I'd like to see a suit that will fit me."

Whereupon the clerk eyeing the tall, skinny figure of his prospect replied: "Hell, so would I." —*Told also on Anthony C. Lund.*

EINSTEIN NEEDED

"Do you know J. Golden Kimball?" was asked of a certain man.

"Be hanged if I know whether I do or not," was the reply. "I've been with him and heard him speak off and on for forty years, and I'm still in doubt."

ANTIDOTE FOR SLEEP

One time President Francis M. Lyman was complaining to me that I upset the authorities too much.

9

I answered him, "Well, you see, Brother Lyman, you talk to send them to sleep and I have to talk to wake them up."

LACKING RESPECT

Brother Kimball was crossing the street in front of the Hotel Utah just as an automobile came swiftly around the corner and almost ran over him. Straightening up and catching his breath, he exclaimed, "Hell of a lot of respect they have for the Priesthood!"

SELECTING A BRIDE

Some select a girl because she has pretty eyes; some because she has pretty hair. I knew a man who chose a girl because she could sing. He married her, and the next morning, when he saw her without any paint or powder on, and saw a part of her hair on the dresser, he looked at her and said, "Sing, for hell sakes, sing!"

DOCTORED POSTUM

Traveling with one of the brethren and feeling the need of a little stimulant, J. Golden whispered to the waiter as his companion's head was turned, "Put a little coffee in my postum this morning, and don't say anything." The waiter returned with the postum but left his discretion in the kitchen. For he blurted out in a voice audible to both, "Which one of you gentlemen ordered coffee in his postum?"

WHOSE FUNERAL

The long distance telephone rang, and J. Golden was heard to say, "Yes, I know the man. Yes, I'll come up and talk at his funeral."

During the services when Brother Kimball was over half way through his sermon, he looked in a certain corner of the congregation and, to his dismay, saw the very man whose sermon he thought he was preaching, and exclaimed: "Bishop, who the hell's funeral is this?"

ANGEL BRIDES

During the course of his remarks at one ward (addressing the young people) he said, "I am reminded that this is the month of June and that it's mating time. I suppose some of you young folks will be getting hitched up to each other. And I just want to warn you not to expect too darn much of each other, and then maybe you won't be disappointed. Now, here, when I got married, I thought I was marrying an angel, and many are the times since I wish I had."

DON'T GET PERFECT

I have often wondered what would happen if a perfect man married a perfect woman. I'll bet he would shoot her inside of a week if she didn't poison him first.

SABBATH BUSINESS

Three men entered the seventies office at Salt Lake City. "Brother Kimball," said the spokesman, "we have come for some books."

"But," responded Brother Kimball, then general secretary of the seventies, " we do not sell books on Sunday."

"We are a long way from home," urged one of the men, "and would very much like to place our order. Can't you possibly take care of us?"

"Sorry," replied the secretary, "would like to accommodate you. I can see your fix, but we have an iron-clad rule; you can see it would not be right for our office to do business on Sunday.—How big is your order?"

CHURCH SLUMBER PARTIES

We went on a six-weeks' trip through the southern part of the state. We held two or three meetings each day. At Kanab conference I listened to Brother Francis M. Lyman for a long time. Then I dozed off and had a dream. I dreamed I was falling over a cliff one hundred feet high. I wondered how long it would be before I hit the bottom. Finally I landed stretched out on the platform, helpless and discomfited before four hundred people. Brother Lyman turned and said,

"Young man, you have ruined one of my best sermons." It cured me of sleeping in church.

"Brother Golden really shouldn't talk that way in conference," remarked one of the general authorities quite seriously to his son following the meeting at which J. Golden Kimball had spoken.

"Father," replied the son respectfully, "do you know how many of you brethren were asleep before Brother Kimball started to talk?"

"How many asleep?"

"Yes," answered the son, "I counted ten. But I noticed that the slumber party was over as soon as the President announced Brother Kimball as the next speaker."

KIMBALL HOSPITALITY

I remember [in those ranching days] one old woman, who walked fifteen miles from a neighboring settlement. She was a perfect stranger to us and said she had heard Elias and me speak in her town of Fish Haven. She was sickly, worn and dirty. "What are you going to do with her, mother?" I asked.

"I'm going to feed her and give her a bath and put some clean clothes on her and let her sleep in my bed," was the reply.

DISPENSING THE BLUES

I was lying in the hospital waiting for an operation. I had been there six days in preparation and in nervous anticipation of the event. The operation was serious. The doctor said I needed "considerable fixing." Later, I learned that over twenty inches of incision was required, most of it in the bone.

The day before the dreadful ordeal, a mutual friend brought Brother Kimball to administer to me. First, he talked and visited a considerable time and then blessed me. There was nothing frivolous about his talk, and yet he soon had me smiling. Later, the smiles were interspersed with laughter. I began to see things in proper perspective and to realize that all was well with the world and that the sky for me, after all, had but one dark cloud in it, which, probably, would soon roll away. I felt I was in the presence of a sane, well-balanced man and a man of exceptionally strong faith. In truth, never did I feel the power of faith more than that day.—*A Debtor.*

FAITH AND HEALTH

I got a telephone message some time ago (I think a year ago, maybe) that I had some relatives in the hospital. They wanted me to hurry there and administer to them. They were two sisters. They were married, and they were not city people. And, by the way, their father and mother were good Latter-day Saints, and these young girls had been taught the faith and they had been active. But they were not healed; so they came to the hospital. When I arrived I found one of them in one room, and she had been operated upon, and was getting along very nicely. The other sister wanted me to bless her before she was operated upon. I asked her how much she was paying for her room. She told me. "And how much are you paying the doctor?"

"Three hundred dollars."

"Well, haven't you got confidence in him? He is charging you enough. Why don't you trust him?"

"Well," she said, "Uncle Golden, I have been administered to, but I was not healed, and I felt forced to come to the doctor."

I said, "I am a little jealous for God, and if I bless you, and you are healed, who is going to get the credit? If the doctor gets all the money and all the credit, and God heals you; I don't think that's fair."

So I blessed her as best I knew how, and I blessed the doctor. I made a full job of it, and blessed the nurse, and asked God that His Spirit might be there and the patient's life be spared, and it was spared.

I realize that hospitals, physicians, and surgeons do wonderful things, and that faith without works is dead. I want to bear testimony to you (and I know it, I don't think it, I don't imagine it) I have seen God heal the sick. I know that where there is sufficient faith there is nothing impossible.

When we were in the South, God had to take care of us, whether it was stormy or sunshine, as we had no choice. I know the Lord can take care of us and will take care of us if we have faith.

QUARTETTES AND APOSTASY

Way back in the nineties, J. Golden Kimball took a quartette and went up North to hold some meetings and rouse the people somewhat, the seventies in particular. In a certain district the spirit of apostasy was entering some of the smaller communities. Attracted by his style of preaching, they came from far and near to hear him speak. At one place, he began by dividing the quartette, having two members on the one side of the house sing, "Come, Come Ye Saints," while on the other side the other two rendered, "O Ye Mountains High."

Immediately he followed with these and other remarks: "Now, what do you think of that singing? Sounds like hell, doesn't it?" Then, he had them all sing together in perfect harmony.

"Now you people up here are working like that first song. Part are pulling one way and part another, and see the result. You have forgotten the Lord and how He has blessed you. When you settled here, there were little drizzling streams coming out of these canyons, hardly enough water to give a canary bird a drink. The Lord has increased the streams and multiplied your crops until you have prospered and become independent. Now you have forgotten Him. And there is contention among you, and you are pulling about the way that first song went."

The leader of the apostate gang, who was at the meeting, must have felt these remarks were aimed directly at him, for every time the speaker made a new point, he would sink deeper into his seat. The next day he remarked to a group of his followers in broken accent, 'What Golden Kimball he say am not true. No da ain't true. But, I'm damn scart it is true."—*From One Who Was Present.*

A BLIZZARD STORY

About 1887 my brother Elias and I loaded a sleigh with provisions and started for Evanston, Wyoming, enroute to Salt Lake City, where Elias was to attend the Utah Legislature as a representative from Rich County. We took our mother along. Elias was on crutches, as he had a severe cut on the foot. We had four fine horses. It was snowing, but we were accustomed to snow storms. We left our home in Meadowville and, after we passed through Lake Town, we wended our way up the canyon. A severe blizzard, with a terrifying wind, set in. We plowed our way through banks of snow. We reached the top of the mountain; night set in and we discovered we were traveling in a circle as the horses could not face the storm. We found a cabin, owned by our friend, James Kearl, and entered. Tearing up the floor, we built a fire and camped for the night.

The next day we reached one of the largest cattle and horse ranches in Bear Lake. It was located on Bear River and owned by three cow-men. We drove to the ranch barn and were tendered a hospitality we have never forgotten. A very large, rough-looking man came outside, and wondered, using a dozen oaths, if we were sane to battle with such a blizzard in weather forty degrees below zero. We told him our mother was under the cover of the sleigh. He took our wonderful mother in his powerful arms (she laughing all the time) and carried her as if she was a child into the house, and placed her gently in a chair with a "God bless you, dear mother." His crudeness, his roughness, and, above all, his generous hospitality exceeded our expectations. He prepared a special bed for mother and treated her as tenderly as if she had been a baby. If she had been an angel, he couldn't have treated her better. He was one of the roughest men I ever met, but his kindness to us and the tenderness with which he treated our mother will linger in my memory as long as I live. Other ranchers along the way were kind and big-hearted, and also took care of us in much the same way. The roads were closed and the snow was so deep that it took us four long, weary days to make that fifty-two mile trip to Evanston, where we took the train for our old home at 36 East First North at Salt Lake, where I now live.

A training of that kind kicks all fear out and you become as tough as a pine knot.

A SICK STORY

Over twenty-five years ago I was taken violently sick at 4 a. m. at my home, my wife and children being absent from home in California. I finally roused Brother Will Spence, my neighbor, who called in several friends nearby, including President George Reynolds, Judge Stewart, and Dr. Samuel Allen, our friend and family physician.

Doctor found my pulse very low, and at once decided that I should go to the L. D. S. Hospital.

An operation for appendicitis—that was the verdict. I discussed with the doctor the cost and finally reduced it from three hundred to seventy-five dollars and even then I thought it too high to just cut the skin and reach in for the appendix; it seemed to be a worthless thing at best.

My family being away at the time, my anxiety was for their welfare and, not being so keen about dying, I admit I was frightened. So I concluded that it was safest to instruct Dr. Allen to choose three of the best physicians, and the four of them, the next morning, were to hold a consultation as to the wisdom of an operation. I felt quite sure four men of any profession could not agree. I was to pay each doctor ten dollars.

In the evening of the day I found myself in the hospital. Apostle Orson F. Whitney came to see me. I said, "Orson, I desire you to bless me. I can't afford to make this great adventure at this time." Brother Whitney replied, "I came for that purpose, but had you not asked I would not have offered to bless you." His blessing was wonderful. I said to the doctor, "Give me a shot in the arm, so that I will not worry all night." I had a restless night. Towards morning the fever left and I knew the crisis had passed.

At 8 a. m., the four doctors, true to their calling, gave me a going-over and concluded that the trouble, appendicitis, had passed. They all agreed that an operation was necessary later. One year later, I had the same pain and agony on the left side. Dr. Allen came. I said, "Surely, I haven't got two appendixes." He said, "No, it's colitis."

Dr. Samuel Allen was one of my best friends, and he always regretted he had not operated on me. I am quite sure the operation would have been successful, but the shock might have finished me.

I now think of the only humorous incident in the Bible: "And Asa in the thirty and ninth year of his reign, as King, was diseased in his feet, until his disease was exceeding great; yet in his disease he sought not the Lord, but turned to the physician. And Asa slept with his fathers and died in the one and fortieth year of his reign."—*II Chron.* 16:12-13.

PRESIDENT KIMBALL'S PROPHECY

In 1929, in a certain outlying ward, they were trying to build a chapel—at least the bishop was. He was doing his best. The people were lagging behind. They had practically forsaken him. I had the contract to help them as builder. It was getting late in the season. The bishop was anxious to finish the chapel that year but was greatly discouraged. One day, I told him I would bring Brother Kimball from Salt Lake to warm the people up if he wanted me to. He responded instantly; so, at the earliest date I had him there.

A special meeting had been called and J. Golden advertised. When the hour arrived, the old meeting-house was filled to overflowing; some were sitting in the windows, others could not get in. They were a pretty rough-looking crowd, in ginghams and overalls and homespuns—good people, of course. After songs and prayer and a short speech by a local man, Brother Kimball's turn came.

"I'm glad to have the opportunity to speak to you people out here, because I believe I can speak your language. For twelve years I lived over in that Bear Lake country when men and horses were about as wild as you ever find them." He told them stories and experiences of that day and then recalled this one about Heber C. Kimball.

[109]

"Father had told us to take our best horse—a beautiful riding horse, cream in color—over to the bishop's office and turn it in for tithing. We boys demurred. 'If we do this, father—'

" 'Do as I say, boys. Take that horse over there before my heart puckers up.' "

"We obeyed."

By this time, the people were getting warmed up to the occasion and greatly interested. "Now," continued J. Golden, "I'm going to prophesy. If you people will get behind your bishop, and help him put this thing over, I'll promise you, you will never miss one cent that you put into this building. Not only that, but it will raise the standard of your community, and you will buy new furniture and furnishings for your homes. And you will get along better and enjoy life more."

The people rallied, got behind the bishop and pledged their full support both in cash and labor. Still the bishop wondered if it could be done. The date of dedication was set for December 30, less than six months away. He couldn't believe there was enough money among the members or time enough to complete the building.

The results were marvelous. Everyone pitched in. The building rose rapidly. It was finished on time—in fact, two weeks early. When it came to settling up the last of the bills, much to his amazement, the bishop found, upon careful checking at the bank, that there was eleven hundred dollars over.

The chapel was dedicated. Again the people turned out in mass. Their standards of living were already improved and Brother Kimball's prophecy was fulfilled to the letter.—*As Told by a Friend.*

Chapter XIV

TRIBUTES FROM FRIENDS

HENRY H. BLOOD
(Governor of Utah 1933—)

From my youth up, it has been my privilege to know President J. Golden Kimball. For half a century, he has been living and teaching those Christian principles of morality and religion which are so essential to our civilization. Upon these broad principles of righteous living we must order our lives as citizens and build our civic structure, if our government is to endure.

Highly endowed with honesty, originality, frankness and other winning qualities, President Kimball's teachings have been unusually effective for general uplift among the people of our commonwealth. For his long and devoted service in the ministry, I greatly admire him. For his excellent contribution to citizenship, I convey to him the thanks and appreciation of the people of our State. I esteem highly this privilege of expressing my sentiments of highest regard for him while still he lives to know them.

ANTHONY W. IVINS

Dear Golden:—

Today, you reach your eightieth milestone in the journey of life.

It has been a long and winding trail toward the land of our dreams, namely, eternal life.

I, too, have traveled over it nearly a year longer than you have. Our experiences have been somewhat similar.

The Lord has been good to me, as I feel that He has been to you.

I am writing this to tell you that you have my full confidence and esteem, and to pray that when you and I finish our mortal lives, which is not likely to be far distant, we may both be approved of the Great Judge before whom we must appear to be judged by our faith and works.

Sister Ivins charged me to tell you she is one of your friends and admirers.

Your brother,
A. W. Ivins.

RUDGER CLAWSON

I have known President J. Golden Kimball for many years. We were boys together, and for a long period we have been associated in the councils of the Church.

Our duty has brought us together in the high privilege of frequent visits to the stakes of Zion for the purpose of preaching the Gospel of the Redeemer and of giving comfort and encouragement to the Latter-day Saints. President Kimball's special calling, as one of the First Council of Seventy and now as the President of that Council, has been

[113]

to look after the interests of the seventies, which he has always done.

My intimate acquaintance with President Kimball has given me an insight into his character. I do not hesitate in saying that he is a man of great integrity, a man who loves the Gospel and has borne a faithful testimony of its truth. He has made many friends in the Church, who love to see him and hear him speak in public. His health for a number of years past has not been the best apparently, yet he has not hesitated to meet the calls and fill the appointments given him.

In conclusion, let me add that I think a great deal of President J. Golden Kimball, and can only wish that his life may be lengthened out for further usefulness and that the blessings of the Lord will ever be found in his habitation.

GEORGE ALBERT SMITH
(Telegraphed from Los Angeles)

J. Golden Kimball was my mission president in the South. I learned to love him for his courage and kindness. His sense of humor drew men to him and his testimony of divinity of the Gospel of Jesus Christ inspired them. He is held in high esteem by thousands who appreciate his humility and humanity.

DAVID O. MC KAY

As I begin to write a brief tribute to my friend and fellow worker, President J. Golden Kimball,

I fancy I can hear him say, "Speak of me as I am; nothing extenuate, nor set down aught in malice." In that wish, which however he would express in his own inimitable manner, we catch a glimpse of the real man. He seeks no undeserved honor, no unmerited praise.

President Kimball is a distinctive character, principally so because of his originality, the source of which lies in sincerity. He believes honestly. He thinks independently. Out of his keenly sensitive nature there springs a humor which reflects his ability to see things in an unusual light or at an unexpected angle.

He possesses many characteristics and virtues which distinguish him among his fellows, one of the most noble of which is his unfaltering trust in God and his unwavering loyalty to the Church. In all of my associations with him I have found him ever a congenial companion, a true and trusted friend. God bless him!

STEPHEN L. RICHARDS

For his genuine sincerity, his rugged honesty, his delightful frankness; for his broad tolerance, his kind, sympathetic nature and fine fellowship; and above all, for his deep and abiding faith in God and his loyalty and devotion to the Church and the people, I greatly love and admire J. Golden Kimball. He has the rare gift of presenting the Gospel in terms that the people understand it, and in such a unique way that they remember his teachings. For half a century he has been devoted to the work of the Master. I regard him as one of His worthy disciples and as an able advocate of truth and right-eousness. May the Lord bless and prosper President Kimball and his family.

MELVIN J. BALLARD

Many years ago, in Cache Valley, as a Ward President of one of the Mutual Improvement Associations and later as a Stake Officer, I had my first opportunity to contact Brother Kimball and to labor with him. The M. I. A. was then undertaking the great mission of enlisting all the young people. His stirring appeals to the younger generation of the Church were responsible for the enrollment of hundreds of them in that section, both boys and girls.

His great sympathy for young people, his entertaining style and method of arousing them awakened an interest in the great M. I. A. cause in northern Utah that resulted in leading hundreds of young people into the activity of that organization.

Brother Kimball was then living at Logan, in the same ward where I lived. I had the pleasure of being his block teacher for several years. I always received a kind welcome in his home and was given every encouragement to continue my labor.

His loyalty to the Church, his sincerity and his deep conviction of the truth of Mormonism have made a lasting impression on great hosts of young people in my day, many of whom are now faithful and devoted workers in the Church.

The Lord has said if one should labor all his days and succeed in bringing but one soul unto Him how great shall be the joy of that individual with that soul in the world to come. If one should succeed in bringing many souls unto Him the joy will be beyond mortal power to comprehend. Brother Kimball can rest in the assurance that he has been the instrument in the hands of God of bringing many precious souls to an awakened interest and love of the Lord's work.

RULON S. WELLS

"As a member of The First Council of the Seventy, what is your estimate of your senior President, J Golden Kimball?" Oh say! Can't you ask me something easier than that? To make an appraisal of his character, his worth, his philosophy is a prodigious undertaking. It simply can't be done. It completely defies analysis. I shall not undertake it. He says himself it requires an intelligent man to understand him. That's where I fall down. And yet I have observed some things about him.

Brother Kimball has many spiritual gifts, among which may be mentioned the gift of prophecy, the gift of healing, the gift of discernment of spirits, all of which have enabled him to render valuable service in his ministry and have won for

[117]

him many appreciative and admiring friends. Many have been raised from their beds of affliction by the power of God through his ministrations. Through the gift of prophecy—a gift inherited from his prophetic father—many have been warned of dangers, both seen and unseen. The gift of discernment of spirits which is also a wonderful gift is one which he possesses in a marked degree. It has enabled him to make wise selections of men for positions of responsibility and to look into the hearts of men—always with unfeigned sympathy—and discover inherent integrity. Even when they have been on the verge of despair and about to give up the fight he has put new courage into their hearts and inspired them with high hope and ambition to carry on the good fight of faith. Brother Kimball is not argumentative, but he discerns the truth by intuition. He does not like to argue, but he meets specious sophistry with a thunderbolt of rebuke through the gift of discernment.

His keen sense of the ludicrous has given him a wide reputation for humor; but his humor is natural, not studied. When he was once put on the program at a meeting of young people for a "humorous address" he made an utter failure of it, because he tried to prepare for it. If they had left him alone and simply asked him to talk, it would have been humorous to their hearts' content. Humor simply bubbles over in him.

In my long association with him as a member

of The First Council of the Seventy, I have learned to love and admire him. I have unbounded confidence in his integrity and devotion to the work of God, and in my most intimate relations with him I have always found him and hold him to be a true friend and brother.

LEVI EDGAR YOUNG

President J. Golden Kimball stands alone as a unique figure. Intensely human, his heart and mind hold treasures of the rarest. Money, place, fashion have no place in his wishes and hopes. He leads his own life, and his intense individualism makes him stand apart. His father had those rare traits of character that stamped his life as an honest, sincere, and an intensely faithful man to his convictions of truth. His mother set her children an example of frugality and work, and spent her life in administering to the sick, and rearing her children in the "fear of the Lord." President Kimball had few opportunities to attend school. He was a child of pioneer parentage, and the first problem of the family was to obtain food and raiment. President Kimball's boyhood was spent in a home where tallow dips were used, and where clothes were made in the "living-room." His education came through the school of experience. He read the Bible, and the divine scriptures helped to mould his character. In his boyhood, he loved the great out-of-doors, and much of his early life was spent in

[119]

herding cattle and riding the range. One day he rode his horse into a clump of quaken-aspen, and opened his heart to his Maker. Not long afterwards he was called to the Council of Seventy, in which position he has been an indefatigable worker.

President Kimball is intensely individualistic. He has always proclaimed the sovereignty of the individual, and Lincoln-like, he has deep respect for the common man. If he hurts one's feelings, he never hesitates to right the wrong. He has his defects, of course, and he frankly confesses them. He never pretends to be what he is not. A sort of permanent happiness and contentment, radiate from him. He has had a wonderfully full life, and the expression of his great wit has brought joy to many hearts.

His love for the Gospel of Jesus Christ our Lord is the most pronounced characteristic of his nature. He has ever been on the battle line for Truth. He has always traveled hopefully toward the goal, and with all his hardships and sorrows, he has enjoyed the journey of life.

I count myself happy in knowing and being associated with such a servant of God. I know him to be one of the purest of human beings. May his life be prolonged in days of richest joy and sunshine.

ELIAS S. KIMBALL

Golden was never unreasonable in his demands, always willing to do his part and to give the other fellow a chance. As square and fair a man as I have ever known. Absolutely true to his friends and genuinely loyal and devoted to the authorities of the Church. He is nervous and high tempered and has made a mighty effort all his days to master himself. No man in the world knows him as well as I do. I love him with all my heart.

FRANK Y. TAYLOR

Like a great many others I have known and admired President J. Golden Kimball for a long time. He possesses many of the characteristics of his noted father. Like him, he understands the Gospel of Christ and has abiding faith in its divinity. Like his father, also, he possesses the singular and marked ability to teach the Gospel to others. He can say things in such a way that the people generally understand and remember his teachings. I regard him as one of the outstanding missionaries of his time, one who is loved and admired by many thousands in and out of the Church, one who will be long remembered for his love of the people and his undying devotion to the work and ministry of the Master. My intimate friendship and association with Brother Kimball has been a source of joy and satisfaction to me.

B. S. HINCKLEY

There is a spontaneity and an originality about J. Golden Kimball which none but those divinely touched with genius possess. His unique personality shines in his every utterance. Packed in his sparkling wit is often the deepest wisdom. Sympathy, pathos, and humor are firmly embedded in his soul. His high voice, his deep, religious convictions, and his rare humor quickly win any audience. Days of tragedy followed by periods of triumph make up the record of his eventful life. Having read the manuscript of this book, I do not hesitate to say that Claude Richards has capitalized these characteristics and presented them in an interesting and admirable manner. I rejoice in seeing Brother Kimball honored by this account of his life and labors while he lives and am glad to know that his life's history, his sayings and his sermons are to be thus preserved for the people.

FRANKLIN S. HARRIS

Everyone who has had an opportunity of meeting J. Golden Kimball has been impressed by his unusual personality. His originality of expression, his independence in thinking, his vigor in the defense of right, his hatred of sham, his loyalty to the Church, are all so characteristic of him that no one who knows him is in doubt as to where he stands. All are aware that any presentation of his ideas on a subject will be both vigorous and interesting, even if not always conventional.

We at Brigham Young University delight in having him come to the Institution and relate his experiences in entering the school and having his ideals raised and his ambition stirred. His experience is similar to that of thousands of others, but he tells the story in a way that makes it seem unique.

J. Golden is a man who will be remembered in the affections of the people after many others have been forgotten. I am very glad that I have had the opportunity of knowing him.

JOHN HENRY EVANS

Bernard Shaw tells us, in one of those self-revealing prefaces to his plays, that an oculist pronounced him one of the rare persons with normal vision, and the great playwright characteristically applies this pronouncement to his mental and moral vision. I should like to apply both the statement and the extension to J. Golden Kimball.

President Kimball, it appears to me, sees things as they are, rather than as he would like them to be or as they ought to be. This is an extremely rare quality. And he has the ability to express what he sees just about as he sees it—another rare quality, as men go.

But the essence of this normal vision and this normal expression is the sense of humor—which keeps the world from going mad. Mark Twain and Will Rogers, who also strip things naked, have not only a sense of humor but a nose for truth. J. Golden Kimball is our Mark Twain and Will Rogers. He tells of things as he sees them, and this is what makes for humor. Others change things before they describe them. President Kimball is the most individual of any Mormon—unless it is his father.

God be praised for men who are *different!*

HUGH B. BROWN

"Happy is the man who has that in his soul which acts upon the dejected as April sunshine upon the roots of flowers . Gifts from the hand are silver and gold, but the heart gives that which neither silver nor gold can buy.

"To be full of goodness, full of cheerfulness, of helpfulness, hope and understanding, causes a man to carry blessings of which he is himself as unconscious as a lamp is of its own shining. Such a one moves on human life as stars move on dark seas to bewildered mariners."—*Henry Ward Beecher.*

J. Golden Kimball dares to be himself. His life is so simple and his words so direct that we never spend time trying to look through the surface to find the man, for there is no veneer—he is solid oak.

He is a philosopher and humorist, with a droll and scintillating way of expressing himself. He was trained in the University of Hard Knocks, and he has a vocabulary all his own. He has kept a sense of humor in the Church, and believes the "trip to heaven" should be a joyous one. Every group is made happier by his presencee, and when he leaves us the angels will greet him with a smile.

He is one of the few remaining examples of the rugged West, as honest as a cactus, as tender as a rose. Through a long life of actual contact with, and deep understanding of his fellow-man, he has achieved the educated heart, which is always set in the direction of true kindness; it functions without deliberate thought.

The young people of the Church love him because he is so human, so natural, so devoid of pretense.

No man will ever fill the unique position held by J. Golden Kimball in the hearts of the people.

LOUISE Y. ROBISON

One of the colorful figures of our community, typifying the past and present, and uniting the best traditions of both, is J. Golden Kimball.

He is of particular interest to women, as the chivalry of his nature gives him confidence in their powers, and enlists his sympathetic understanding. He believes in women! Mothers instinctively feel a trust in his counsel and advice, and an appreciation of his kindly interest in their sons and daughters, with whom he is especially influential.

His heroic struggle against physical disabilities, his determined effort to carry on, are living examples of fortitude. Though not so strong in

[125]

body, he reflects the rugged strength of faith characteristic of his illustrious father. He stands a valiant, uncompromising defender of truth. Free from intolerance or bigotry, his faith, coupled with his courageous heart, has motivated him through the years. His hatred for any form of hypocrisy, his sympathy for frailties of humanity, his desire to help the weaker, his invaluable sense of humor have greatly endeared him to the people.

RUTH MAY FOX

I deem it a real privilege to be asked to pay a short tribute to President J. Golden Kimball, one of God's noblemen. I have always admired him for his frankness, his loyalty to the Church, and his fine geniality.

In August, 1903, I had the pleasure of accompanying President Kimball through the southern settlements. We were away from home almost four weeks so that we became quite well acquainted. After leaving the railway our mode of travel was rather primitive compared with present day facilities. The authorities of one stake would send us about half way to the next stake by team where we would be met by another team to proceed on our journey. Noticing this arrangement I wondered, aloud, how we should get home. President Kimball answered in his characteristic way, "Sister Fox, don't worry, they always see that we get out."

Visiting Mutual Improvement Association

Conventions in Panguitch, Kanab, St. George and Parowan was our chief objective, at least so far as I was concerned. We held between fifty and sixty meetings. At these meetings President Kimball made a great impression upon the young people. His work among them has always been very effective. I am sure he will never be forgotten.

In one of his sermons President Kimball spoke of the prevailing custom of sending flowers to the funerals of deceased friends, and remarked that personally he would prefer that if anyone thought enough of him to buy flowers for his bier, he would rather have them while he was living. So as we rode along in the wagon while President Kimball was talking to the driver, I composed the following lines:

NOT WHEN I'M DEAD

If you have kindly words for me, O give them to me
    now,
While the tempest raves about me and the storm
    beats on my brow;
               Not when I'm dead.
If you your sweetest songs would sing about my
    silent bier,
'Tis now I need your tender strains my drooping
    heart to cheer;
               Not when I'm dead.
If lovely flowers you would strew upon my lowly
    bed,

[127]

I need their dainty fragrance now to soothe my
aching head;
        Not when I'm dead.
And yet there is one little thing which I shall dearly
prize,
Far more than any solemn pomp that mortals can
devise
        When I am dead.
'Tis this that one of Zion's sons for whom I've labored here,
Whose feet I may have guided right shall drop one
grateful tear
        When I am dead.
For this I consecrate my all, gladly my life lay
down,
That by the grace of God that tear may glitter in
my crown,
        When I am dead.

MAY ANDERSON

I recall attending a conference-convention at
one time in the Young and San Luis Stakes. Brother
J. Golden Kimball was also assigned but was unable
to make the strenuous trip. Word had reached the
various communities in Colorado that Brother Kimball was coming and the people turned out en
masse. Such disappointment as was registered when
they found he was not there was one of the greatest
tributes that I have ever seen paid to anyone.

The people love J. Golden Kimball. To them

he is pure gold. They love to be near him and shake his hand. They love his integrity, his rugged humor, the testimony he bears. There is only one J. Golden Kimball and wherever he goes a common prayer is echoed in the hearts of his multitude of friends: "God bless that man."

A TRIBUTE IN OIL

In honor of President J. Golden Kimball's eightieth birthday, a group of his relatives and friends presented him with an oil painting of himself. The portrait, life-size and three-quarter length, was painted by Gordon Cope. From the *Salt Lake Tribune,* we quote these lines of comment:

"The portrait is declared to be a striking image of the noted churchman who is known and admired throughout the West as a wit and philosopher. The artist is Gordon Cope, formerly of Salt Lake City, who came here from Denver especially for this work. Viewing the portrait sometime after his last sitting, Mr. Kimball is reported to have made the following characteristic remark: 'I didn't think it possible to do so much with such raw material.' "

The idea of making the portrait originated with his son, Max Kimball, and his nephew, Ranch S. Kimball. A committee was appointed, consisting of Benjamin L. Rich, Jessie R. S. Budge, and Ranch S. Kimball to contact President Kimball's many friends and accept contributions from them. The painting now hangs in President Kimball's home and is cherished by him and his family as a tribute of esteem and affection.

SHIRLEY PENROSE JONES

[On his eightieth birthday, June 9, 1933, under the leadership of Benjamin L. Rich, a group of business and professional men at Salt Lake City, admirers of J. Golden Kimball, complimented him with a dinner at the Hotel Utah. Indicative of his popularity, it is related that sixty men were invited to this function and eighty-two came. Following is one of the principal toasts.—*Author's note.*]

Occasionally a community produces a man of such lovable and genuine characteristics as to arouse in the hearts of all a possessive pride, as though each person in that community acquired an individual distinction by the very fact of that man's existence. He becomes a community asset, to be quoted on occasion when a final word is needed to end an argument, to be exemplified when in doubt of a course to follow, and to be extolled to the stranger as an example of local excellence. Such a community is ours, and such a man is our guest today. In honoring him we do honor to ourselves. Words are poor vehicles to convey our sentiments. Much more eloquent is the presence of this group on this, his natal day. Men have assembled from the various walks of life, with no thought of creed or other affiliation, to bear testimony by their presence to our belief that Brother J. Golden Kimball is in fact and deed our brother.

As we all know, he was born in this city eighty years ago, in 1853, six years after the advent of the pioneers. He has seen our city grow from a frontier village of muddy streets and insignificant buildings to a modern metropolis, with conveniences and comforts as existed only in the courageous vision of such men as he. He has lived our history. The struggles to subdue the desert and tame it to the will of man are struggles of which he was and is a leading actor. When we travel our magnificent roads through valleys and mountains of unsurpassed beauty and grandeur, we see only the results of a dread. But those same journeys, to our guest, must bring pictures of days that tried the souls of men, of people who were ruled by faith, so that heartaches never became despair, and clouds never obscured the sun of that day. Thank God for the life and example of men like J. Golden Kimball.

At the early age of twenty-two he moved with his mother, then a widow, and her other children into Rich County, and in that cold outpost set to work to further extend the settlement of this community. In his youth and young manhood he was, first, a teamster, next, a rancher and cattle-raiser, then, a merchant; and finally, he was called to the pursuits that are his heritage by birth and character —a guide and teacher in the enrichment of life. He performed valiant service as a missionary for his church through years when his body was racked with fever, which could not daunt his spirit. He was called to the First Council of Seventy forty-one years ago, in 1892. For more than half a century his life has been devoted to the service of his fellow men, without thought of gain or profit to himself, except the joy that comes from bringing happiness into the lives of others. His name is a household word throughout this entire mountain region. His words of comfort and advice have been, and are, guideposts in the lives of thousands of our people. Many of us in this very room have frequently ordered our actions in compliance with his counsel.

Brother Golden, as we affectionately know him, is a true product of the West, with a humor as dry as our desert sands but as refreshing as our canyon breezes, with a philosophy as beautiful as our twilights and as brilliant as our noon-day sun. He has endeared himself to us for the high quality of his mind, his patience, and straightforwardness. But above all he is a true and loyal friend.

CHAPTER XV

J. GOLDEN KIMBALL'S OWN FUNERAL SERMON

Sentiments from J. G. Kimball, Sen., written down with a desire that they be read at the time of his funeral services.

I am indeed proud in saying, I am a soldier of the Cross, a special witness for the Lord, being clothed upon with the spirit of my appointment and having the desire and being prepared to go to the front—when called—and be one of the soldiers on the firing lines.

I say this with that kind of gladness and gratitude which admits of little pride. I say it because it has been said to me and expressed to me in silent pressures of the hand and uttered to me by eyes full of interest and pleasure.

To say that all this makes me happy would not be to say all that I feel. I account it an honor in occupying a place in the hearts of the people, of being welcome in God's name into the affectionate confidence of the Latter-day Saints, and of my friends who are not of the Church. I believe this to be the greatest honor to be worked for and won under the stars. Were I permitted to live, I would desire to continue to perpetuate this communion with my God, my Redeemer, my people.

[133]

To do this successfully, I know I must draw directly upon the world's experience and upon the results of my own individual thinking, acting, living. I know that no truth can be fully understood and appreciated by a soul that has not learned it in some way through the things he has suffered.

The world cares little for theorists and theories. I come to the matured age of fifty-eight as a pilgrim with shoes worn and dusty with the walk on life's highway, with a body too small for my spirit.

These feelings were not conceived in my mind, but they spring from the mixing and associating with the people. I now give to the people their own, and my soul cries out, "God save the people, not any one man, but the people." I have given to them all I have received—that which was in me came out of me; freely I received, freely I gave.

May my God in His great justice and mercy forgive me my many mistakes, blunders and foolishness, together with my "twadling nonsense," and grant me pardon when all my transgressions are paid to the "uttermost farthing" and I am forgiven. He will then take me into a glory and kingdom suited to a humble, penitent sinner.

I feel sometimes like the little freckle-faced, red-headed boy who was asked by his teacher, in Sunday School, to tell how thankful he was to the Lord: "Teacher, I don't know what to be thankful for; God purty nigh ruined me."

I was chosen and sustained as worthy of being one of the general authorities of the Church, a member of the First Council of the Seventy. This has come to me, not through any of my seeking, but no doubt to do honor to our illustrious father and to perpetuate his memory amongst the people. Even though I may not have been called by direct revelation, I am sure I was chosen by the Lord's servants, who hold divine authority, and I have been sustained by the people in conference assembled.

At a semi-annual conference of the Church held in April, 1892, I was set apart to this most humble calling by Apostle Francis M. Lyman. I have done fairly well and in a weak way have tried to be a faithful, loyal soldier; and while I am a very poor follower, yet to date I have not been an insurgent, but a progressive.

As to my patriotism, it calls to my mind a story. "During Sherman's famous march to the sea, General Longstreet saw just before him on the road—screened by a bush—a poor abject-looking mortal, engaged in a soliloquy. 'Here I am a poor miserable beggar. My shoes are gone, my clothes are almost gone; I'm hungry, I'm weary. My family have been killed or scattered and may be now wandering helpless and unprotected in a strange country. I love my country. Yes, I would—I would die—yes I would die willingly, if it were necessary, because I love my country. But if this

war is ever over, I'll be d_____ if I ever love another country.' "

I feel just such patriotism for my church and
my people. I, too, have suffered much for my religion and I love my church. I, too, would die—
willingly if necessary—but if this fight is ever over,
I do not hanker for any more battles.

Believing I am a soldier, I ask as an evidence
of the gratitude of my comrades and people to be
buried like a soldier.

1. My fellow comrades are to preside and ar-
range the services.

2. Martial music.

3. Violin solos of the inspiring kind, with
quartettes and songs that are befitting the occasion.

4. Short prayers.

5. Brief addresses, remembering always that
these services are for me and no one else.

6. No person to speak who did not love and
understand the deceased.

7. The subjects uppermost in the minds of the
speakers must be:

    a. What was his character and what
was his general influence, taken as a whole,
through the course of years among his people?

    b. Did he have any special attraction for
the narrow and intolerant?

    c. Was he tolerant, charitable, intelli-
gent, unselfish, and self-sacrificing?

[136]

d. Was the Golden Rule his great morality and his practical guide?

e. Did he believe that justice means a free and equal chance of life's happiness to all, and that there can be no rest this side of justice?

ANSWER: Yes, I believe in all this and have endeavored to train myself along these broad and generous lines. My failure in not reaching my goal has been due to my weakness and not to the fact that I did not believe it.

I believe this great goal is to be won through the grace of God and by the influence of His Holy Spirit, by the morality of toleration, freedom of thought, brotherly love, and charity to all men—not the charity of alms-giving, but that charity which is forgiveness and love.

My closing testimony is that I have unfaltering faith in God the Father, and in His Son, Jesus Christ, my Redeemer, and in the Holy Ghost.

I am conscious and as far as I know anything, I know Joseph Smith was, and is, a Prophet of God and that this is the Church of Jesus Christ. And, please God, every step of my way shall be on high firm ground and in the open. I know not how else to fight.

My love, confidence and affection for my family cannot be questioned. They have been true, kind, and generous, and my impatience has made it somewhat difficult for them at times. But with it all, I love them to exceed all else, excepting my God and my Master.

The above statement and sentiment must not be taken as an indication of insanity or premonition. My fad is to preach my own discourse, and then it will be satisfactory to the one most concerned.

J. G. KIMBALL.

March 8, 1912.

Tabernacle Talks

Abridged by Claude Richards and Approved by
J. Golden Kimball

INTRODUCTORY

There was so much lively, interesting, and worthy material in the Talks that the task of reducing them to their present proportions became an arduous one. In justice to the speaker, be it said that many excellent passages were left out, in order to tempt the average reader, who, in the midst of a busy life, we assume, is neither overburdened with time nor has the inclination to read large books.

A few talks have been eliminated—not many. The average talk has been cut about one-half. Because of so many eliminations it has been impossible in all cases to preserve a smooth reading of the text. When the reader encounters abrupt places, we trust he will overlook them. While some of these are the result of abridgment, others come from the characteristic disposition of the speaker to turn suddenly from one topic to another. His moving-picture mind explains this.

To remove ambiguities and make the meaning clear, it has been necessary to do considerable editing. While attention has been paid to grammar yet the greater effort has been to preserve the style and individuality of the speaker. Wherever there has been a conflict between grammatical construction and style, the latter has usually been given the right of way. To preserve the integrity of the individual talks it has been found necessary, occasionally, to repeat some of the speaker's ideas and utterances.

These talks reflect the major effort and thought of a whole lifetime of an interesting, intelligent and gifted man, a man possessing a spiritual yet practical and humorous turn of mind, a man of keen observation and extensive and varied experience covering our day and the pioneer period preceding it, a man who has spent his strength diligently for half a century in the service of the Master, for the good of the people.

Therefore, let us not pass too hurriedly over the things he has to say. His excellent teachings, enlivened by his native sense of humor and originality, surely are worthy of one or more thoughtful readings. In this day of mistaken values, chaos and temptation, may we not welcome the friendly teachings and counsel of inspired spiritual men like J. Golden Kimball?

TALK ONE

October, 1897

BLESSING OF REAL COMFORT

I feel very humble, my brethren and sisters. I have discovered in my short career that I don't amount to very much, that all that I have tried to do within myself I have failed in. The only blessing of real comfort that I have received is in laboring in the ministry. Some men are more easily tied than others, and, as far as I am concerned, I desire to be free in what I say, and I hope that I may be moved upon by the Holy Ghost. For I can testify to the children of men that I know what the Holy Ghost is, that is, I know what its influence is. I know that I have felt that joy, that peace, that satisfaction, that burning within me that comes from the influence of the Spirit of the Lord.

HOME MISSIONARY WORK

I have labored for the past six weeks in company with Apostle Lyman through the southern part of the state, largely in the interests of the Young Men's Mutual Improvement Associations, and I discover in associating among the people that there is a great missionary work to be performed here at home. There are something over twenty-five thousand young men, from fourteen up to my age, and only a very small percentage of that number are laboring earnestly and ardently to gain information and knowledge pertaining to this great work. Talk about your missionary fields of labor, talk about the nations of the earth; I comprehend that the angel came with its message that the Gospel is to be preached to every nation, to every kindred, to every tongue and people; but I want to testify to you, my brethren and sisters, that the rising generation at home are being neglected. They are not being reached by the Priesthood of God; and if there is any place on the great earth where there needs an awakening and an uplifting, it is right here in Zion. And, I want to say to you, the fathers and the mothers are helpless, and they know not what to do.

I know the cause, too, and the sin will rest upon the parents. They have not followed this counsel, to instruct their children when they are young. President George Q. Cannon said we were in bondage, to a certain extent, because we had not followed counsel, and I want to testify that it is true. And I want to say there is a great sin resting upon some of the fathers and mothers, because they have not taught their children faith, repentance, baptism, and the reception of the Holy Ghost when they were eight years old. And they are now reaping the sorrow of their neglect. We need missionaries. I take the position that we need one hundred to start out with, to commence this mission here at home; and I don't know, before they get through with it, but they will have to preach on the street corners like the elders do in the states and in Europe.

WE MUST STUDY

In associating among the people, we discovered, and I want to testify to what one of the brethren spoke in reference to that matter, that our people are not a reading people. They do not diligently read the Bible, the *Book of Mormon,* and the *Book of Doctrine and Covenants.* We have, however, been sustained by the people of the South, and in the Stakes of St. George, Kanab, Panguitch, and Parowan; we have met with a very kindly reception, and I believe there has been a reawakening.

We believe that men who are aged should study just as much as young men. I want to ask the Latter-day Saints if that is a true doctrine, that when a man gets old he should quit learning and stop studying, and cease to progress? I want to read you what the Lord has said in this line, speaking to Oliver Cowdery: "Behold, you have not understood. You have supposed that I would give it unto you when you took no thought save it was to ask." Have you misunderstood, my brethren and sisters? Have you fancied that all you have to do is to "ask and you shall receive, knock and it shall be opened unto you, and if you lack wisdom,

[145]

ask of God who giveth to all men liberally and up-
braideth not," and that you can sit down and make
no other effort? As one of the brethren expressed
it: "I fancy that the minds of some of the people
are chloroformed." And we have imagined that
we would be saved in our ignorance, and when the
Lord has said, "Whatever intelligence you attain
unto in this life will rise with you in the resurrection."

Now, He taught this lesson to Oliver Cowdery: "But, behold, I say unto you, that you must
study it out in your mind. Then, you must ask
me if it be right; and if it is right, I will cause that
your bosom shall burn within you; therefore you
shall feel that it is right."

Now these are the last days spoken of by the
prophets; these are the "perilous times." And I
want to say to you that mountains of obstructions
will be placed before this people, and if you have
not been tried, you will be; if you have not been
tested, you will be, before you gain eternal life.
And before we pass our opinion unwisely, as we do,
it is well for us to "study it out in our minds."

I am fearful that some of the Latter-day
Saints simply come to the leaders and listen to the
servants of God, and they never study; they never
go to the written word, and compare it with the
servants of God in their doctrines and teachings,
and consequently they are unable to judge right-
eously, and they are losing confidence. Their con-

fidence is being shaken, because they are unable to judge, because they have not first studied it out in their minds . . . because, as a people, we are mentally lazy. I will say that because I do not expect to preach here again for a long time.

A WONDERFUL PEOPLE

But I pray the Lord to bless this people. Why, you are, nevertheless, a wonderful people. The Lord has blessed you as He has blessed no other people. He has given you the Holy Ghost. Remember how particular He was with His apostles, with His servants that He sent out to preach the Gospel. He promised them the Holy Ghost, "whom the world cannot receive," and we are in a different situation from what the world is. As Paul says: "What! know ye not that ye are the temples of the Holy Ghost, and that ye are not your own; and if any man defile the temple of God, him shall God destroy, for the temple of God is holy, which temple ye are."

THE SECOND GREATEST SIN

Now I want to say to you people, in soberness, and with consideration—I don't want to be an alarmist, I don't want to be a revivalist; but I want to say to you, the great sin that is creeping in among this people, together with other worldly sins, is the sin of adultery. This is creeping in amongst us, and we, seemingly, cannot help ourselves. But I

[147]

want to say to you, there needs be an awakening. I want to tell you there needs to be a fear planted in the hearts of the young people. Take the *Book of Mormon.* Read what Alma said to his son Corianton, who had left the ministry, and had followed after the harlot, Isabel. He told him what a terrible crime adultery was, that it was *next to the shedding of innocent blood.* O, I am fearful that our young people do not comprehend that great sin that is creeping in amongst us; and, as the Prophet Joseph said, a man that commits adultery, and repents not according to God's word, cannot enter into the celestial kingdom of God. If he enters any kingdom, it will not be the celestial kingdom. I pray that our people may be moved upon to be a virtuous, to be an honest, to be a faithful people; this is the prayer of my heart, in the name of Jesus. Amen.

TALK TWO

April, 1898

FINANCES AND FAITH

I have the idea, but it is not yet clothed. But I pray the Lord that He may move upon me, through your faith and prayers, to explain my views upon a certain subject. I am very much interested myself in the financial welfare of this people, because I realize from my own experience that when men are in financial difficulties, and their honesty is in question, and they are unable to fulfill their agreements, it is very difficult for honest men who are sensitive to the reproach of the children of men, to feel joyous and happy, and to appreciate the blessings with which they are surrounded. I want to say to you that the sun does not shine brightly to such men, the grass is not green, and sometimes, I fancy, they hardly feel that water runs down hill. It is a most terrible condition to be in.

EMPLOYMENT A BLESSING

One of the great difficulties that menace this people is lack of employment. I know how some of us worship gold and silver, but I tell you that is not so great a problem among this people as em-

ployment. I am not in much doubt that the time
will be in these United States when the people will
worship work more than they do money. And it
is one of the demands that I make upon this people,
that they see to it that the people of this Church
are employed. If you have large farms, and you
are poor and poverty stricken with so much land,
see to it that the people are given employment.
Then the people must see to it that they are willing
to take the produce of the country as pay for their
labor, and not ask the farmer to give them gold and
silver, which it is very difficult for him to get.

I tell my brethren, "when you have not employment for me, say the word, and I will take my
family by the hand, and I will again be a pioneer in
the land." We have hundreds of brilliant young
men, also, men with experience; but they are hanging around these streets and starving to death. Do
you know what is the matter with us: There is a
great deal of pride connected with it. It is not a
difficult thing to live in a log hut if you have never
had anything better, but it is a difficult thing to
drop to a log house when you have been living in a
castle. But our pride has got to be humbled. There
are a great many of us that ought to be sent out.
Talk about missionary work; they ought to call
out of this city five hundred and send them on missions to colonize and build up the tens of thousands
of acres that are in this great State of Utah. If the
State of Utah is not good enough for you, go to

Canada. That is a wonderful country, and you can get rich and prosper if you keep the commandments of the Lord. Then you can come back to Salt Lake City, and put on all the style you want to, if you pay for it.

ALL NOT WELL IN ZION

"And Zion cannot be built up unless it is by the principles of the laws of the celestial kingdom; otherwise I cannot receive her unto myself."

"And my people must needs be chastened until they learn obedience, if it must needs be by the things which they suffer."

Now, Zion will be redeemed, and I want to say to you, my brethren and sisters, that all is not well in Zion. But if you wish to be popular you want to say that all is well in Zion. The Lord requires it at the hands of this people that they pay their tithes and their offerings, and that they see to it that they impart of the abundance which the Lord has given, to those that need work, and give them employment.

WORK FOR ZION

Now I want to prophesy, as the son of a prophet, that if this people want to be blessed they must labor for Zion; for if you labor for money you shall perish. You are under covenant, and it is a demand that God makes of the people that they redeem Zion. You have got to be generous, and you have got to place all that you have and are upon

[151]

the altar and learn to live the law of the celestial kingdom.

"But," says one to me, "you would not preach that way four years ago when you had something." Well, if you have got to learn to preach the way I am doing, you will learn it just the way I learned it. You will pay for it. The Lord will take from you what you have, if you don't humble yourselves, and He will chasten you. You will be called upon to place all that you have and are upon the altar. And, if you do not have your feet right and know that this is the Church of Jesus Christ of Latter-day Saints, when you are asked to give up your means, you will flounder and lose the faith. But if you have not got anything you will be just as Peter was. I am in the same fix; if I leave this Church, where in heaven will I go? That is the way I feel.

BLESSINGS OR JUDGMENTS?

I feel to bless the people. I feel that you are being blessed and that you will continue to be blessed as long as you keep the commandments of God. When you cease keeping the commandments of God, then the judgments of God will commence at the house of the Lord, and I pray that that may be averted. I pray that we may not pass through the experience that the people had in Kirtland because they transgressed the laws of God. May the Lord bless you. Amen.

[152]

TALK THREE

April, 1899

WONDERFUL PROMISES

Our people should follow the instructions that have been given them and keep out of debt. I call to mind a saying of the Lord: "I am bound when ye do what I say, but when ye do not what I say, then ye have no promise." He says to the young people: "He that seeketh me early shall find me, and he shall not be forsaken." The Lord has made great and wonderful promises to His people.

SHAKING HANDS

I desire to call your attention to an incident that occurred when I was laboring in the Southern States, in 1884. I went there in 1883. The year 1884 was the time of a sad experience in that mission. It was then that some of our elders lost their lives by mob violence. It seemed that there was bitterness on all hands. We had but few friends. I was at the office in Chattanooga under Elder Roberts at the time. I picked up a *Chattanooga Times* one morning, and I was very much delighted to see in print these words, speaking of Elder John Morgan. It said, "To shake his hand was to be his friend." I have never forgotten it. When you shook John Morgan's hand and he looked into your

[153]

face, you always knew that you were his friend. John Morgan understood that principle.

Some of our people are becoming careless in the shaking of hands. I have shaken hands with some men, when I would just as soon have put my hands into a bucket of ice water as to shake hands with them. They may have been friendly, but had no means of showing their feelings. Great sermons have been preached in this Church by the simple shaking of hands; and you who have been in holy places, you who have been in the holy temple, know what it means to shake hands.

I witnessed a play in the theater at Los Angeles, and was very much taken up with it—*Julius Caesar*—and when I saw the mimic representatives of great Romans walk up and shake hands, I presumed every one in that large theater was impressed with the idea that it meant friendship.

But we have been too much carried away with temporal matters. When our elders come home—we have probably eight hundred who return every year—they ask me what is the matter with the people. They discover it whenever they shake hands with you. When you meet the elders that come home and shake hands with them, they will hardly let go of your hand, they are so friendly, and you can feel it in your hearts that they love you. They do it from the bottom of their hearts. You who have lost children know when a person comes up to you and sympathizes with you on account of

[154]

your loss, taking you by the hand and looking you in the face, notwithstanding he may not utter a word, you feel that friendship, that sympathy that pierces to the innermost recesses of your hearts. If one who has passed through the terrible experience of losing his wife comes to sympathize with another man who has lost his wife, in shaking hands both experience a feeling of friendship and sympathy that cannot be expressed in words.

SYMPATHY AND LOVE

Brethren and sisters, we can afford to be sympathetic; we can afford of all people on the earth to be filled with sympathy and compassion. I am not concerned very much about what other religionists do. I am not concerned about the Christian Scientists; I have little to say against them. If they do any good that is their business, but no church or lodge can find a more successful way of making inroads among our people than by getting them to extend the hand of sympathy, love, and affection in their trials and tribulations. We who hold the priesthood—elders, seventies, teachers, and deacons—ought to perform our duties. Our hearts are not always as they should be; we do not always exhibit the sympathy, love, and affection that we ought. I am sorry to say that some of my acquaintances, some who are near and dear to me, have been won from our Church through love and sympathy.

[155]

J. GOLDEN KIMBALL

STOP AND SHAKE HANDS

My brethren and sisters, I have this to say in conclusion: Even if you are in a hurry, stop and shake hands before going on, but do it right; have the spirit of God within you, and when you greet them say, "God bless you."

I know a good old sister who is working for her living. She would not let the Church support her; she is too proud. She is over seventy years old. She said to me that when an apostle took her by the hand and said, "God bless you," it was worth more to her than all the money they could give her.

I remember Apostle Erastus Snow, and I will never forget him as long as I live on the earth. He stopped long enough to take me by the hand as a boy, after my father was dead, and said, "God bless you." There are others that have done so, and they stand foremost in my mind, and I remember and esteem every one of them. We should learn to love and honor each other. We should have the spirit of God burning within our hearts. You can make more converts in this way than any other. God bless you. Amen.

TALK FOUR
April, 1901

I thank God, the Eternal Father, that we have young men, honored of the Lord, that can preach and testify just as well as apostles and prophets. I desire to say to the rising generation, you do not have to be apostles, you do not have to be presidents of stakes, nor bishops to enjoy the gifts and blessings pertaining to the Gospel of the Lord, Jesus Christ. And I say to you that some of you—and I may be among that number—place too much stress upon the positions that men hold in the Church. And we fancy in our weakness that we cannot be saved, that we cannot serve God, that we cannot be faithful and true and enjoy revelation from God unless we have high office in the Church. There is danger in exalted position, and where "much is given much is required." The poorest man in all Israel, though he may carry a hod and be dressed like a pauper, is entitled to revelation from God, and he is entitled to lay hands on the sick and have them recover through the power of prayer and faith.

COURAGEOUS MISSIONARIES

Judgment comes with age, as a rule—not always. We young men that have responsibilities

[157]

placed upon us oftentimes have a great deal of courage, but may lack judgment. The point I want to get at is this: we must have some very brave and courageous men. Apostle Grant, with the assistants that will go with him, may open up a mission in Japan. Some apostle may be sent to Russia to open the door in that great nation, and it may be the privilege of some of us to go and get killed after the doors are opened. The Gospel will never be preached to every nation, kindred, tongue and people without lives being lost, nor without your eating "the bread of adversity" and drinking the "water of affliction." And we may not all be successful, but when a man is willing to lay down his life, and takes his life in his hands and labors for the Kingdom of God, he can do no more. And I tell you that great good will come out of it. I admire courage and bravery as well as judgment and wisdom. We have to have brave men and courageous men, and we young men have to learn, and the only way we can learn is by trying, like Brother Grant. My heart swelled within me when I heard him sing today.

FORGIVE MISTAKES

As long as a man has a righteous object he has a right to make an effort, and if he makes any mistakes, it is my duty to reach out to him my hand, even the hand of charity. And if you Latter-day Saints do not do it, and some of us young men fail because of your severe criticisms and your unkind statements, God will hold you responsible.

MYSTERIES VS. IGNORANCE

We have seen men handled because they waded into mysteries, and, of course, it was proper and right when they waded into mysteries and preached false doctrines that they should be handled. I can see the righteousness of it, but I wonder if any man has ever been handled in the kingdom of God for not knowing anything and for never trying to learn and to do things. I am in favor of some of them being handled right away. I pray the Lord to bless you. Amen.

TALK FIVE
October, 1901

FAITHLESS YOUTHS

I realize that there is a very great work for us to perform, not only among the nations of the earth preaching the gospel to every kindred, tongue, and people, but also among the young people of this Church. Only the other day, as I was walking down the street, I came to an old gentleman, who was tottering towards the grave, and, after I had shaken hands with him, he said, "Brother Kimball, I wish you would send a missionary to my home; I have three sons and several daughters that need to be labored with."

A day or two after that, an aged gentleman came and introduced himself to me, and said he was a member of the Church of Jesus Christ. He paid his tithing, he said, and tried to do his duty. He had four sons and several daughters, and I believe that he said there was not one of them that had very much faith in the Church, and he wanted me to explain to him why it was. I rather evaded answering him, as I was not acquainted with him, with his environment, or with his home circle.

In associating with the young people I discover that this is not general; but there are many of our young people, who, for some reason, are bewildered and dazzled with the things of the world that are being introduced so rapidly among us. I can see only one course of safety for the young people of this Church, and that is to teach them until they have an abiding faith in God the Father, in His Son, Jesus Christ, and in the Holy Ghost.

MISSIONS BUILD FAITH

After this brother talked to me, I thought of your sons that are sent out to preach the Gospel. Some of them mere beardless boys, and yet when the call comes for them to go to the nations of the earth, father or mother may have had some doubts, but they were soon removed, and the boys came to the city, were set apart and received a blessing. The stenographer took the blessing and sent it to their home address. They received perhaps twenty minutes' instruction and were then sent forth to the world. I have seen a few of such boys go to Australia lately, and if my memory serves me, there have been over five hundred of your sons ordained seventies since the last October conference. We do not fear nor tremble for these boys. We tell them to be careful about some things. We advise them to see everything that is good in the world and try to understand it, but to avoid wine and women as they would the gates of hell. It is very seldom that any of them fall by the wayside. Only once in a great while do we hear of an elder going astray. I am more familiar with the Southern

[161]

States Mission than any other, and though hundreds and hundreds of the elders have labored in the South, very few have fallen that I know of.

Why can't we get our young people to have that same spirit at home? Even though the things of the world are introduced among us, why is it that we cannot stand on the same ground that our elders do in the nations of the earth? If we have faith and the Spirit of the Lord, the things of the world do not dazzle or tempt us.

PRIESTHOOD FIRST

I pray the Lord to bless you, that you may go to your homes and breathe the spirit of this conference into the hearts of the children of men with whom you associate, that there may be an awakening among the Priesthood of God. I desire to say to this great congregation that the Lord never intended His organized priesthood to fall in behind the auxiliary organizations of the Church. There should be a greater effort on the part of those who look after the priesthood quorums to see that they stand foremost and ahead of all the auxiliary organizations of the Church. I comprehend the great work that is being done by the Sunday School, by the Improvement Association, and by other associations, and I regret that it has to be said that some of our priesthood quorums are not doing their duty.

May the Lord bless you. Amen.

TALK SIX

April, 1902

THE LORD QUALIFIES HIS SERVANTS

I feel, my brethren and sisters, that life is too short and our time is too brief to be spent in making apologies or excuses, or for expressing myself as being surprised at almost anything that happens pertaining to our calling in the holy Melchizedek Priesthood, for we never know where lightning will strike.

We are not acquainted with those that will be released, or with those that will be sent to the nations of the earth, but we believe that the inspiration comes from God. I do know and testify that when a man is appointed to fill a place, notwithstanding the fact that he may not have all the qualifications, nor be endowed so richly as some other man may be, and the people may be surprised at the appointment, yet the Lord is able to qualify him. It is marvelous in my sight how men that are called by divine authority increase in wisdom and knowledge, how they progress, and how well they fill their positions when they have the spirit of their office and calling.

TURNING THE OTHER CHEEK

It takes a great deal of wisdom and courage to go among the children of men and have the finger of scorn pointed at you and be as unpopular as a Mormon elder is. Educated as we are, and breathing this mountain air for twenty years, it takes a little training before you can turn the other cheek and treat those kindly who spitefully use you. It takes a little education to learn how precious are the souls of the children of men in the sight of God. So we need some older men to put their hands on us younger boys and hold us down. We are a good deal like Peter. I was that way. I would have cut more than one of their ears off, if there had been someone to stick them on again. That is the spirit of young men at first, but after awhile they moderate.

You will be surprised how I will moderate in the next ten years, I will be as mild as a summer's morn, because I will commence then to look for death. But I expect to live a number of years yet, and I hope the fire won't entirely burn out of me. I had one of the apostles tell me, "Brother Kimball, if you don't quit making so much noise, you will burn out." "Well," said I, "I want to burn out, and give room for somebody else, as I believe some men live too long."

ROCK OF SALVATION

I desire to call your attention to a revelation, and I have tried to understand the part which I shall read:

[164]

Remember the worth of souls is great in the sight of God;

For, behold, the Lord your Redeemer suffered death in the flesh; wherefore He suffered the pain of all men, that all men might repent and come unto Him.

And He hath risen again from the dead, that He might bring all men unto Him, on conditions of repentance.

And how great is His joy in the soul that repenteth.

Wherefore you are called to cry repentance unto this people;

And if it be so that you should labor all your days in crying repentance unto this people, and bring save it be one soul unto me, how great shall be your joy with Him in the kingdom of my Father?

And now, if your joy will be great with one soul that you have brought unto me into the kingdom of my Father, how great will be your joy if you should bring many souls unto me?

Behold, you have My Gospel before you, and My rock, and My salvation.

I believe with you, my brethren and sisters who have a testimony, that your feet are planted upon the rock of salvation, and that you know that Jesus is the Christ. I believe that you will be saved in the Kingdom of our Father. I believe that a greater part of you will be true, will be steadfast, will be firm, immovable, and unshaken. You are not dazzled nor bewildered by these allurements that are finding their way among this people. You have got past that. You no longer have on your shoulders young heads; you no longer care for society, worldly society; you no longer hunger after the things of the world. You have been able to stamp under your feet these appetites and these weaknesses that young men have not yet overcome. When you came into the world, men were not so bewildered with the things of the world. These things have come with luxury and riches.

SONS AND DAUGHTERS

Now, after having referred to you older brethren, how you are fortified and fastened, how faithful you are to keep the commandments of the Lord and pay your tithing; what about your sons and daughters? Are they converted? Are they fastened? Can you handle them? We are doing a great missionary work at home. In every stake of Zion home missionaries are sent out among the people to preach; and we preach, and we preach, and we preach, and we preach most eloquently. But, these boys are not there. Possibly not twenty percent of them are at your meetings when the home missionaries talk. Of course, there are some exceptions. Now, what are you doing about them?

We preach daytimes, and I believe ardently that we sleep too much nights. I remember Brother Lyman saying, "Young man, how old are you?" "I am over forty." He said, "I thought so, because you commence to hunt for an easy chair even now." At forty we commence to hunt for an easy chair, and so when night approaches, it seems that we parents all go to bed, that we may rest. I rather believe the idea that if the presidents of stakes and bishops of wards would appoint missionaries to walk the streets at night, there would be a marvelous work done in Zion. The devil does not do his dirty work in the daytime, when the sun shines, but he is getting so he does some here under the blazing electric light.

Are we going to watch our children? I remember being in a far-off settlement not long ago, where they see few, if any, of the leading brethren, and yet they number over twelve hundred. They have a great many young people, and when I retired to my bed after the meeting I was kept awake all night long by the boys and girls running the streets of that settlement. I got up towards morning, looked at my watch, and it was then four a. m., and they were still roaming the streets. While it may have been harmless and they may have been pure in their intentions, I tell you, in the name of Israel's God, it is one of the criminal things that are going on in this land. The devil is breathing in the hearts of our young people, and the very air is stagnated in some of our larger cities with the spirit of immorality. No greater sin can find its way in the hearts of our young people.

I tell you, it is your duty and it is my duty to go out as missionaries; not to preach these things from the pulpit, not to talk to our sons and daughters publicly, but privately, and point out to them, in a proper way, the great and abominable evil of secret sin. Some of you in your far-off dis-

[167]

tricts are not burdened with what we call civilization and the things of the world; but you are
menaced, and the greatest danger that menaces you
today is immorality and secret sin.

MISSIONARY COURTSHIPS

You know how we guard our missionaries.
The elders yesterday pled with a number of missionaries till tears came to my eyes. "Don't allow
any woman to take your honor. Don't allow any
woman to take your arm. Keep them at arm's
length. And as you expect to honorably fulfil
your mission and have the Spirit of God burning
in your hearts, see to it that there are no courtships,
that there are no arrangements made of any kind
to enter into matrimony; but come home clean and
pure and sweet before the Lord." As one missionary said, when he returned home from his first mission, he was about to step over his mother's thresh-
hold and his mother said, "Hold on, my son, have
you come back to me as pure and as good as when
you left?" He was able to say, "Yes, mother, I am
pure; I am clean before the Lord;" and she threw
her arms open and took her son in her embrace.

FORTIFY YOUTH

Brethren and sisters, are we going to fortify
the youth of Israel and the daughters of Zion, that
they can withstand these men who seem to think
that it is their special mission and that they are justi-

fied in coming among our people and ruining our daughters and leading away our young men? God bless you. Amen.

TALK SEVEN
April, 1903

WAYS OF MEN

The few moments I occupy I very much desire to enjoy the Spirit of the Lord. I realize that the ways of the Lord are not in harmony altogether with the ways of men. I have labored in the ministry long enough to know that should I be favored to enjoy the Holy Spirit and speak the things that the Lord shall give unto me; they will not be altogether in harmony with people who do not enjoy that spirit. I believe it is proper for us to be conservative and consistent in all that we say and do, but I confess to you that my time is too short on this occasion to prepare your minds for what I may say, for I have not an entire conception of just how I am going to come out in fifteen minutes from now.

BIBLE MISUNDERSTOOD

I have thought some little lately about the Bible, which we claim to be the word of God, "as far as it is translated correctly." Taking that statement into consideration, there are no people on the earth that quibble so little about the Bible as do the Latter-day Saints. I am strongly impressed with the idea that the Bible can be understood only

[170]

by the same spirit with which it was written. If that statement be true, I am impressed with the idea that the Christian world have not got very much of it, or else they would understand it more alike. There are said to be six hundred or more denominations. I have never found out exactly how many.

WORD OF GOD

Now, we have the *Book of Mormon,* and if there is anything on earth that has made trouble for this people, it is that book. It is largely the means of costing the lives of the Prophet Joseph Smith, his brother Hyrum, and hundreds of others belonging to this Church. But I am prepared to testify that it contains the word of God. We have also the *Book of Doctrine and Covenants* and the *Pearl of Great Price,* which are accepted by this people as the revelations of God; and they have made an endless lot of trouble for this people, because they are the word of God. There is only "one of a city and two of a family" that are willing to accept them; so you need not think I am going to get discouraged because they do not believe all I say, and you need not think I am going to stop talking if permission be given me, because some people do not believe all I say.

POPULARIZE MORMON CHURCH

Brethren and sisters, I believe I will tell you how to popularize the Mormon Church. If you want to be popular, I can tell you how to be so.

[171]

The "Josephite" church has started out in about
the right line to accomplish their purpose, by cut-
ting out a number of truths that Joseph Smith revealed to the Saints, and in this way they are trying to popularize themselves. Now, if you will
stop sending out these fourteen hundred elders,
testifying that Jesus is the Christ, that Joseph
Smith is a Prophet of God, that we have apostles
and prophets inspired of God, that we enjoy revelation, that the signs follow the believer, that the
sick are healed by the laying on of hands, that we
have divine authority from God; then you will be
popular. Are you prepared to do it? If you will
stop going into these temples and receiving your
endowments and being married for time and all
eternity, that will help a little.

If the Lord cannot take care of His Church
and His people and look after their interests, then
we have been mistaken. I tell you we have friends
and we have men in the world who have the Spirit
of God, who will rise up and protect this people.
I am not numbered among those who think that
we have no friends, for we have friends. But,
brethren and sisters, you are not of the world, and
therefore the world hateth you, speaking generally.
If you want to be popular, stop doing the things
that I have mentioned and deny their truth. But
if you want to stay with this Church, be true to
your covenants. The time will come when you will
be—as you are now—a light set upon a hill. I tell

you, all the devils in hell cannot destroy this Church. And the devil never has been entirely comfortable since that temple [the Salt Lake Temple] was completed.

THE SEVENTIES

I would like to call your attention to another subject. I happen to have a little information on paper this morning, which is rather unusual for me. I desire to call your attention to some of the labors of the First Council of the Seventy. Listening to all these presidents of stakes, you would think that their stakes were the only stakes in Zion; and I rather approve of that style. I believe that you ought to love that which is your own. I am learning that slowly. If you have got anything that is not presentable, for heaven's sake, do not say anything about it; someone will find it out soon enough.

There is nothing that has been done for years by the First Council, under the direction of the Presidency, that has done as much good as our inquiring after these brethren. I wish we had the time to inquire after every one of the seventies, especially those that are nearly dead. It would doubtless start their blood circulating, and teach these seventies the fact that they are witnesses of the Lord Jesus Christ to the nations of the earth. Also that it is their privilege to preach the Gospel continually, and that they ought to be out of debt and prepared to go. . . . Out of 497 seventies only five declined to go on a mission; and I believe if we had fully understood their letters and had started the presidents to labor with them, there would not be found probably more than one out of the whole number who would decline to go. I tell you, it is a remarkable thing. The other Christian churches cannot show anything like it.

HELP MISSIONARIES

I have not time to talk much about missionary work. All I have to say, brethren, if you cannot go on missions; if you are too rich to go, or you have too much business, or you have positions in the Church that prevent you from going; then, for heaven's sake, help those who do go. The Church must be protected in its business, in its wards, its stakes, and its church schools. I believe in protection—if I am among the number protected; [laughter] but inasmuch as this Gospel must be preached, you men that stay home must help carry the burden, and not have our brethren mortgage their homes and sell out everything to do this work. There are not two rich seventies in the whole number we have reported to the missionary committee of the apostles. They are all poor men, and some of their letters would bring tears to your eyes, when they write to us explaining the little they have. But they say, "I am ready to go; I know God Almighty will bless us."

MISSION A BLESSING

I will rob you of a little time for the purpose of reading you what the Lord told my father, and I take it as a testimony to me that there is nothing that brings a greater blessing than preaching the Gospel to the nations of the earth.

Far West, Apr. 6, 1839.

A word from the Spirit of the Lord to My servant, Heber C. Kimball:

Trouble not thyself about thy family, for they are in my hands. I will feed them, and clothe them, and make unto them friends. They never shall want for food, nor raiment, houses, nor lands, fathers nor mothers, brothers nor sisters, and peace shall rest upon them forever, if thou wilt be faithful and go forth and preach My Gospel to the nations of the earth.

I stand before you as a living witness of its truth. I have traveled among this people for eleven years. I have received honors and blessings from among this people, because of my father. I have found fathers and mothers, brothers and sisters. I have found friends everywhere I have been among this people. And I attribute the greater part of it to the fact that my father fulfilled that commandment. His children have never wanted for bread, and I tell you, in the name of Israel's God, they never will. They will be mighty poor, but they will always have bread. God bless you. Amen.

TALK EIGHT
April, 1904

THINK FOR YOURSELVES

I am ready to confess that I am keyed up to a pretty high tension, and the only thing I am afraid of is that I will say just what I think, which would be unwise, no doubt.

I feel a good deal, or at least I imagine I do, like a man does when held up by a burglar, and he is looking into the muzzle of a six-shooter. I would quietly and willingly hold my hands up, but, during the time, would think very profoundly of what I would do if given my liberty. We are in a similar position today, but all the men in the United States cannot prevent us from thinking, and they are not disposed to do so; but some people fancy because we have the Presidency and Apostles of the Church they will do the thinking for us.

There are men and women so mentally lazy that they hardly think for themselves. To think calls for effort which makes some men tired and wearies their souls. Now, brethren and sisters, we are surrounded with such conditions that it requires not only thought, but the guidance of the Holy Spirit. Latter-day Saints, you must think for yourselves. No man or woman can remain in this Church on borrowed light.

APOSTATES

Our special mission and calling is to see to it that all peoples and nations hear the glad tidings of great joy. Personally, I have no feelings against the gentiles and those who are not of our faith, and I can say it honestly, thanking the Lord that I am broad-minded enough to carry the olive branch in my hand and preach the Gospel of peace to the nations of the earth. But when it comes to apostates and our own people lifting up their voices against us, I tell you there is not influence enough to restrain me from rebuking them. I am not willing to fold my hands and stand silently by and hear apostates abuse our leaders and people. Why? Because they know better. They have been taught, nurtured and warmed at our hearths, and they know they falsify the truth.

TRAITORS

I will say to the Latter-day Saints, I have no use for a traitor, unless he will speedily repent of that great sin. I do not believe the Lord will give to a traitor salvation, unless he repents. The people of these United States have no use for a traitor. The Masons have no earthly use for them, neither have the Methodists, Baptists, or any other Christian people, and I join them in the cry against traitors and those that love to make lies.

I will now read to you a few words from the sayings of the Prophet of the Lord, at a meeting held in Nauvoo, Illinois, July 2nd, 1839, with the twelve apostles and some of the seventies who were about to go on their missions to Europe.

O ye Twelve! said Joseph, and all saints! Profit by this important key—that in all your trials, troubles, temptations, afflictions, bonds, imprisonments, and death, see to it, that you do not betray heaven; that you do not betray Jesus Christ; that you do not betray the brethren; that you do not betray the revelations of God, whether in the Bible, *Book of Mormon,* or *Doctrine and Covenants,* or any other that ever was or ever will be given and revealed unto man in this world, or that which is to come. Yea, in all your kicking and floundering, see to it that ye do not this thing, lest innocent blood be found on your skirts, and you go down to hell. All other sins are not to be compared to sinning against the Holy Ghost, and proving a traitor to thy brethren.

SPIRITUAL UPLIFTING

I pray God to bless you, my brothers and sisters. I wish there was more time for us to speak to the people. I say to you, as a servant of the Lord and as a watchman upon the towers, it is high time that we were looking up. I tell you, if there is anything on earth that we need in the Church, in this day in which we live, it is not money or temporal power, but it is a spiritual uplifting, and it must be taking place in Zion, or else there will be a falling away.

EXAMPLES TO YOUTH

Now, brothers and sisters, in your comments and conversations and in expressing your views, see

[178]

to it that you do not express yourselves thoughtlessly before the rising generation. Don't pass your opinion too quickly, and by doing so cause the young people to fall away from the Church, for they have not received the testimonies that you have. You have a great mission to perform at home. See to it that you do not "lift up the heel against the Lord's anointed," crying out that they have transgressed. For the Lord says, "Those who cry transgression do it because they are the servants of sin, and are the children of disobedience themselves."

May the Lord bless, direct and prosper this people, I ask in the name of Jesus. Amen.

TALK NINE

October, 1904

PRAY TO THE POINT

I feel a good deal, at this time, as the chaplain did in one of the Utah legislative assemblies when my father put him on oath. Father was a little acquainted with him. They had crossed the plains together, and father knew what a long and tedious prayer he usually offered, so father said, "Will you pray briefly and to the point." Well now, I feel that I will have to talk briefly and to the point.

TRUE CHURCH

I was born in this Church, and I thank God for it. It comprises everything that is good, everything that is pure, everything that is elevating, notwithstanding all that is said against it.

JESUS IS THE CHRIST

We must have a knowledge that Jesus is the Christ, or we cannot stand. Latter-day Saints who have failed are those who have not obtained a knowledge that Jesus is the Christ; all such are liable to apostatize. I am afraid there will be a lot of apostates, and that worries me.

CANNOT DESTROY CHURCH

You can't live on borrowed light any longer. This Church has passed through many close places,

[180]

and, as my father said, it will pass through many other close places before victory and triumph are given to you or given to the Church. I know a good deal more about this Church than the man did, one of those strangers that came in our midst, who went on a hill here recently and stood in an ant bed, and, when the ants commenced to bite, he commenced to curse the Mormons. I suppose he thought they were Mormon ants, and he held us responsible for them.

Now there are a lot of people talking about us, and we have a great deal of cheap notoriety, but I am not at all concerned about it. I am not worrying about it; I don't stand with bated breath for fear this Church will be destroyed. This is the work of God; this is the Church of Jesus Christ. There are not devils enough to destroy it, and it can't be destroyed by men. If it could have been destroyed, some, who claim to be members in the Church, would have destroyed it years ago. I don't care how much harm is committed by pretended members of this Church, they can't destroy it; they will destroy themselves. I care not how many apostates attempt it, they cannot destroy this Church.

APOSTATES UNRELIABLE

Now, I want to serve notice on all Catholic, Methodist and Presbyterian churches—I don't suppose they will take my advice; they never have done up to date, but I would like to continue giving

[181]

them good advice—I would advise them never to receive a man into their church that has been a Latter-day Saint and apostatized from the Church. Such individuals will never make good Catholics, good Methodists, or good Presbyterians. They will be agitators, and make a deal of mischief in those churches, because they will be so restless and unsettled that no one near them will have any peace or rest. And they will get to asking a lot of questions. The first thing they will ask is, "Where do you get your authority from?" and that will worry you a little. And they will ask other hard questions, and make trouble and mischief. And then, they are no account, anyhow, as members of any church.

You never saw an apostate in your life that was a Latter-day Saint and did right up to a certain time and then apostatized, that has ever settled down and been satisfied in any other church in the world. They are not even satisfied with spiritualism, notwithstanding they may talk with spirits and get a great amount of information. They won't stay with that sect.

And, by the way, I would like to serve notice on the Republicans and Democrats that the individuals of whom I have been speaking will never be good Democrats or Republicans either; they will not stay with their party.

Now, I want to serve notice on apostates. I am willing to carry the olive branch in my hand when I associate with the children of men in the world. I have nothing but the kindliest feelings towards them; but when an apostate lifts up his voice against this people, when he makes dastardly charges against the Latter-day Saints, he lies, and I have no patience with him. I have breathed this mountain air so long that I feel inclined to discard a little of the Gospel and knock such men down, and repent afterwards. I want to say to an apostate, and to any man that has been born and bred in the Church, he is a coward to lift up his voice against 300,000 people [1904], with over 100,000 children among the number. If apostates had their way, the whole United States would be against us.

Persons who have lived in this country and received all that they own from this people, and who lift their voices against us, are cowards. Whenever any man or woman wants to leave this Church, they have a right to do so, and it is our duty to treat them right, to extend to them every courtesy and kindness, and be their friend, if they refrain from lying and persecuting us. This is God's work, and, just as sure as He lives, and as we breathe and have a being, this work will come off triumphant. There may not be very many of us left, but, let the number be ever so few, it will succeed.

COUNSEL OF CHURCH AUTHORITIES

I want to say in conclusion, the only discipline I have had was by my own father, up to fifteen

[183]

years of age. For twelve years after that time I was under no responsibility, but, since then, I have been in business of different kinds: I have been a farmer, a stock raiser, a real estate man, and an implement man. I knew Brigham Young almost as well as I knew my father. I knew Daniel H. Wells, a counselor of Brigham Young and associate of my father. I have known all these brethren down to President Smith, and can testify that all the counsel and advice I have received from them has been a savor of life unto my soul. It has been a godsend to me, and I am grateful that I have been favored because of my association with men of God, who have given me counsel, such counsel that, if I follow it, will bring me back into the presence of my Eternal Father.

NEVER SPEAK AGAINST THE WORK OF GOD

Now, that is my testimony to this congregation. If you have got anything to say in favor of this people, whether you are in the Church or out, say it fearlessly. My father said to one of his grandchildren, who is living in Arizona and didn't take any active part in the Church: "Billy, these are my words to you, don't you ever lift up your voice against this people." Speaking to me about my father's advice to him, he said, "Golden, I never have, and I thank God for it." I repeat the advice; never speak against the work of God, nor against His people. May the Lord bless you. Amen.

[184]

TALK TEN
April, 1905

BLOWS FOR BLOWS

I once read a beautiful article about anvils and hammers and I copied some of its sayings. But I have never used them, although I have carried the copy until it is nearly worn out. I now quote as follows: "Every man in the world who gives blows must take blows, and until a man becomes as good an anvil as he is a hammer, he fails to be thoroughly fitted for his work."

RESTRAINING PASSION

Now I grant, my brethren and sisters, that sometimes we have to endure many things, and I presume that if we live the Gospel of the Lord Jesus Christ we shall have to endure all things; but it requires a very prayerful heart to enable us to endure some things. I realize that the Congress of the United States, and the committee on privileges and elections, have their duty to perform. I do not object to those things, for it is a doctrine of the Church that we sustain the law of the land, and we have done it. But the thing that I object to is, for every little gutter-snipe, that comes into the country, to think that he can kick and maul and abuse us.

I occasionally feel a little like Joe Rich did

once when they abused his father, Apostle Charles C. Rich, who spent a great part of his life as a pioneer in that hard country of Bear Lake, who used to come over the mountains on snow shoes in order to attend conference, who used to grind his wheat in a little coffee mill in order to have bread, and whose wives and children lived in log houses with dirt roofs for many years. Joe went down to a certain newspaper office and demanded retraction. He told them if they didn't retract he would turn the whole family loose on them, and that he was the smallest one in the family and the biggest coward. The retraction came. I am not saying this to be sensational. I tell you, if it were not for that man of God, Joseph F. Smith, restraining his children, and they being obedient unto him, there would be some men horsewhipped today. But, he is a servant of God. I have known him all my life. I have known every man who has presided over this Church from President Brigham Young down, and I know they have been men of God.

WE MUST HAVE BACKBONE

We have no small mission to perform. I honor Joseph Smith the Prophet, for his bravery, for his courage, for his manliness. He had a message to deliver that was in conflict with sin and wickedness, and it came in conflict, also, with all the man-made religious organizations of the world. But God had revealed it to him, and he would not deny it, though it cost him his life. Do you think we can continue proclaiming this message—can we elders continue telling the world that God did appear to Joseph Smith, and that He did reveal these things, and expect they will receive us with open arms? Never. And, notwithstanding that it is our mission to treat them kindly, to carry the olive branch in our hand, to preach the Gospel and to deliver this message, at the same time, brethren and sisters, we must have backbone.

I am going to read some more to you: "I think there is a contemptible, quiet path for all those who are afraid of the blows and hammers of opposing forces. There is an honorable fighting for any man who is ready to forget that he has a head to be battered and a name to be besmattered. Truth wants no champion who is not as ready to be struck as to strike for her."

Any of these backboneless people, any who are afraid that God's work will not triumph, had better get in the background and let those that have courage stand in the front of the battle. Of course, I might be the first one to run, I have not been tried very much yet; but I know I will be tried if I stay in this Church. I know that I cannot live on borrowed light. You can talk and preach and expound until you are black in the face, but if you do not know that Jesus is the Christ you will never stay in this Church.

As far as I am concerned, I want to be broad-

[187]

minded enough to open my arms to the stranger, and to treat him kindly, but, I will not sustain a man who will lie and abuse and deride this people.

AUTHORITIES KIND

May God bless you people. May He bless the authorities of the Church. It is not often I bear my testimony, but I want to tell you today that I know this work is true. I know that Joseph Smith is a Prophet of God. I honor and love him and his memory, although I never saw him. I have been acquainted with all the Prophets of God from the days of President Brigham Young down. They have been kind to me in my childhood and in my manhood. It does not matter much to me where the place is that they have gone to, but I do not want to go with any others because I would be lonesome. God bless you. Amen.

TALK ELEVEN
October, 1905

CHILBLAINS SERMON

Arising to speak to you at this time puts me in mind of a story I read not long ago. It was during the Civil War, when some soldiers were around a camp fire, trying to keep themselves from freezing to death. A preacher came along to hold services. He looked around among the soldiers, and said, "I will take for my text, Chilblains." So he instructed the soldiers what to do, which was to put soft soap in their shoes, place them on their feet and wait till their feet were healed. And then he would talk to them about the Lord the next time he came. You can't talk to people when they are uneasy, not if you are like I am. You can't preach to people when they want to go home. Now if any of you want to go, please go, and the rest of us will stay till we get through.

AFRAID OF JUSTICE

I am not going to announce any blood and thunder doctrine to you today. I have not been radical for four long months, not since I had appendicitis. I came very nearly being operated upon. I thought I was going to die for a few hours.

People said to me, "Brother Kimball, you needn't be afraid; you'll get justice." "Well," I said, "that is what I am afraid of." Well now, the Latter-day Saints need not get frightened they will get justice. You have been fed on rich diet during this conference, and now I will give you a little coarse food to help you out.

HARDEST CHURCH TO STAY IN

I am not exercised about the triumph of this work. I am not lying awake nights any more, wondering how the Lord is going to do it. Notwithstanding the fact that I am laboring in the Church, I don't know what the Lord wants in all things. If I did I would be willing to try and carry it out. The Lord's ways are not as man's ways, and He does things so differently from the way we want to do them that many of us are oftentimes surprised, and it requires constant faith to stay in this Church. I believe it is the hardest church to stay in that there is on earth, because you have always got to keep exercising faith. I remember hearing of a man that apostatized from the Church, and he was asked what was the matter. He said, "Well, I have got tired exercising faith."

YOUR DUTY IN THE CHURCH

I say, we need not be anxious about the triumph of this work; we need not be so exercised about it that we will lie awake nights. But I tell you, every man and woman in this Church should be exercised and anxious about the salvation of the souls of the children of men, and about the preaching of this Gospel. Look at our Savior; think of the anxiety He had for the souls of men. Just think of the sleepless nights He must have spent. I cannot be converted to the idea that the Savior sweat great drops of blood because they were going to crucify Him. But, He so loved the souls of the children of men, and His sorrow was so great for them, that He sweat great drops of blood. Now, you need to get a little bit anxious, and go home and get a little healthful exercise, and not sleep too much. Lie awake a little and think about your duty in the Church.

DEBT

Now, brethren, the Lord bless you. You shouldn't get yourselves tied up by debt. Of these seventies, 8,000 men, I am sorry there is not more than one out of a hundred that is prepared to go on a mission, because of debt, or infirmities. When a man claims that he would lay down his life for this work, that he would place all that the Lord has given him on the altar, and you invite him to go on a mission, you sometimes find him full of sorrow and trouble, and in debt. It is the most inconsistent thing in the world.

MISSIONARIES TO PREPARE

I believe there was a time in the history of this Church when it was necessary to send all kinds of men to preach the Gospel. God magnified them, and made them marvelous; but I tell you He does not look upon ignorance now with any degree of allowance. There is no need of our priesthood being ignorant; there is no need of our priesthood going out as the fishermen went out. They ought to go out well equipped and fitted for the work of the Lord as special witnesses of Christ. I know what the Lord wants in this respect, just as well as if He gave me a direct revelation; and when missionaries are wanted they should be found in the seventies quorums instead of any other. The Lord bless you. Amen.

TALK TWELVE

April, 1906

LONG FACES

In standing before the Latter-day Saints this afternoon, I desire to say those things that are timely, and to speak under the influence of the Holy Spirit. Notwithstanding the seriousness of the occasion, having met as a part of the great Annual Conference, we need not pull long faces and put on an air of self-righteousness, thinking it indicates faith and is more pleasing to the Lord. The Lord has said, "Cease from your light speeches and excess of laughter," but He surely is pleased with pleasant countenances and a happy people, although wit and humor may be out of place in houses of worship.

I read somewhere the following: "Many persons who never had a bright idea in their heads, or a generous sentiment in their hearts, assuming an air of owlish wisdom, affect to disdain wit and humor, having never heard of the great truth enunciated by Charles Lamb: 'A laugh is worth a hundred groans in any market.' The idea is propagated "that mental dryness is indicative of wisdom." I realize that my reputation for wisdom has been greatly injured by repeating jokes in my public utterances and that, because of my calling in the ministry, I should, in the estimation of some people, be as solemn as an owl.

It seems to be the destiny of the children of men to suffer sickness, sorrow, pain, and poverty, and to die. With our most perfect organization, priesthood and authority, we still have troubles, and skeletons in our closets. It is considered a good thing to look wise, especially when not over-burdened with information.

IMPRISONED SERVANTS OF THE LORD

I desire to make a statement here in explanation of something that I said in the conference meeting on Friday.

I have learned that some of the greatest miracles and most marvelous events have happened to the servants of God when they were placed in jail for righteousness sake. Some of the greatest revelations that God has ever given in this age and dispensation were given to the Prophet of God when he was in jail, in trouble and difficulty. During his time of sorrow and loneliness, God the Father, came to him, by His Spirit, and he received marvelous revelations. I read in the Bible about Peter being imprisoned, and an angel of God coming to his rescue. He was taken through the great iron gates, and escaped when his enemies were desirous of taking his life. I read, also, about the Prophets of God in the days of the *Book of Mormon* history. Prisons were broken down and mani-

[194]

festations of God were made apparent to the servants of the Most High.

An incident happened in the Southern States Mission, which I will relate. It transpired in the days of President John Morgan, and occurred at a time when the State of Tennessee passed a law that any man who advocated or preached polygamy was to be arrested and punished. Enemies to the elders entrapped the brethren into a discussion on this most unpopular subject, and the elders defended the principle from a Biblical standpoint. A complaint was filed, and the elders were arrested. They were short of room inside the jail; so the brethren, two in number, were confined in two steel cages on the outside, near to each other. The imprisoned servants of the Lord were not orators or singers. The people from far and near, hearing of Mormon elders being under arrest, gathered to see these peculiar individuals. The brethren sang hymns and testified of the truth of the Gospel, etc. It is claimed they had congregations of three hundred, and I have been told that the people had never heard such wonderful preaching and singing. The elders almost regretted receiving their freedom. So, I am almost inclined to advocate putting our elders in jail once in a while, when they are unable to get a hearing in any other way.

TRIALS OF THE SAINTS

Now, I will read to you to show that there will come sorrows to the Latter-day Saints, trials, and tests. Every man in this Church will be tested to the core; they will be proved as Abraham was proved, and when the Lord is satisfied that they love Him and will keep His commandments, then He will come to their rescue.

GREAT SIFTING TIME

I will quote to you a prophecy. In 1856, a little group of friends convened in the Endowment House, and were engaged in a conversation on the isolated condition of the Latter-day Saints:

Yes [said Brother Heber, by which name he was so frequently called] "we think we are secure here in the chambers of the everlasting hills, where we can close those few doors of the canyons against mobs and persecution, the wicked and the vile who have always beset us with violence and robbery; but I want to say to you, my brethren, the time is coming when we will be mixed up in these now peaceful valleys to that extent that it will be difficult to tell the face of a saint from the face of an enemy to the people of God. Then, brethren, look out for the great sieve, for there will be a great sifting time, and many will fall, for I say unto you, there is a test, a *test,* a *test* coming, and who will be able to stand?

THE TEST

My mother has told me that the last time father took a walk down Main Street, after he was stricken with paralysis, he returned with difficulty back to his home, the residence which still stands on the hill, and he said to her, "Oh, the test, the test, the test, who will be able to stand?" Mother said, "What is the test?" He replied, "I don't know, but it is only those that know that Jesus is the Christ that can stand."

NOW APOSTATIZE AND GO TO HELL

As I have said, this is the Church of Jesus Christ, and each of us has individual work in it. If the Latter-day Saints do not know that Jesus is the Christ, and that this is His Church, I tell you, in the name of the Lord, you will not stand; you will be among the number that fall.

I remember hearing about a saying of President Young to a brother who was terribly tried. His case came before the High Council, and the council had decided against the man. You know it happens sometimes, when the decision is not in your favor, you feel disgruntled. And some leave the Church because of the actions of men; they feel they have been dealt with unjustly. Brother Brigham, on the occasion referred to, said to the brother in sarcasm, "Now apostatize and go to hell." And the brother ejaculated, "I won't do it; this is just as much my church as it is yours, and I am going to stay with it."

Well, that is Mormonism. It is our church, as long as we keep the commandments of God; and we can be put out of it only through apostasy, rebellion, or criminal actions. Now, let us stay with it, and, like my brother Andrew, always tell good things about Zion and let other things alone. The Lord bless you. Amen.

[197]

TALK THIRTEEN

October, 1906

My brethren and sisters, I hope you have confidence in me, and that I can hold your attention for a few moments. I feel happy, just as happy as a man can feel with the rheumatism.

COST OF THE CHURCH

I now want to ask you Latter-day Saints if you have counted the cost of establishing this Church? Have you considered that it has cost thousands of men and women who have been valiant in the truth and died in the faith? The country is fairly strewn with the bodies of our people from Salt Lake City to the East. Construction is very difficult, destruction is easy. Ordinary men can criticize and destroy. It has required much sacrifice and constructive effort to establish this Church.

LORD WANTS HIS PEOPLE

I feel grateful this day, my brethren and sisters, that I have the confidence of my brethren; I must have it, or I would not have been called to address you. I want also the confidence of the Saints. I say, God save the people; what can He do without them? The Lord can accomplish great things, but He wants the people, and He will never be satisfied until he secures the hearts of the children of men.

STOP SELLING INHERITANCES

I desire to call attention to a thought that is in my mind—it is not new, however. I desire to advise the Latter-day Saints to stop selling their inheritances. I call your attention to the fact that this earth is your habitation, that this earth is your heaven, or will be. This earth is hell, too, and there is a big lot of people in this hell now; their lives are such that this earth is of that character to them. They have no peace of mind, no rest of body, and I pity them. This earth is your habitation while you are in the flesh. If this earth is to be your heaven, I think you had better have an inheritance here, don't you? I do not believe the doctrine for one minute that you people or myself (and I think I am as good as some of you) are going immediately after death to the arms of Jehovah. It will take some of us a long time to get there. You had better be very good and take care of this earth.

My father had an inheritance in Independence, Missouri, and it has never been sold by him or his heirs to any living man. The time will come, as sure as the Lord reigns, when father will claim that inheritance. He had an inheritance in Salt Lake City, on the hill, a whole block, including where the Lafayette School is now built. I was born in the Kimball mansion, which now stands on the same block. I have a small place on that block, at least large enough to bury me in, and it is about all I can do to hold it. Why? Because they tax me almost more than human nature can endure, and the end is not yet! Are you going to get frightened and run away somewhere? Are you going to sell your inheritance every time you meet a difficulty? If the pioneers had done that they would have been going yet; but they stopped in this barren waste, and they made it habitable for you and me. I tell you, God is not pleased with some of this people, because they are selling their inheritance for a mess of pottage. I sold part of mine, and I confess that the money went through my fingers like water through a sieve. I don't know where it went, but I know I haven't got it. That is exactly what will happen to every Latter-day Saint who sells his inheritance. The Lord wants you to stay in this country; He does not want you to break for the woods. You have a right to every particle of land that you can secure legitimately and pay the taxes on.

SECURE WASTE LAND

Now, I am going to give you a little fatherly advice, and I believe you won't take it. I advise the Latter-day Saints, as Brother Smoot did, to take up and secure the wasteland throughout the State of Utah and other sections where Latter-day

Saints reside. If the Saints will keep the commandments of God, if they will raise grain enough, build
up cities, emigrate the people we are converting in
the world, eliminate selfishness and avariciousness,
and divide up the land and make homes for the
people; if they will bless the land and dedicate it
to the Lord, let our friends come in here, and leave
our gates open to the strangers; the bowels of the
earth will be opened, and there will be produced
therefrom riches more than we can contain. The
time will come when the strangers will have little
use for their money, they will come to this people
for bread, and we will feed them and treat them
kindly, notwithstanding some of them have acted
miserably mean. Do you believe that doctrine?
My father predicted it years ago, and some people
are laughing over it now. I have heard some of
them pooh-pooh it; but I stand as a son of my
father, as a witness of the Lord, and testify to you
that the time will come among this people when it
will be fulfilled.

PREACH THE GOSPEL

Don't you go off in wild speculation, or have
part in wildcat schemes. You are advised to raise
grain. You had better secure an inheritance; get
your titles and pay for the land. I say to you, in
the language of the Prophet Joseph (I suppose I
dare quote his words): "Be honest, be frank, and
stop bowing and scraping to gentile sophistry." Go

along and do your duty; follow counsel, and preach the Gospel to the nations of the earth. See that this Gospel is preached to every creature under heaven. I repeat to you the words of a promise made to my father, "Trouble not thyself about thy families, for the Lord will give them food and raiment, houses and lands, fathers and mothers, brothers and sisters, if you will teach My Gospel." God bless you. Amen.

TALK FOURTEEN
April, 1907

SALVATION INDIVIDUAL WORK

I am a strong advocate of individuality and agency. I value it above everything that I can conceive of, except salvation. I am very doubtful if a man can be saved in the Kingdom of God who has no individuality, and does not assert his agency, because salvation is an individual work.

WAIVE RIGHT TO SIN

The chief point I have in mind at this time is that when we became members of the Church of Latter-day Saints we waived certain rights and privileges. At least that was my understanding when I became a member of the Church.

Now, as I said, I waived certain rights when I became a member of this Church; I waived the right of sin. I have my agency and individuality; but as long as I am a member of this Church, I waive the right to sin, to transgress. When you joined the Church, became members of it, you also waived the right to do a great many things. You have no right to commit adultery or to be immoral. You have waived the right to break the Word of Wisdom. And in many other things we have waived our rights, and sometimes I feel muzzled when I wrestle with my nature and human weaknesses. You know there is no other man just like me in all Israel and probably you are glad of it.

SELF-RIGHTEOUSNESS

I am having a pretty hard time wrestling with myself. I don't feel self-righteous, I feel more like that poor fellow who stood on the street corner and bowed his head and said, "O God, forgive me, a poor sinner." I feel confident, when I think about the matter carefully, that some people become self-righteous in their own estimation, because they keep one or two or more commandments, and then they commence to exercise "unrighteous dominion" when they find a transgressor in the Church. Now, Latter-day Saints, such people have "sinned and come short of the glory of God," and stand condemned before the Lord unless there is such a thing as repentance and forgiveness of sins.

SALVATION

It is a question, how long will it take for me to secure salvation? The Lord only knows; I don't: I am not competent to tell whether I will be saved or not. I am making an effort for salvation, and as I said, I waived a great many rights in order to become a member of the Church. I have trampled ambition under my feet, for I have an ambition, and it takes me all the time to keep my feet on it. I am sometimes afraid of my friends, because if one doesn't qualify every statement he makes, he may be like one man said of me in the North Country: "Well, he didn't say it, but he intended to, and if he will say to me that he did not intend to say it, then I will take back everything I said against him."

FEW ARE CHOSEN

I wish to properly express my thoughts and feelings on this occasion. I will read to you from the *Doctrine and Covenants*:

"Behold, there are many called, but few are chosen, and why are they not chosen?"

I have been surprised that I was chosen, but there will come another time of choosing, and I don't know whether I will be among the number then or not. You don't know, either.

FRUITS OF THE HOLY GHOST

Experience teaches me that when I have been angry, I am quite sure I did not have the Holy Ghost, and I was not in any proper condition to administer reproof. It took me quite a long time to learn that. When I became excited, fanatical, and over-zealous, I mistakenly thought it was the Spirit of the Lord, but have learned better, as the Holy Ghost does not operate that way. My testimony is that the internal fruits of the Holy Ghost are joy, peace, patience, long suffering, and kindness.

[205]

TRYING TO BE SAVED

Now, I am speaking of myself; I am not criticizing others; I am talking about principles. I stand before you a transgressor, but I am trying to be saved, and that is all God asks me to do. Any man who tries to do the right thing and continues to try, is not a failure in the sight of the Lord. Dreyfus, a Jew of the French Army, was falsely accused by his associates because of jealousy and hatred, and it resulted in his losing his appointment, being disgraced and banished. He was afterwards proven innocent and reinstated with honors. His experience and sorrow would not be as great or as serious as mine would be, if, for cause or otherwise, I was to lose my priesthood and appointment. Such things have occurred through sin, or apostasy, and sometimes it may be because men holding the priesthood have exercised unrighteous dominion, and have accepted statements made by tattlers, and thus became suspicious, prejudiced, and unfriendly.

GOD IS MERCIFUL

My brethren and sisters, I want you to be good to me, and help save me. If I can be saved it is an encouragement to every man, woman and child in Israel to make the effort. If you have weaknesses, try to overcome them, and if you fail, try again; and if you then fail, keep trying, for God is merciful to His children.

[206]

SALVATION

I have learned the lesson that nothing on earth would be a greater failure to me than to fail to keep my family in the Church. They were God's children before they were mine, and I think the Lord will look after their interests and save them in His own due time. If Golden Kimball can't be saved in the flesh, after all the struggles and efforts he has made—and I have made a few sacrifices—then I believe God will save him on the other side. And it may be that his earthly father will come to his rescue, and lift up his voice to God in behalf of his child and plead for his salvation. It may take a hundred years to save me, but if I get through in a thousand years it will be a most profitable investment.

I have no fancied notions; I have gotten rid of tradition, and of a few false ideas that rested upon me. I do not expect to become a God, right away. No, it will take a long time; I am too ignorant. When I stand before my Maker, in the other world, I will be like some of those poor elders who have been laboring in missions; I will speak with a stammering tongue, and God will look upon me, no doubt, as a child, mediocre in intelligence compared with those who have preceded me.

I pray the Lord to bless you. Amen.

TALK FIFTEEN
April, 1908

INTELLIGENCE IN PREACHING

I have been in California for a few weeks and I tell you I am in sympathy with Elder Robinson, and my heart goes out to the elders. If I had been called upon in Ocean Park to stand before the intelligent class of people there, I don't know what I would have said. We need intelligence, and pure knowledge, to preach the Gospel to the nations of the earth.

HATS OFF TO PIONEERS

This work is true. The character of this people is a marvel to me and it has a pathetic side to it. I have traveled among this people from Mexico to Canada, and I know whereof I speak. I say to the young and rising generation: I am willing to take off my hat to these horny-handed, white-headed, broken-down men who have made it possible for us to exist in this mountain country. I say, God bless these aged men.

If you want examples, any object lessons, go down to Saint George and see what it has cost to settle that country. It is a number of years since I was there, but I found ninety widows. Some of the best men in the whole earth have died to make that country habitable.

Then I would like to take you on a trip down to Arizona, in the St. Johns country. I preached faith there once, but I want to tell you I haven't got enough faith to stay in such an undesirable country. You talk about good people; you talk about righteous people; I tell you there are people in this city who are not worthy to unlatch their shoestrings. That hard country, and their obedience to the Priesthood of God, has made those men great characters. You can't discourage them. They will build a dam across the Colorado River every five years, if it washes out the next day. That is their country; there, they worship God. Then you go up into the Big Horn country, then up into Canada, and then think what it has cost to make this country what it is.

But, every time some of us weak-kneed young fellows encounter a difficulty we break for the woods, and we give up our rights and sell them for a little pottage. I tell you that the Almighty is not pleased with some of the rising generation. They stick up their noses at these homely men. It is such homely men and women of character who have made this country, and this Church, what it is today, and I say, God bless them.

TRANSGRESSORS MISERABLE

Brethren, I want to call your attention to one thing: I am a sort of transgressor. My father died when I was fifteen years old. I have not committed any crimes, but there are some things in my history that I regret. Environment has a great deal to do with a man, and men who have colonized these out-lying districts do not look upon some habits as seri-ously as men who have never indulged in them; if they did, it would be an injustice to themselves. You never saw a man in your life do a wrong thing who was happy over it. You never saw men vio-late a commandment of God and feel jubilant over it, for when they get the Spirit of the Lord they feel miserable about that transgression.

SPIRIT OF REPENTANCE

I say to you Latter-day Saints, and I say it to myself: I have preached this Gospel for fifteen years, and I now understand the doctrine of repent-ance. A man can't repent simply because an apos-tle tells him to repent; he can't do it until he gets the spirit of repentance, which is a gift from God; and some of us don't get it very quickly. Some of us don't get the spirit of repentance and see things right until our hair is gray.

SALVATION COSTS ITS PRICE

Brethren, let us be tolerant; let us be kind and considerate. It is the proper thing to despise sin and wickedness; but I think it is wrong to despise the man that has a weakness and make him feel that he is good for nothing, and that there is not much chance for him. I think I can safely say to you Latter-day Saints: You will all be saved, every one of you; the only difference will be this, some will be saved sooner than others. Every man that has transgressed and done wrong must pay the penalty of his transgression, for salvation costs something, and you have to pay the price or you don't get it.

Now, brethren, let us be kind and considerate to one another.

The Lord bless you. Amen.

TALK SIXTEEN
April, 1909

JOSEPH A TRUE PROPHET

I have read about the Prophet Joseph Smith.
I have the story of the Prophet, and it is a wonderful story for a boy to tell. About those two personages that came to him, also John the Baptist, Peter, James and John. To me, it is very wonderful. Do you believe it? If that is not true, Joseph Smith was the biggest fraud that ever came to a people on earth. There has never been a more sacrilegious thing uttered by man, if it is not true. Now, I say, do you believe it? Do I believe it? I believe everything that has been revealed to the Prophet Joseph Smith. If any principle that has been revealed to the Prophet is not true, then it is all wrong, as far as I am concerned. There is no use of mincing over it. Every Latter-day Saint in the Church should receive every truth, or else none of it. I believe it all. I believe every word of it.

I believe all that God has revealed, as fast as I can understand and comprehend it; and I believe that God will reveal many great and important things. I am not sure if we will be prepared to receive all or not. Joseph Smith said the Lord had revealed things to him for which, if he had repeated them to the people they would have taken his life.

It is a good thing he didn't; we have more truths and doctrine than we now live up to.

REPENTANCE

"We believe in being honest, true, chaste, benevolent, virtuous, and in doing good to all men." I accept that with all my heart. A man must be honest, and he must be true, and he must be chaste and benevolent, virtuous, and continue doing good to all men. What can God do for a man who is not honest? You may baptize him every fifteen minutes, but if he does not repent, he will come up out of the water just as dishonest as ever. What can God do for a liar who refuses to repent? Can the Lord save him? He can't claim salvation. Baptizing him in water will not settle the trouble, unless you keep him under. [Laughter]

What can the Lord do with people who are not virtuous, unless they repent? You cannot change the laws of the Lord. Men may deceive men; they may deceive apostles; they may deceive the President of the Church; they may even get into the temple, but that would not make them virtuous. You may confer the Holy Ghost upon them by the laying on of hands, but the Holy Ghost does not remain with the unrepentant; it will not remain in an unclean tabernacle. To deceive men is easy, but I want to tell you in the name of Israel's God, and this thought should be burned into the souls of our sons and daughters, that unless they

[213]

repent of all their sins and cease immoral practices, they cannot remain in the Church of Jesus Christ of Latter-day Saints. The Holy Ghost will not stay with them; they will not have the testimony of Jesus. This doctrine is true.

INTOLERANCE

I have tried to be generous in my sentiments, and be on the right side. I have tried to be tolerant, not intolerant. I have tried to respect men's opinions, for I have discovered that we do not always see things alike. We may, as far as the Gospel is concerned, but we are a long way from it in other things. In temporal things we do not sufficiently respect each other's opinions. Are we going to sit in judgment upon men? I am not in favor of it. I am not in sympathy with men who are intolerant; I am afraid of them.

Now, brethren, let us repent if we have got any bitterness in our hearts toward each other—let us be generous, and forgiving. No man has any influence or power for good when angry. It is "amen to the priesthood and the authority of that man when he uses unrighteous dominion," etc. It doesn't matter who he is. When a man has the Holy Ghost his heart is full of meekness; it is full of love unfeigned. He loves the souls of the children of men and he realizes how precious they are in the sight of God. May we as Latter-day Saints enjoy the fulness of the Holy Spirit, I ask it in the name of Jesus. Amen.

TALK SEVENTEEN

October, 1909

TEMPORAL SALVATION

Now, I want to confess to the people that I have been thinking along certain lines, and I came to the conclusion that if I were called upon, I would speak upon the temporal salvation of this people. Some of us—I plead guilty—have sold our inheritances for a "mess of pottage"; and in doing so we are without excuse, for we were warned by the servants of the Lord to hold secure our inheritances, as we were only stewards over the same.

A MIGHTY PEOPLE

I will now read something I have copied. On August 5th, 1842, the Prophet Joseph Smith prophesied that the Saints would continue to suffer much affliction and would be driven to the Rocky Mountains; some would apostatize; others would be put to death by their persecutors or lose their lives in consequence of exposure or disease; but, he said, "Some of you will live to go and assist in making settlements and building cities and will see the Saints become a mighty people in the midst of the Rocky Mountains."

They had not been here very long before the gold fever broke out in California, and some of our people were tinctured very badly with the spirit of money getting. Now, listen to what President Brigham Young said—it was his admonition to the Saints who desired to go to California: "The true use of gold is for paving streets, covering houses and making culinary dishes. When the Saints shall have preached the Gospel, raised grain and built cities enough the Lord will open up the way for a supply of gold to the satisfaction of the people."

I am very glad that the Prophet Brigham Young emphasized the true use of gold and silver. I have heard it preached hundreds of times—the effects of speculation among this people; that it would tend to break them up and lead them from raising grain, building cities, and making preparation for the tens of thousands of people who will desire to come to these mountains for safety.

LOSING OUR HERITAGE

We have our own people scattered all over the world, and which of you has land to divide among them? Are we properly supplied with grain? I say to the Latter-day Saints, that we are not doing our duty in regard to temporal affairs. We are not looking after the streams of water; we are not securing titles to land. So it is all over Utah; we are sleeping in our trail, and we are in a sort of Rip Van Winkle condition as to our rights—some of us.

SPECULATION

My brethren and sisters, I am a practical man, and I wish you to know that I have been a pioneer;

[216]

I know what it costs to make a home. I fought my battles years ago, in as hard a country as has ever been settled by our people. I know it requires ten years of hard labor, and economy, to succeed as a pioneer. I desire it to go down in history to my posterity, that, while I have made a number of failures, I did not fail as a pioneer. When I left that country, I could have bought out a dozen men who had been raised and remained in Salt Lake City; I mean young men who worked behind the counter. But I lost it all through speculation. That is what I want to talk to you about. Speculation—there is nothing more dangerous to the people and to the Church of Latter-day Saints, unless it be immorality and wickedness. I point you back in history to Nauvoo. What did the spirit of speculation do? According to the history, it nearly destroyed the people.

Take Heber C. Kimball's family as an illustration. My father died in 1868. When his administrators divided up the estate there was not a single silver dollar given to any of his children, to my knowledge, but there was some property. Our father selected land on the side hill, among the rocks—he wanted to get away from the center of the city. He owned what is known as the Capitol Hill. He left his children that real estate. There was one lot that was given to my mother's family, and I owned one third of it. I received twenty-five thousand dollars, and I have been sorry twenty-five thousand times that I ever sold it. [Laughter] I am thankful we had sense enough to keep sufficient ground to bury our posterity on. We have paid taxes on it ever since I was fifteen years old, and I still hold it.

What about the other property? There is now hardly a Kimball to be found on the Capitol Hill—unless it be those that are dead. Some of the Kimballs sold their lots at fifty dollars each; today the same lots are worth four thousand dollars. If Heber C. Kimball's family had kept their inheritance they would all be wealthy now. And what about the families of other pioneers who came here and fought this great battle? Many of their children are in very nearly the same predicament.

I predict to the Latter-day Saints, as a watchman upon the towers, if you follow that foolish example you will "hew stone and draw water:" You can write that down.

God bless you. Amen.

TALK EIGHTEEN
April, 1910

To begin with, I came to this meeting prepared to speak, expecting to speak; and came provided with some information. Having done my part, the rest depends upon the Lord and His Spirit, and the attention that I receive from the people.

SPIRIT OF GOD

They say, we ought to have three kinds of speakers: One on premisement, one on argument, and one on arousement. Now, I have been on "arousement" for a great many years.

I don't know whether I can interest you or not, but I am going to try, with the help of the Lord. I have a theme. This is something I hardly ever have. I never took a text in my life and stuck to it. This may be an occasion of that kind; but I am willing to say anything the Lord wants me to say, and I don't care what it costs. I have never been afraid of the children of men when I had the Spirit of God. I never was afraid of a mob in the Southern States when I had the Spirit of God, but I was scared pretty nearly to death after the Spirit left. It takes lots of courage to say always what you think. One trouble is, we think things sometimes we ought not to say.

[219]

REVELATION

I desire to talk to the people on revelation. The seventies have been studying revelation, and I have condensed the lessons. It is not original; I never read anything that is.

What is the definition of revelation? "Revelation is the name of that act by which God makes communication to men." How was revelation received in this dispensation? My intention is to compare notes and see how we conform to the old methods of the prophets in receiving revelation. That is, in what manner was revelation received?

The Prophet Joseph Smith received revelations in every way that the Lord communicates His mind and will to man. Like Moses, he knew the Lord face to face, stood in His very presence and heard His voice, as in the first communication the Lord made to him, usually called the Prophet's First Vision; as also in the vision given in the Kirtland Temple, where he and Oliver Cowdery saw the Lord standing on the breastwork of the pulpit, and heard Him speak to them.

He received communications from angels, as in the case of Moroni, who revealed to him the *Book of Mormon;* John the Baptist, who restored the Aaronic Priesthood; and Peter, James and John who restored the Melchizedek Priesthood. Also, the communications from angels, mentioned in what is usually called the Kirtland Temple Visions. See *Doc. and Cov.* Sec. 110.

[220]

He received communications through the Urim and Thummim, for by that means he translated the *Book of Mormon,* and received a number of the revelations contained in the *Doctrine and Covenants;* among others, sections 3, 6, 10, 11, 12, 14, 16, 17.

He received divine intelligence by open visions, such as is contained in sections 76, and 107.

He also received revelations through the inspiration of God operating upon his mind; and, indeed, the larger number of the revelations in the *Doctrine and Covenants* were received in this manner.

Now then, how did they receive them in the days of the Bible? The world is so bitterly opposed to revelation, let us compare notes and we will see that the divers manners in which revelations were given in ancient times, and the various ways in which the prophets in olden times received revelations, agree with the various ways in which God communicated His mind and will to Joseph Smith. I quote the following from the "Annotated Bible," published in 1859:

The divine communications were spoken to the prophets in divers manners: God seems sometimes to have spoken to them in audible voice; occasionally appearing in the human form. At other times He made use of the ministry of angels, or made known His purposes by dreams. But, He most frequently revealed His truth to the prophets by producing that supernatural state of sentient, intellectual, and moral faculties which the scriptures call "Vision." Hence, prophetic annunciations are often called visions, that is, things seen; and the prophets themselves are called seers. Although the visions which the prophets beheld and the predictions of the future which they announced were wholly announced by the divine spirit, yet the form of the communications, the imagery in which it is clothed, the illustrations by which it is cleared up and impressed, the symbols employed to bring it more graphically before the mind—in short, all that may be considered as its garb and dress, depends upon the education, habits, association, feelings and the whole mental, intellectual and spiritual character of the prophet. Hence the style of some is purer, more sententious, more ornate, or more sublime than others.

Also, the Rev. Joseph Armitage Robinson, D. D., Dean of Westminster and Chaplain of King Edward VII of England, respecting the manner in which the message of the Old Testament was received and communicated to man, said, as late as 1905:

The message of the Old Testament was not written by the divine hand, nor dictated by an outward compulsion. It was planted in the hearts of men, and made to grow in a fruitful soil. And then they were required to express it in their own language after their natural methods and in accordance with the stage of knowledge which their time had reached. Their human faculties were purified and quickened by the divine Spirit; but they spoke to their time in the language of their time; they spoke a spiritual message, accommodated to the experience of their age, a message of faith in God and of righteousness as demanded by a righteous God.—Quoted from Seventy's Third Year Book, by B. H. Roberts.

JOSEPH SMITH A TRUE PROPHET

I have something I want to call your attention to. If this was the last sermon I would ever preach in the flesh, and the last testimony I would ever bear to this people, it is my desire to tell you what is ingrained in my whole being. I believe Joseph Smith was and is a Prophet of God, and I believe it as fervently and honestly as any man in all Israel. I may not have received the revelation and inspiration others have, but I have the testimony of its truth in every fiber of my being.

Joseph Smith had revelations, and they are written and received by the Church. My testimony is that they are true. I have witnessed the fulfillment of many of them. I do not know how I could get a better testimony.

BRIGHAM YOUNG A BUILDER

But President Joseph Smith is dead, and Brother Brigham Young was his successor, and I have the same testimony as to him. I knew him from the time I was a small child, and I testify of his greatness and of his bigness. He was a different man from the Prophet Joseph Smith, who was the great architect of this work under the Almighty. Brother Brigham Young was a great builder, and he builded well and firmly, and as a Prophet of the Lord he continued where the Prophet Joseph ended. One reason why Brother Young was so great was that he had great men beside him, he had men who were tried as gold seven times, who never faltered or fell by the wayside; they held up his hands, no matter how much their hearts were tried. That is my testimony, and I knew nearly every one of them. President Brigham Young is also dead.

PRESIDENT TAYLOR

Then comes President Taylor, a most magnificent specimen of manhood, a man of God that I always honored. Never was I in his presence that his bigness and majesty did not impress me. His personality was wonderful. The first time I went into his presence was in answer to a call to the Southern States as an ambassador of the Gospel. I never could forget him or the impression that he made upon my soul. But he is dead.

PRESIDENT WILFORD WOODRUFF

Then came President Wilford Woodruff. I have personally stood by the side of that good man. Thank God his time was not so precious that he could not sit by me for a few moments—and when I rose to go, the testimony of the Spirit was the same; he surely was a Prophet of God. He is dead also.

PRESIDENT LORENZO SNOW

Then came President Lorenzo Snow—I have the same Spirit and the same testimony concerning him. No man was ever kinder to Golden Kimball than Lorenzo Snow. He put his arm around me before he died, and said, "I need you, I need your help, God bless you." That is the only time I have ever felt like a full grown man. I felt like I was eight feet tall, that God needed me. I have felt big only once, and that was the time when I thought God needed me in this great work.

PRESIDENT JOSEPH F. SMITH

We now have a living prophet, and his name is Joseph F. Smith. This may be my last discourse on this subject. I am not a man that caters to men; I have no ax to grind. I don't want any place only what God wishes to give me; all I expect is a salvation and possibly it will be a scratch if I get it. When I do get in I have paid the price, and am under obligation to no man on God's green earth, if I pay the Lord the price. My father paid full value, and his election was made sure. If I get the same salvation, I expect to pay the same price. I haven't paid it yet. I am entitled to only a little, and God will give me all that belongs to me.

President Joseph F. Smith is the prophet of this Church, and he is the man who is appointed. When the Lord wants to give this Church a revelation, or give it instructions, He will give it through Joseph F. Smith, the Prophet. He will not give it through me, and He will not give it through an apostle. The apostles are prophets, seers, and revelators, and as such we sustain them. God does not give His revelations through the Twelve for His

Church; He gives them through His living prophet that is appointed, as the Prophet Joseph Smith was. I am satisfied I have got this thing figured out about right.

In conclusion, there are a lot of things that we are troubled over. I have spent a few sleepless nights myself, regarding the doings and actions of men who were in authority, but have concluded I am not responsible for anything I may regard as irregularities. I must not lift up my "heel against the anointed and say they have sinned when they have not sinned before the Lord." If the Lord cannot care for His Church, what can I do?

I am going to trust in the Lord, and I am going to trust in His Prophet, Joseph F. Smith. You look all over Israel. I have looked over it, and I know it from Canada to Mexico. We are God's people. Brother Joseph F. Smith is the biggest man in the Church today, and there is not a man in all Israel that has the record he has—a cleaner, a sweeter, a better record. He is the President of the Church of Jesus Christ of Latter-day Saints, and God knows he has earned the place, and the Lord has preserved his life for the appointment.

APPOINTMENTS NOT ENOUGH

I have learned that appointment does not give a man knowledge. My calling gave me no knowledge at the time I was chosen and ordained one of the First Council of Seventy, but it gave me an appointment, opportunities, and many privileges. I have gained knowledge and information just the same as you have got yours. I have an appointment that you have not got, and anyone of you had better not try to get into my shoes; if you do, I will kick you out. [Laughter] Neither am I going to try to get in an apostle's shoes. I am going to let the apostles alone, further than to try to sustain them. As I said once, I say again to all Israel: If the Lord, through His servants, the prophets, places a child in the apostleship, with the help of God I will try to sustain him, if I can. Therefore, O Israel, we must sustain the living prophets. The dead we honor, but the living are chosen, ordained, appointed and sustained, and it is to the living we look for counsel, reproof, and instruction. The Lord bless you. Amen.

TALK NINETEEN

October, 1910

PATIENCE OF THE LORD

In thinking about the mission of our Savior, I desire to give a little evidence for my faith in God the Father and in His Son, Jesus Christ.

I love the Lord because of His great patience. When I think of His patience in creating this world in which we live, which they claim took six thousand years, that of itself appeals to me. When I think of the patience of the Father and His Son with me, one of His children; how, through His providence, His care and protection, and the whisperings of the Holy Spirit, that I have been able to do as well as I have, I feel to thank Him for His kindness unto me. Sometimes I marvel that I have done as well as I have.

The Lord is very patient with His people, with His children. I often think of the time when I was in the South, laboring as an elder in Virginia. The president of the conference in which I was appointed was called into Colorado to continue teaching the people. He shed tears, because he wanted to stay in the Southern States Mission, and "bind up the law and seal up the testimony"; he wanted to condemn all the people and close up the mission so

[228]

the end would come. That was in 1883. We have had a great many elders who would have closed our missionary labors, as far as the world was concerned, but the Lord is not so short-sighted and impatient; He has all eternity, and He proposes to save His children, "excepting the sons of perdition." Some of us become very impatient with each other because we fancy we are better than others, and we become angry with our fellow-men because they will not do as well as we do.

I love the Lord because He causes it to rain upon the just and the unjust, because the sun shines for them as brightly as it does for any of His children. And while He is just, He is merciful.

I thank God the Eternal Father that up to the present I have had the spirit of repentance, and while it has kept me pretty busy repenting, I hope I will always have that spirit. If it were not for repentance and forgiveness, I would become discouraged and discontinue my labors.

OUR SAVIOR

I am going to read to you a little that has been culled from the Bible as to the mission of Christ. I would quote it, but I never dare quote scripture, for after I get through quoting you wouldn't recognize it. [Laughter] I am a little like father, when he used to quote scripture, he would say, "Well, if that isn't in the Bible, it ought to be in it."

[Laughter] So it is not safe for me to quote. Speaking of the mission of our Savior:

Is He not that Mighty Prophet that should come unto the world?

At His birth the air was filled with angels and over Whose couch hung a celestial star.

Before Whose infant feet the three wisest men of the world, representing the family of mankind, bowed in adoration and worshiped, as to God.

This is He whom John the Baptist proclaimed the Lamb of God, which taketh away the sin of the world.

At Whose baptism the heavens were opened above His head, and the Spirit of God descended upon Him in the form of a dove, while the voice of the Lord, like the voice of many thunders, proclaimed from the clouds, "This is my beloved son."

At Whose words the tempest became still, the billowy waves placid, the winds hushed. Who healed the sick and leprous by a word; Who by a look reanimated the lifeless limb of the paralytic; raised the daughter of Jairus; healed the Centurion's servant; restored to life the son of Nain; cast out a legion of devils out of Beor, the Levite; restored the deaf and dumb; gave also to His apostles the same power to do miracles. Feeds at one time four thousand men, and at another time five thousand from a few pounds of bread or a few fishes which a lad could carry in a basket.

Moses and Elias came from the regions of the blessed and held communion with the Savior.

Who calls forth, from the tomb of corruption, Lazarus to life and health.

Who, when praying, was answered by a voice from heaven in the hearing of many people. "I have glorified my name, and will glorify it again."

Was it not the Savior, at whose trial nothing could be found against Him and Who, when delivered to execution by Pilate to save himself and appease the Jews, was publicly declared to be an innocent man by the Procurator, who in calling for water and washing his hands and saying that he was clear of His blood for he found no fault in Him.

Who was He, at whose crucifixion the heavens grew black as sackcloth, the sun withdrew its light, the stars shot from their spheres; the lightning leaped along the earth, the earth itself quaked, and the dead sprang from their graves.

Who, on the third day, burst the bars of the tomb, received as He walked forth the homage of an archangel; Who appeared alive to His mother, to the women of Galilee, to Mary, Martha, and Lazarus, and to the apostles. Does not this prove Him the Christ, the Son of the living God?

That to me is evidence, preponderous evidence; it satisfies me but as J. B. Holland said, in one of his writings:

Better have faith in a fable which inspires to good deeds, conducts our powers to noble ends, makes us loving, gentle, and heroic, eradicates our selfishness, establishes within us the principle of benevolence and enables us to meet death with equanimity, if not with triumph in the hope of a glorious resurrection and a happy immortality, than the skepticism of kingly reason, which only needs to be carried to its legitimate issues to bestialize the human race and drape the earth in the blackness of Tartarus.

CLEAN HEARTS OF THIS PEOPLE

My brethren and sisters, I believe in this work. I believe in the Prophet Joseph Smith. I want to sustain the Priesthood of God. I love the people,

[231]

and I say, God save the people. When I look over this body of men, I do not discover that you are very distinguished in appearance. Why, you are no better looking than I am, and I look pretty bad. [Laughter] I am only a remnant of what I ought to be. I am not very well groomed, and I do not look distinguished; neither do you. [Laughter] You can't boast very much about your appearance. We are a hard-working people, and we would not take a very good picture, unless you take the better side of us. But I tell you, in the name of the Lord, we have got clean hearts; we love the Lord; we love truthfulness; we desire to be honest, truthful, and virtuous. You can't judge us by our appearance. If you knew the hearts of this people, there would not be the bitterness there is against the Latter-day Saints.

LOYALTY AND INTEGRITY TO CHURCH

I pray the Lord to bless you. With all of my weakness, with all of my difficulties, I would like to see the color of the man's hair, and I would like to look into the eyes of the man that questions my loyalty and integrity to this Church. You may have to be patient and long-suffering with J. Golden Kimball, but don't you question my integrity. I think I have given some evidence of my faith, loyalty, and integrity. I learned it by being a stranger in a strange country. I learned it by traveling without purse or scrip, and I want to tell you, in the name

[232]

of Israel's God, the Lord is amply able to provide for His servants. You do not have to "trust in the arm of flesh." The Lord has answered my prayers; He has opened up the way before me; He has raised up friends upon the right hand and upon the left. That is how I secured my knowledge and information. I know, just as well as I ever expect to know (until I see with my eyes) that Jesus is the Christ, that Joseph is a Prophet of God, and that this is the Church of Jesus Christ of Latter-day Saints. I sustain the Church. I support as best I know how the Presidency of this Church, the Council of the Twelve, and the general authorities of the Church. The Lord bless you. Amen.

TALK TWENTY

April, 1911

SALVATION

Now, why should we not have faith in God the Father and in Jesus Christ? We all have an equal chance; He is no respecter of persons; He is a God of truth. We never need be in doubt about those matters. I think some of us are mistaken; I think we have gone off wrong; I think that we expect salvation without doing very much to get it.

It is all in vain for men to think that they merely need to have faith, and repent, and be baptized, and receive the Holy Ghost by the laying on of hands, and then their salvation is made sure. There never was a greater mistake. "It is in vain for persons to fancy to themselves that they are heirs with those, or can be heirs with those, who have offered their all in sacrifice, and by this means obtained faith in God, and favor with Him, so as to obtain eternal life, unless they, in like manner, offer unto Him the same sacrifice, and through that offering obtain the knowledge that they are accepted of Him."

For a man to lay down his all (his character and reputation, his honor, and applause, his good name among men, his houses, his lands, his brothers

[234]

and sisters, his wife and children, and even his own life, counting all things but filth and dross for the excellency of the knowledge of Jesus Christ) requires more than mere belief that he is doing the will of God. It calls for an actual knowledge, does it not, Latter-day Saints? A man who gets off on this is in a very sad condition.

LUKEWARM MEMBERS

Some of us know how a man feels who hasn't that spirit—one who has become careless and indifferent. The Lord knows if there is any one I sympathize with it is a man who is not doing his duty, and who is a member of this Church, because I know how he feels. I am going to tell you how he feels, because I know whereof I speak. I have been in that place, in the history of life.

A man who considers his religion a slavery has not begun to comprehend the real nature of religion. To such men, religion is a life of crosses and mortifications. They find their duty unpleasant and onerous. It is to them a law of restraint and constraint. They are constantly oppressed with what they denominate a "sense of duty." It torments them with a consciousness of their inefficiency and with a multiplied perplexing doubt of the genuineness of their religious experiences. They feel themselves enchained within the bounds of a religious system. That is the feeling of every man who is careless, and every man who is indifferent.

[235]

Are they happy in that condition? I say no; only those are happy who are doing their duty.

LOVE CHRIST

The question is, do we really love Christ? That is the whole question. I am made to feel more and more that the religion of the Latter-day Saints is to be tested in this generation. Our fathers died for the faith, and so with our mothers, and we are living on the faith of our fathers and mothers—a great many of us. We have never made the sacrifice, and we are unwilling to prepare ourselves for it.

Now, brethren, I plead for fraternity; I plead for love of each other. If we can't find friends among the Latter-day Saints, and those who will speak a good word for us, even when we are "unwise," without putting in those infernal expressions, "Yes, he is a good man, but if—" I wish to the Lord you would leave those things out. I repeat, if we can't find friends among our own people where can we expect to find them? The Lord bless you. Amen.

TALK TWENTY-ONE
October, 1912

GIVE US MEN LIKE OUR FATHERS

If I were to put up an appeal to the Lord for the present generation, I would say, "Give us men, men like our fathers, and women like our mothers, men and women who had faith in God, whose religion was love and sacrifice, and who were willing to lay down everything for God." They were men who were clean, who were pure, who were courageous, and who were not afraid to do right when they knew it was right. Now, that is the kind of men we want. That is the kind of men we hope that our children will be.

HALF-WAY MEN

But, there is another class of men, I call them half-way men; I pray God I may never be found among them. I would rather be dead than to be numbered among half-way men, persons who have plaster-cast expressions on their faces and are without hearts, without souls, without love and bigness. They are the hypocritical class, such as were found among men when Jesus was on the earth. They have the presumption and nerve to want everything on earth as a reward for their assumed generosity.

[237]

They call it alms-giving or helping the poor; some call it religion, but that is a misnomer.

That kind of people are a spineless class, self-righteous, intolerant, and the cause of endless mischief. They never fight in the open. They are demagogues and place hunters. They are perched upon every anthill, croaking out their stump speeches for this or for that man to hold office. They never give it a thought whether such a man will do good for the people or not. They are parasites who feed and fatten upon the people. "They want us to beat in the brush while they bag the game." Some of this is not original, but it is mighty good. [Laughter] When it comes to self-sacrifice, fighting for the truth, they are like the dying man who was asked by the minister, "Will you denounce the devil and all his workings?" The dying man looked up in a feeble and distressed way and said, "Please don't ask me to do that. I am going to a strange country, and I don't want to make any enemies." [Laughter]

FOR OR AGAINST GOD

"Rock-a-bye baby in the tree top" won't work out our problems. There is no use crying, "All is well in Zion," because it is not true. The question is, who is for God and who is against Him? This puts me in mind of another story. In the midst of an election in Denver, a little girl sat in a church with her suffragette mother, listening to a minister who was preaching with much earnestness and emphatic gestures. When he had finished, the little girl turned to her mother and asked: "Mother, was he for or against God?"

MORMONS A VALUABLE HERITAGE

The Mormon people are a valuable heritage to the race. We have had physical vigor, which must be one of the foundations for the mental strength of any lasting race of people. Our lives have been ruled by high impulses. There is only a generation or two between us and our pioneer fathers and mothers. It is physically impossible for this type of man to be produced in any other way than by developing the possibilities of this splendidly endowed earth. Buckskin men are not developed indoors. We cannot evolve men like Washington, Boone, George Rogers, David Crockett, Joseph Smith the Prophet, Brigham Young, or the other pioneers, under the present environment and educational system. Some one said, "We run our children through a course of education covering from eight to twelve years, then they are turned loose and called educated."

BONDAGE OF LUXURY

Now, my brethren and sisters, with the help of the Lord let us endeavor to uplift the present generation, that they may have breathed into them the spirit of their forefathers, that they may have courage to resist evil, live a better and cleaner life, find out what is right and then stay with it. Unless this generation will get the spirit of our forefathers, what can God do to preserve the Constitution? Unless the children of this nation rise up and get away from the bondage and serfdom of luxury, of ease, of comfort—you can't evolve true men with that kind of environment—it can't be done. That is the appeal I make to the present generation.

YELLOW STREAK

I tell you, God can do nothing with a half-way man. You never saw one of them in your life that gave evidence of a yellow streak in him that ever amounted to anything. I sent one of my sons to do a certain thing. He did not get what he went after, but he held up his colors and fought to a finish. There never has been a time in my life when I was so proud of my boy; he did not show the yellow streak. That is the way I feel towards the Kingdom of God.

TESTED MEN

I don't know of a man in all the world that I could sustain easier than the man who has fought his way up these mountains and over the valleys, through hardships, sufferings, and privations, like the President of this Church has. If any man on this earth has a right to his position today, and has earned it, he is the man, and there are others with him.

I was conversing with a prominent stranger yesterday, and he told me he was prejudiced when he came here, and I said: "I wish you had known our leading men. I wish you had been acquainted with Brigham Young and Heber C. Kimball; you would have liked them." He said, "Do you think so?" I replied, "I know you would or else you are not a man like I am." [Laughter]

I pray God to bless you, my brethren and sisters. I may be near the finish of my labor, but let it come and let come weal or woe, life or death; if God will give me His Spirit, and I retain the courage of my convictions; I will be true to God and defend the Church of Jesus Christ of Latter-day Saints. The Lord bless you. Amen.

TALK TWENTY-TWO
April, 1913

FAMILY RESPONSIBILITY

There is a great responsibility resting upon us fathers, and upon the mothers, and I do not think there has ever been a time in my life when I have felt the responsibility to be so weighty and great upon me in all my labors in the Church as it is at the present time with my own family. They are not many in number. But there are enough of them, and about all I can handle.

I think you will find somewhere in the Old Testament that "the fathers have eaten a sour grape and the children's teeth are set on edge." I have to confess to you that I have eaten some sour grapes in my day, and there is a problem regarding my children. And while I am interested in my children and family, I have similar interest for your children and families. I will read some scripture that I thought of today. I have heard it many times; it is found in *Matthew*, 8th chapter and 11th and 12th verses:

And I say unto you, that many shall come from the east and west, and shall sit down with Abraham, and Isaac, and Jacob, in the kingdom of heaven.

But the children of the kingdom shall be cast out into outer darkness: there shall be weeping and gnashing of teeth.

PARENTAGE AND SALVATION

I am very proud of my parentage. I do not think any one appreciates his parentage more than I do. But, I want to say to the Latter-day Saints that pride in parentage won't save you. If we get salvation, we must keep the commandments, and serve the Lord. Knowledge pertaining to the Gospel of Jesus Christ does not come through ordination, nor by appointment, nor by lineage, nor through father and mother, though they are helpful. But no matter who my father and mother were, or how devoted and faithful they have been; no matter how much work they have accomplished, and how much Gospel they have preached to the children of men; I tell you if Heber C. Kimball's children are saved in the Kingdom they must keep the commandments of God, or they won't be saved. If they don't accomplish it here, I am glad to know they will have another chance.

LAXITY TOWARD CHILDREN

I don't want to be radical, but I think we are in great danger; I think it is wrong for us to sit down quietly and feel satisfied that "All is well in Zion," that our children and children's children are not in constant danger. There was a time in the peaceful valleys of these mountains when we were as one great patriarchal family, when it seemed practically safe for our children to run hither and thither, when it was just as safe in this great city

[243]

of Salt Lake as it is in your distant country places to leave your doors open. I was born right up here on the hill and have known this city all my life; it is not safe anymore.

There are no people, I think, in the known world, where there is more laxity and freedom given to the children than there is among the Latter-day Saints. I want to warn the people that there is great danger on every hand. I would just as soon think of putting my daughters in a den of lions as to send them to Salt Lake without some one to look after them. When I say that, I am not saying anything against the people of Salt Lake. I am not saying there is not as good a class of people in Salt Lake, as good Latter-day Saints, and as pure a lot of people as can be found in the world. But, I tell you there is no longer safety for your children, if you don't look after them, I don't care who you are, apostle, or prophet, evangelist, pastor, or teacher. The responsibility rests upon us to look after our children, and I appreciate the responsibility.

TEACH CHILDREN GOOD PRINCIPLES

My heart has not been broken yet over my children, but I realize the danger; and whenever one of my boys goes away I am concerned; I am full of anxiety, I have little peace or rest of body. All in the world I can do with my boy, my oldest boy, who is away now at work, because I cannot get him work here—and that is a responsibility resting upon us, to provide employment here for our boys and girls, so that we won't have to send them away off; we should regard that as a part of our religion;—all in the world I can do for my boy is to teach him good principles. I do a great deal of writing. And I just put a little good counsel in here and there, and hope he will catch it, and get his feet anchored, and realize the danger that menaces him on every side.

PRIVATE WORSHIP

I believe in public worship; it is part of our religion; it is part of the revelation to this people that they shall attend to their public worship. But I don't believe that public worship is the only worship acceptable to our Heavenly Father. It is along that line I would like to talk to you a few moments, that is, about private worship.

Jesus lays great stress on private devotion. "When thou prayest," says our Master, "enter into thy closet, and when thou hast shut thy door, pray to thy Father which is in secret." The reason this thought has come to me is because of my own household. It is not because I am intending to criticize your home, or render judgment as to the way in which you manage your household, but because I have a household of my own. The question is as to private devotion. Now, Isaac's closet was a field, David's closet was his bed chamber, the Lord's closet was the mountain, Peter's closet was the house-top. Now, the question is, can God be nearer to us while we are praying in solitude than when praying in congregations? Do we need to go to church to find God?

PRAYER IS NECESSARY

Some say, why is prayer necessary, since God presumably knows, without being told, the wishes of all men? God assuredly does know the wishes in the hearts of all men. Is not the impulse to pray a natural one, springing from love for the Lord? And is that impulse given to all of God's children? Yes, if the person loves the Lord he will have a great desire to communicate with Him. But if this love is lacking, is it not almost useless to force it?

PRAY FROM THE HEART

Now, there is the question. I am trying to get my children to pray. When I was a boy, my father did most of the praying in the home, and when I got to manhood I did not know just how or what to pray for. In fact, I did not know very much about the Lord, because my father died when I was fifteen years old. But I can remember how he prayed, and I have been sorry, many times, that I can't pray like my father did; for he seemed on those occasions to be in personal communication with God. There seemed to be a friendliness between my father and God, and when you heard him pray you would actually think the Lord was right there, and that father was talking to Him.

[246]

Can you pray that way? Are you on friendly terms with the Lord? I don't mean that we should get too friendly and try to take advantage, like children do with parents, but that we should manifest reverence and love for the Lord, asking only for what we need, and not for what we want. I think if you will just ask the Lord for what you need each day, and you will believe that the Lord is near and can answer your prayers, then there may be friendship between you and God. Well, then, learn to love the Lord.

LOVE FOR THE LORD

But, how is this love to be cultivated? Now, there is the question, can we sit down and teach our children? How are you going to cultivate love for the Lord? In other words, how is this love to be obtained?

If you cannot understand what God has done for you, and you cannot learn to love God; then you cannot pray to Him. I may be wrong in stating that you can't pray. You might practice until you can, but you don't feel satisfied after you have got through praying, and you don't feel like your prayers have ascended to the Father, because your prayers are not built on love and gratitude.

Now, how are you going to cultivate love for God? You don't know much about Him. He has not communicated much to you. Perhaps some of our children have never had a prayer answered.

We must study, think, reason, try to comprehend the goodness and the wisdom of God, and the knowledge you obtain will help you to appreciate what God has done. You cannot then fail to love Him, if you can only get impressed with what God has done for you.

GOD SHOWS NO FAVORITISM

I love God for one thing, if nothing else: That He gives to every one of His children, black or white, bond or free, an equal chance. I like equality of opportunity, and whenever parents make a favorite of a child, I feel sorry for the favorite. If you want to destroy your family, show favoritism, and do not give every child an equal chance. We parents have got to learn that lesson. Not to favor the child because we love it, but favor each and every child alike; that is a sacred obligation. God does that with all of His children, and if there is any disadvantage or any wrong, we do it against each other—God does not do it.

SIMPLE PRAYERS

Prayer can be made in a simple, humble manner, without using a multitude of words. A person does not love the Lord just because He created him, or because He has given him health or wealth. Your love may become weakened when illness and sorrow come to you. I hear people pray, "I thank thee, Lord, for health." They ought to be thankful; it is the greatest blessing we can have.

DO YOU FORGET GOD IN YOUR TRIALS?

But what do you do when you are sick? Do you forget God? What do you do when you accumulate a little means? I haven't been in poverty all of my life; neither have I been raised with a silver spoon in my mouth. I went out and fought my battles in the North Country. I know what it costs to earn your bread by the sweat of your brow. I was mighty grateful for what I acquired, because I worked for it. I never grafted men for it, but I lost it. Now, have I forgotten God, because I lost it? Is my love and gratitude to God on so small a foundation that just as soon as I lose my health or wealth, I will forget my Maker?

I have had a little experience along that line, when I went into the South and got poisoned from the crown of my head to the soles of my feet with malaria. I have now got appendicitis on both sides. Am I going to forget God? Am I going to say that God has not been good to me? Why, no; I feel that I have been favored above the whole Kimball race; I have got opportunities and privileges some of them have never had. Am I going to forsake my God? No, I have learned to love Him—not as well as my father loved Him, perhaps, but I am learning to love Him.

Now, what do you love God for? We should love the Lord for justice, for His perfection and mercy, because He manifests His love by giving His children an equal chance in life's labor. We

[249]

should ask for what we need, and find pleasure and
spiritual enjoyment in it.

LEARN TO PRAY

I know that we have got to teach our children to pray. I remember an incident that happened upon the ill-fated *Titanic*. Those people
were in distress on that great ocean—I have never
seen the ocean, but I have always been afraid of
it. I read about a group of them that climbed onto
a raft, some of them rich and wealthy, some of them
as good people as ever lived, and they wanted to
pray. The band was playing, and the end was about
to close upon them. They wanted to offer the
Lord's Prayer, but they did not know it; and some
one had to lead them, and they followed in saying
the Lord's Prayer. They did not know how or
what to ask for. They were so frightened, perhaps,
and so unaccustomed to pray that they could only
repeat the Lord's Prayer, and some one had to lead
them. Now, I would like to learn how to pray before I get in such an emergency.

I want to ask you Latter-day Saints if you can
have private devotion in the home unless you are
agreed and unless you have everything in order? Do
you ever try to pray in the morning when the children have only fifteen minutes to get to school?
I thank the Lord there is one place where my children are always on time; whether they get their
breakfast or not, they get to school. Did you ever

know children to lose their breakfast to get to prayers? The father almost needs the patience of Job to get a family together for morning prayer. That is pretty plain talk, but you seem to understand what I mean. I guess you have tried it.

PRIVATE DEVOTION

Don't forget private devotion; learn to pray in your home and get in communication with God, as my father did, right up there on Gordon avenue. In that little bit of room there, my father communicated with God, and God answered him. I have got it in writing. I am a living witness that it has been fulfilled.

GOD COMMUNICATES WITH HIS CHILDREN

I will tell you a story, and then I will quit. Father had men working for him for a good many years, and he had one he called Colonel Smith. It was in the days of hardships and poverty, and men had great difficulty. They employed a great many people, the brethren did; that was a part of their religion. He employed the colonel, who had been a soldier in Great Britain. And on one occasion he went to father for a pair of shoes, and I guess father felt pretty cross, and answered him a little abruptly, perhaps. So the colonel went home feeling bad, and when he prayed that night, he made a complaint to God against father, saying that "Thy servant, Heber," was not treating him right.

When he came past that little place on Gordon avenue, next morning, father came out and said, "Robert, what did you complain against me for? You come in and get your shoes, and don't do it again?" Now, how did he know that Colonel Robert Smith, who lived away down in the Nineteenth ward, had filed a complaint against him? Don't you think that we can get on friendly terms with God? Not on familiar terms, but friendly terms? I tell you, God will answer your prayers. If there was any one thing I knew better than another, when I was traveling in the South, it was that God answers prayers and softens the hearts of people towards you. May the Lord bless you. Amen.

TALK TWENTY-THREE
April, 1914

CLEAN TOWN CONTEST

I am very thankful this morning, notwithstanding the condition of my physical body, that I have been busily engaged cleaning up my own dooryard. I could not get the boy to do it, so I got busy and did it myself. [Laughter] I am pretty near dead tired as a result of it; but I am grateful for this suggestion to the Latter-day Saints, as to the Clean Town Contest.

In our beautiful Utah, many of the homes and farms are old-fashioned. There is very little intense farming. Some people declare that nearly everybody is slipshod; barns, houses, out-buildings are fast going to ruin. The front yards are weed-grown; the fences down and hid by weeds; no flowers, no lawns, no vegetable gardens, no family orchards, or if there is, the trees are old, sickly, and neglected. The fact is, no more beautiful valley, no better place has God's people ever found. No people have been more greatly favored during the last year as to climate. The past winter has been unexcelled, it has been just lovely. There is no need to go to California, or to the East, North, or South. I have made enquiries, and am posted.

[253]

As the saying is, we have all countries and climates "skinned to death."

NOT AFRAID OF WORK

What we need is old-time enthusiasm. We should make a strong appeal to the rising generation and get the boys and girls to use their heads, and go to work with their hands. We need practical education, ambition, push. The whole family ought to work, none should be ashamed of work; but all should roll up their sleeves and dig. The key to success is: "We're not afraid of work." There should be no aged father or mother bent with hard work, who could say: "Our boys and girls are educated so much that they go away from the home and farm and forget us." We appeal to their children to give them a lift occasionally. Let the cry go out to all and create a desire among the citizens of our cities and towns to clean up and beautify the old homesteads and surroundings. Some of our homes, outbuildings and fences need whitewashing awfully bad.

BEAUTIFUL HOMES

I visited my mother's home town in Hopewell, New Jersey, in 1884; and I found there was no home, no outbuilding, no fence that was not painted, or whitewashed.

Now, brethren and sisters, wake up and make a good try-out in following this suggestion. No greater blessing can come to this people than a thorough and general cleaning of homes and surroundings.

The Lord bless you all. Amen.

TALK TWENTY-FOUR

April, 1915

TALK ABOUT REAL THINGS

To speak to people in the open is new to me, but there is something about it I like, and that is, if you don't care for what I say, you can return home. [Laughter]

What I want to talk about are real things, not something that I do not know anything about. When I get through, I will have told you something I know, so that you can go home and think about it. I am going to talk about things that have happened since I was born, not something that happened eighteen hundred years ago, or that will happen hundreds of years in the future.

TEMPLE STONES SPEAK

When President Brigham Young came with the pioneers, he was sick and prostrated in the wagon in which he was riding; but he rose and saw this valley, and said: "This is the place; drive on!" He did not preach for an hour over it. When he came upon the ground where this temple now stands, he dropped his cane, and said: "Here, we will build a temple to our God." They got busy; they prayed about it, they fasted, and then they built it. It took them forty years. When I think about that building, every stone in it is a sermon to me. It tells of suffering, it tells of sacrifice, it preaches—every rock in it preaches a discourse. When it was dedicated, it seemed to me that it was the greatest sermon that has ever been preached since the Sermon on the Mount. When I get up on the Capitol Hill, and see that great building—a great pile of granite, etc., that will cost two million and a half—there is not a stone in it that whispers! It is speechless. It does not tell of suffering or of faith the way the Temple does. Any man who will come to the Bureau of Information and listen to the guides will learn that every window, every steeple, everything about the Temple speaks of the things of God, and gives evidence of the faith of the people who built it.

SAVED BY GULLS

When I see this monument here [indicating the Sea Gull Monument standing on the Temple Grounds] I notice that many of you men pass it by as if it told no story. When I think of that monument, it tells me of suffering, it tells me of a people that were about to be destroyed by famine, it tells me of crickets that were destroying and eating up everything. The people prayed, they fasted, and they got busy; every man, woman, and child killed crickets. But they could not kill them all, so God came in and helped them. He sent the gulls, and they ate the crickets, and the people were saved.

WORK FOR THE HUNGRY

That Tabernacle preaches the same kind of sermon. I helped haul sand for it, when I was a boy. Every Saturday we had to haul sand, and that is how I learned something about these things. You see this wall surrounding this block—do you think we built it to keep the Indians out? I want to tell you we built it to give employment. And when people were out of work, and hungry, we found something for them to do. If we could not find anything else to do, we built walls. That is what you want to do now—give service, give work.

When Christ gathered the people together, they were hungry; and then the Master fed them. And after they were filled He gave them the Bread of Life, and told them the truth. If people are out of employment, find something for them to do, and then bless them.

GO ON A MISSION

Think of what this people have done, not what they have preached, but what they have accomplished, and what they have suffered. I desire to say to you seventies, get ready and after a while we will sing the hymn, "Hark, Listen to the Trumpeters. They Sound for Volunteers." Now, we will not say to you what the Savior said to the young man: "Sell whatsoever thou hast and give to the poor, and take up thy cross and follow Me, and I will give you the greatest of all gifts that God has ever given His children, which is eternal life." All we ask you to do is to give whatsoever you have to your family, and pick up your valise and go on a mission. Do you want eternal life? Almost everybody here would be awfully keen for it, if it did not cost anything. We would accept the whole world if it did not cost anything; I would be willing to take half of it myself. [Laughter]

ETERNAL LIFE

The greatest of all gifts is eternal life, but we have to pay for it, just like our fathers and mothers did. We will have to pay for it with service, and with sacrifice, as there can be no blessings obtained without sacrifice. I know what is the matter. We think more of automobiles, we think more of oriental-rugs and hundred-dollar gowns than we do of salvation. I know you have faith, many of you; and now we want to begin to hold on with both hands and make this fight for the Lord. I prophesy that hundreds of you, thousands of you, will go into the world on missions.

PREPARE FOR MISSION

Now, my brethren, every man who holds the holy Melchizedek Priesthood, and is a special witness for God, should get ready for a mission.

[259]

Begin to pay your debts and train your family
and get them so that they will be glad to have you
go. Stop writing letters to the First Council, making a lot of excuses that your wife is sick, that you
are in debt, or that you are sick. What is faith for?
Who is the Great Physician? Why don't I get well?
Because I haven't faith enough. I am trying to hurry
up and get well so that I can go.

WORLD BELONGS TO VISIONARY MEN

You must look into the future; this world
belongs to the visionary men. Brigham Young had
vision. He said that this city would reach to the
point of the mountain south, and I am a witness
that it will come true. People did not believe it.
Joseph Smith had a vision, a revelation that we
would "come to the Rocky Mountains and build
great cities, and become a mighty people." We
have started to fulfill that prophecy.

SEVENTIES MUST COMFORT THE DESOLATE

Now, brethren and sisters, we have prophets,
we have apostles, we have the gifts and the blessings. You seventies must go out and heal the sick;
you must go out and comfort the desolate; and you
must go to the nations of the world, after this war
is over—it cannot last forever. You seventies will
go—this prophecy will come true, otherwise we
will make high priests of you, and ordain other
seventies who will go. The Lord bless you. Amen.

TALK TWENTY-FIVE

October, 1917

THIRST AFTER RIGHTEOUSNESS

I am not accustomed to speak in audiences out of doors. I have always had them closed in where they could not get away. [Laughter] Brethren and sisters and friends, I want to bless you people, in the name of the Lord; for he surely ought to bless a people who hunger and thirst after righteousness enough to stand up as you have stood and listen to the word of the Lord.

WHY FEAR DEATH?

Why fear death? That is what I am talking about to myself all the time. People have been looking for it in my case for a considerable length of time, but I have fooled them up to date; and I am trying to learn not to fear death. A great man said when he went down with the ship. "Why fear death? It is the most beautiful adventure of life." He must have been exalted by a spiritual enthusiasm such as elders have when they go out into the world in the service of the Lord. They feel as Christ felt when he said, "Think not of your life, of what you shall eat, or of what you shall drink, or of your body and what you shall put on." I want to say,

on the side, that is about all we are thinking about
—at least some of us.

SUFFER TO FIND FAITH

My brethren and sisters, the short time I occupy I want to say to you that my knowledge is
very limited, and it does not take me very long to
tell it; but what I do know, I know as well as any
man in this Church from the least to the greatest.
Why do I know it? Because I have learned it
through the things which I have suffered. We have
to suffer sometimes to find things out, until our
hearts are twisted, before we are meek and humble
and have faith in God.

ON THE LORD'S SIDE

I remember reading a story. The incident
happened during the Civil War, when a large committee of Christian ministers came to Washington
to wait on President Abraham Lincoln. After they
had performed their duties, one of the Christian
ministers turned to President Lincoln, and he said,
"I hope the Lord is on our side." That is what all
these nations are hoping, that the Lord is on their
side. And President Lincoln said, "Well, I am not
much concerned about the Lord being on our side,"
which was quite a shock to the ministers. "I am
not concerned about that. What I am most concerned about is whether we are on the Lord's side."
That is what I want you to be concerned about, you

men who hold the holy priesthood; you want to remember, in this great rush and hurry, not
to be too much taken up with man's business,
but you want to be exercised more about "our
Father's business."

BEAUTY OF HUMAN LIFE

I am going to ask you a few questions, and will
let you answer them. If you don't know enough
to answer them, then you don't know as much as
I do. [Laughter] I am going to ask you this question: Do you know of anything—you can think
about your money, your wives, and children, and
everything else—but do you know of anything in
all this beautiful world more important than human life? If you do, just hold up your hands.

SALVATION THE GREATEST GIFT

I am going to ask you another question: Do
you know of any gift in all this world, or blessing,
that is greater than salvation? No, because God
said in the revelation that "salvation is the greatest
gift of God to His children." These are reasons why
you ought to be in the service of the Lord. That is
why these presidents of missions and elders are
blessed. And that is why we are able to come home as
I did from the South in 1884—and it is one of the
greatest truths I ever told in my life, although I
never had as hard a time in all my life as I had in
the South, and when I think of it now, I actually

shudder—and yet I came home to you people and I looked you in the face and I told you it was the happiest time of all my life, and I never lied, either. That is what you get for being in the service of the Lord.

THE LAST DAYS

As a servant of the Lord, I only want to repeat what the servants of God have said: "These are the last days, spoken of by the prophets, when perilous times shall come."

CONSTRUCTIVE LEADERSHIP

There has never been a time such as the present in the history of the world, when men ought to be talking big things, thinking big things, doing big things, and overcoming their selfishness. It is a day of destruction, and leaders must be raised up who are constructive. Constructive work sometimes means destructive—you tear down to build up; you change the old for the new. Leaders must have a knowledge of mankind in order that the Lord's plans may be carried out.

The German nation is one of the greatest nations today when we consider her social and industrial condition, although it is founded on militarism.

CHURCH A PERFECT ORGANIZATION

The Church of Jesus Christ of Latter-day Saints, as it has been organized through the Prophet

[264]

Joseph Smith, is more perfectly organized and greater than any other organization upon the earth.

When you contemplate this great organization you find prophets and inspiration which is not founded on militarism, but brotherhood, fraternity, and "love-one-another," which is in accordance with the teachings of Jesus Christ. The great test was: "By this shall all men know that ye are my disciples, if ye have love one for another."

If you have not love for one another you have not the spirit of the Gospel.

May the Lord bless you. Amen.

TALK TWENTY-SIX
April, 1918

This is the first time in twenty-five years of missionary service that I have been honored to preside at a public meeting connected with the Semi-annual Conference of the Church, and I would like to preside with a good deal of dignity, and have tried to do so.

WRITTEN DISCOURSES COLD

I am a little nervous when given an opportunity to speak, knowing that what I say will be taken down by a stenographer, and when my discourse is written in cold type, it doesn't read well or sound good to me, as it has but little spirit, and no feeling in it. I am now speaking of my discourses.

NOT UNDERSTOOD BY ALL

My purpose is not to discourse on wonderful things that I have achieved and experienced, but my wish and desire is to reach the hearts of men. I only wish I were better understood; but unless men are of my temperament and see things as I see them with a moving-picture mind, they can not comprehend things in the way I do.

SALVATION

I may not stand blameless before God at the last day, but I am not afraid to meet my God and be judged by the Lord as to my desires, efforts and works. I understand the Gospel of Jesus Christ well enough to know that God is perfect and deals out justice and mercy to His children; Jesus Christ is the door to the sheep-fold, and with all my many imperfections and weaknesses, if I am invited by the Master to come in at the door, all men who try to block my way will get run over and pushed aside.

HAS RESPONDED TO CALL

I do not trust in man, but I honor and respect men who hold the Priesthood of God. I haven't given my life for this work, but have shown forth a willingness to place the little I have on the altar. I haven't been called, nor asked to do anything, that I have not responded to. No appointment has been given me that I have not filled, in my way, and to the best of my ability.

I can do anything I am set apart to do, if I have the spirit of my appointment and am humble and prayerful.

SPIRIT OF PROPHECY

I know the sick are healed through the laying on of hands, as well as any man in all Israel, as I have witnessed the healing of the sick. I know we have the spirit of prophecy, for I have tried it out, and it works all right, if you get the spirit of prophecy.

[267]

TRUST THE LORD

If you can grasp my meaning you will know exactly how I feel towards the Church and the priesthood. The Lord knows I love the Church, her people, and my country, and I have no fear that the Lord cannot overrule and overturn nations and people, until they shall repent and serve him. The Lord has taken care of me, and I have learned to trust Him, as He is a good Master, and He is full of mercy, justice, kindness and love.

JOY OF SAVING A SOUL

Brethren and sisters, this work is true, for I have worked and labored in it until I know of its truth. I am now going to ask you a question: "Do you know of anything in all this great universe that is dearer to the Father than a human soul?" You don't, do you? Of course, you don't, as the Lord said in the *Doctrine and Covenants,* "And if it so be that you should labor all your days in crying repentance unto this people, and bring save it be one soul unto Me, how great will be your joy with him in the Kingdom of My Father."

ADVERTISE THINGS OF GOD

To be saved in the Kingdom of God is the greatest of all the gifts of God; for there is no gift greater than the gift of salvation. Then "soul hunting" is of far greater importance than spending one's life in money seeking and the accumulation of wealth. I can see that the things of God must be made more interesting than the things of the world, that the things of God must be better advertised than the material things of the world.

BLESS THE CHOIR

I almost forgot the one thing I desired to say, and that is: God bless the choir, the singers and the musicians. I know as well as I know anything that the Lord will bless Brother Evan Stephens; and as a servant of the Lord, I promise him he shall have the Holy Spirit to comfort and console him, and he shall not be lonely or desolate among this people. God bless all these sweet singers he is training. Little do you people know what it costs in time, effort, and study to acquire the art to sing. If we as a people put forth a tithe of the effort they do to sing, in studying the word of God, we would be the most intelligent people in the world. The Lord bless you. Amen.

TALK TWENTY-SEVEN

October, 1918

SPIRIT OF GOD

I often wonder when you do have the Spirit of God. I used to think I had it in the Southern States, when I became excited and sensational, and my face was red, and the cords of my neck swollen —I thought then, in my ignorance, that it was the Holy Ghost. I learned differently afterwards. I am sure that was not the Spirit of God. I have learned since that the Spirit of God gives you joy and peace and patience and long-suffering and gentleness, and you have the spirit of forgiveness and you love the souls of the children of men. I have learned that the Holy Ghost is the spirit of prophecy and the spirit of revelation.

I think of my father—our father, the father of a great race of people—he prophesied once somewhere on these temple grounds, when the people were in poverty, when they were almost disheartened, and things looked so dark and dreary before them. Heber C. Kimball prophesied that goods would be sold as cheaply in Salt Lake City as in New York. After he sat down, he said to Brigham Young, "Well, Brother Brigham, I have done it now."

Brother Brigham said, "Never mind, Heber, let it go."

They did not, either one of them, believe it. [Laughter]

After the meeting adjourned, Apostle Charles C. Rich, I am told, went up to Heber C. Kimball, and he said, "Heber, I don't believe a word you said."

Heber said: "Neither do I." [Laughter] But he rounded it out: "But God hath spoken."

It was not Heber at all; it was God who spoke through Heber as a prophet. A short time after, the prophecy was literally fulfilled.

So that sometimes, and very often, the servants of God speak by the Spirit of God, but some of the people haven't got the same spirit, and do not believe the servants of God. Now, brethren, I want to express to you this thought, that it is just as necessary for you Latter-day Saints to have the Spirit of God as it is for the apostles and the seventies and the presidents of stakes and the bishops. For when you speak, or when the servants of God speak under the influence of the Holy Spirit, it is the word of God to the Latter-day Saints. I do not care whether you like the mannerism or the crudity of the speaker. That does not make any difference whatever; it is the word of God to you.

TRUE SERVANTS OF GOD

The Lord said, not only to the seventies but to the Priesthood of God: "If you desire to serve God, you are called to the work." I have that desire burning in my heart like a living fire, and so has every other man who holds the Priesthood of God and has the spirit of his appointment. Again, in that same revelation, the Lord tells us what qualifies us for the work. It is not money. What is it? It is faith, hope, charity and love, with an eye single to the glory of God, and any man who holds the Priesthood of God, who has those gifts, is qualified and fitted for the work. All he needs is to be called to the work by those holding divine authority.

GREATEST GIFT IS SALVATION

In conclusion: I have worked in the Church, perhaps not as well as I might have done, but I have staked everything on it. As I told a man one day, I had fifty-two cards in the beginning. I never played cards in my life—only smut. But to illustrate: In the beginning I had fifty-two of them—that is a deck, I think. Some of you seventies are better informed, perhaps, than I, but at the present time I have only one card left. Do you know what I have staked it on? Eternal life; and if I fail in that I have failed in everything. Why? Because "salvation is the greatest gift of God to His children." Of all the gifts and all the blessings that God can give to His children, the "greatest gift is salvation."

HUNDREDFOLD PROMISED SERVANTS OF GOD

If you leave your father and if you leave your mother, your wife and your children, and your flocks and your herds, and all that you have, and go out as a witness for God, He has promised you an hundredfold. All the investments I ever made in my life, except the one of two Liberty Bonds, have been failures. All I got out of them was experience; the other fellow got the money. [Laughter] But this investment we have started for, the Lord has promised us an hundredfold, and I pray God that the Spirit may burn in the hearts of the Priesthood of God that every man shall understand for himself, as I understand for myself, that the Priesthood of God is "inseparably connected with heaven." That is what places us in communication with our God.

PROPHETS OF GOD

I know, as well as I know anything, that this is the Kingdom of God, that this is the Church of Jesus Christ of Latter-day Saints, that Joseph Smith is a Prophet of God. I have always sustained the Prophets of God, and I never talked with one of the Presidency of the Church that I did not rise to my feet and know that they were Prophets of God. The Lord bless you. Amen.

TALK TWENTY-EIGHT

June, 1919

MEMORY OF PRESIDENT JOSEPH F. SMITH

As stated by President Seymour B. Young, it is desired that the First Council of the Seventy speak in memory of President Joseph F. Smith. I have known President Smith from my early youth, and have listened to his teachings, as an apostle and as the President of the Church, during the greater part of my life.

I remember, in the early days of my youth, of the people of this Church looking forward hopefully when the time should come that the prophecy made by the servants of God would be fulfilled; viz, that President Joseph F. Smith would become the President of the Church of Jesus Christ of Latter-day Saints.

I can think of no man who has been President of the Church, who has had greater opportunities and advantages than he has had. President Smith was chosen and ordained an apostle in his youth. He was favored, as I remember it, by being sent on a mission to the Hawaiian Islands, when he was fifteen years old. He was hedged about and privileged in associating with great men, and his life and labors were in the service of the Lord, as a special witness and an apostle of Jesus Christ. President Smith was trained, instructed, and prepared for this great appointment as prophet, seer, and revelator by the greatest men who ever lived, in my judgment, in the history of the world.

CHURCH OF GOD

I am proud of the fact that I am a natural born heir, and was given birth in this land of liberty and freedom. We are not called upon to cry out, "All hail to the king." I thank God, I belong to a church which is the Church of Jesus Christ of Latter-day Saints. It does not belong to President Joseph F. Smith, and he made no such claim, but it belongs to God the Father and to His Son, Jesus Christ.

NO KINGS IN CHURCH

There are no such things as earthly kings in Christ's Church. There never will be any kingmen in Christ's Church. For when His disciples came to Him, He tried to teach them the great lesson: "Whosoever will be greatest among you, let him be servant of all;" and when these same apostles asked the Savior, "Who is the greatest in the Kingdom of Heaven?" He called a little child to Him and said: "Except ye be converted, and become as little children ye shall not enter into the Kingdom of Heaven." Joseph F. Smith was like that. He was a man of great integrity also. Few men had greater integrity or greater faith. He loved God with all his heart, with all his soul, and with all his might; and that is all a man can do.

PLACE TRUST IN GOD

Time will not permit me to say more. I have always honored and respected and sustained President Joseph F. Smith, and I am glad of it. But I discovered, in the time that I have labored in the Church, that he was human just like the rest of us. I want you to learn the lesson: Disappointed be the men who trust in man. You want to learn that lesson, if you are to be tested and meet difficulties, or you will stumble and lose faith. I place my trust in God, the eternal Father, and it is my business to get a clear and true conception of God, and of Jesus Christ, and to realize that these men whom we have sustained are servants of the people. They are servants of God, and we sustain them, and we uphold them. . . . If there were no people, there would be no need of a Church, so that we all say—at least I do—God save the people. God bless you. Amen.

TALK TWENTY-NINE

October, 1919

LOVES GOD

I presume there are very few who are here present who are not aware of the fact that I was born in these valleys of the mountains. Have I not given evidence to the Latter-day Saints during the twenty-seven years of my ministry? Have I not been frank and honest and clear in my statements, and have you felt any doubt in your minds that I do not believe, and am not honest and truthful, and believe with all my heart and with all my soul that God is the Father? I may not have a perfect and true conception of God, but I love God; I love Him for His perfection; I love Him for His mercy; I love Him for His justice; and notwithstanding my many weaknesses I am not afraid to meet Him. For I know that He will deal justly with me; and the great joy I will have is that He will understand me, and that is more than some of you have been able to do. [Laughter]

LOYALTY TO CHURCH

I believe with the same love and faith that Jesus is the Christ, the Redeemer of the world; I believe that Joseph Smith is a Prophet of God. And

[277]

there is no man living who reads the things that God has revealed through the Prophet and the sayings of the Prophet with more joy and more satisfaction and more happiness than I have in reading of the Prophet of God. My father breathed it into my very soul, and I thank God that I am a son of one of God's servants, and that no man can place a finger or make a statement that my father did not uphold the Prophet of God, not only Joseph Smith but Brigham Young and all the others who labored in the Church. Now, friends, if you want to question my loyalty and patriotism you can get a row any time you want it. [Laughter]

SUSTAINS THE CHURCH AUTHORITIES

I sustain President Grant. When he became President of the Church of Jesus Christ of Latter-day Saints, I told him I sustained him with my full faith and confidence; and that is the best I can do. I propose to stand behind him and his Counselors and the Twelve Apostles. As I told an apostle once: "If God Almighty puts a child in the Council of the Twelve, and He will give me enough of His Spirit, I will sustain him. I pray the Lord to bless you. Amen.

TALK THIRTY
April, 1921

NOT YET DEAD

My brethren and sisters, I have been hanging on the hook so long during this conference that I am nearly exhausted. I have had some wonderful thoughts, but have waited so long they have nearly all oozed out of me.

When I came in the Tabernacle yesterday afternoon, I was met by one of my old missionary friends. He said, "Hello, Golden, I thought you were dead." Now, I want to notify my friends (and I have some good friends—I have tested them out; I know them) not to worry about me. When I am dead—and it is an awful job to get there, I have found that out—when I die, I have made arrangements for a brass band. I like the idea of lots of noise and confusion, people inquiring, "Who is that?" "Why, Kimball's dead." Then the people won't worry any more about me.

A MIGHTY GOOD WORLD

My brethren and sisters, I attribute my partial recovery (and I hope I will continue to improve) very largely to the kindness and sympathy of my brethren, the Presidency of the Church, the Council of the Twelve, and the First Council of the

[279]

Seventy and other friends. I came home last October to attend conference and was taken sick, and remained at home nearly two months. When I got around and thought of my brethren and their kindness and sympathy for me, I want to tell you, brethren, I felt this was a mighty good world. I have repeated hundreds and hundreds of times, while I was sick, the words of Frohman when he went down to his death. He said, "Why fear death? It is the most beautiful adventure of life." I want to tell Frohman I have not got that in me yet. I think this is a pretty good world. I think I am safer here among my brethren who know me, although we have had an awfully hard time getting acquainted.

FAITH TO BE HEALED

Brethren, I have had a pretty lonely time. I have had a pretty hard struggle. I haven't suffered much pain. I have got a pretty good brain, but it has not been big enough to handle my body; I have tried to direct and control my body, but it wouldn't obey. I have been administered to by some of the best men in this Church; no better men ever lived than the men who have administered to me; but I am sorry to say, and ashamed to say, I did not have the faith to be healed. There is not a man in this Church who knows any better than I do that God the Father and Jesus Christ, the Redeemer, are the great Physicians. I have unfaltering, unwavering faith in God the Father and in His Son, Jesus Christ.

I have got the gift to heal others. I have seen wonderful healings. Few men have seen more, unless they were better men. I have witnessed all kinds of diseases healed, but I could not get the faith to be healed. I failed. I just had enough faith to keep alive—that is all. I talked with President Grant, and I thought climate would help me; I was a little short of faith, so I tried climate for nine months. As I told you, I came back last October sick and I went back again and tried climate again. Now I am on my feet.

SERUM AT FIVE DOLLARS A SHOT

I went to a specialist; I had an X-ray taken of my lungs; I was scared to death he would find something, but I thought I would test him out. My family wanted to know what was the matter. Well, I found one of my batteries somewhat damaged; that is, they told me so. Then he shot me full of serum and full of iron and strychnia, at five dollars a shot. They pretty near broke my heart when I got through with that specialist.

I did not want to go to him, but to please my family I went. They are very anxious for me to live, for some reason. I hardly know what it is. I have been awfully neglectful of them. My family have been secondary to my work.

ABOUT FAMILIES

I hope the brethren will be awfully careful what they say about families. I hope they will be very tender of men's feelings when they talk about our children and about parents being responsible for their children—that their sins will rest upon them. God knows, I have got all I can carry without packing anyone else. Now you want to be awfully careful and awfully tender of those things, because in the wisdom of God, He will gather our children together. They are God's children. My children are God's children. God is just as much responsible for my children as I am.

Now, brethren, I want to say to you—I do not know whether you know it or not—there are a lot of things you do not know that you ought to be told —if there are any people who are neglected in the Church of Jesus Christ, it is the families of the leaders of the Church. They go out and tell you how to take care of your families and they are away from home and their families take care of themselves. You want to be careful.

HUNGRY FOR THE WORD OF GOD

Brethren and sisters, when I am satisfied, everybody is satisfied. I can see a hole in a doughnut. I have always grieved over a doughnut. My mother was a doughnut maker. When she showed me those doughnuts, I grieved over the holes. Some of the people say there is no hole in a doughnut, but I never could agree with them. I always see the hole and forget about the doughnut. I think we have some faults and some failings. I have been worried a little. While I have been absent I was afraid that we might get too material. I have been a little afraid of God's people and myself, afraid that we would trust too much in money and forget God, and I came to this conference hungry, hungry for the word of God.

While in San Francisco, I attended the Latter-day Saint Church on Sundays, I took part in the worship of the people. I have watched those young elders carefully, for over a year, off and on, and have seen them develop and grow and become men. But I was hungry for the words of Ruth. I never quoted them before; maybe I cannot now. She said:

Whither thou goest, I will go; and where thou lodgest, I will lodge; thy people shall be my people, and thy God my God:
Where thou diest, will I die, and there will I be buried.

That expressed my feelings.

WE ARE GOD'S PEOPLE

I have never felt better, I never felt surer, in all of my ministry for over twenty-eight years in this Church, that we are God's people, that God is sustaining President Grant as prophet, seer and revelator. He is sustaining his Counselors and the Twelve Apostles.

[283]

PRAY FOR THE AUTHORITIES

By the way, in conclusion, I would like to admonish you people not to pray only for the Presidency and the Twelve, but once in a while pray for the First Council. I don't know of any other council that needs it worse. We need your help, we need your assistance, we need your faith to prepare that great body of seventies to fulfill their appointment in this Church. I know as well as I know that this is my right hand that if you call that body of priesthood to the foreign ministry, they will go. If you will call them and get behind them, I promise you in the name of the Lord they will go. I know it. God bless you. Amen.

TALK THIRTY-ONE
October, 1921

CHERISHED ASSOCIATIONS

Now, brethren and sisters, I shall address you for a short period of time, only a few minutes—although it seems a long time to you, and does to me; certainly it will before I get through. My voice has been heard among this people for nearly thirty years. I think I have been in the ministry here at home for nearly that length of time. I would not give my experience and the association I have had with the brethren of the authorities for all the riches in the world.

TRYING FOR HONEST MIND

I hope, brethren and sisters, that during these thirty years, I have created an impression in your minds—at least I have tried to do that—that I am trying to be honest. I am trying to be truthful. I am trying to be sincere and loyal and unafraid. There is nothing that I desire more, outside of the Spirit of God, the honoring of the priesthood, and the sustaining of this work, than to have an honest mind.

It seems to me during the past few years that the minds of many are warped. We do not think honest; we do not hear straight, nor do we see straight. I am sure, from the experience I have had in the Church, that the Lord can do very little for a man who persists in being dishonest and untruthful. And, of course, it goes without saying that no man or woman in the Church of Jesus Christ can be immoral and have the Spirit of God to be with them.

I read in the *Doctrine and Covenants* the message that was given to the elders in early days. The Lord said: "But with some I am not well pleased." Now, what was their trouble? "Because they will not open their mouths, but hide the talent which I have given unto them because of the fear of man. Woe unto such, for mine anger is kindled against them, and it shall come to pass if they are not more faithful unto me it shall be taken away even that which they have."

CHAFF ONLY REMEMBERED

I realize, my brethren and sisters, that during the past thirty years I have said some foolish things. I have, in my own way, given the people a good deal of chaff to get them to take a little wheat, but some of them haven't got sense enough to pick the wheat out from the chaff. If a man in this Church ever does say a foolish thing, they will remember it to the very day of their death; and it is the only thing some of them do remember.

BURN ALL BUT CHURCH WORKS

I found out some things by reading the *Doctrine and Covenants*—which, by the way, I do read.

I am familiar with the Bible a little, and the *Book of Mormon*, the *Doctrine and Covenants* and the *Pearl of Great Price*. I have wished, sometimes, that there would be a big fire and burn all the rest of the books so that we would read these books more.

I don't believe the man lives, unless God inspires him, who can ever breathe into a book what you can get out of the Bible, *Book of Mormon*, *Doctrine and Covenants* and *Pearl of Great Price*. That is my testimony. Joseph Smith said that a man will live nearer to the Gospel of Christ reading the *Book of Mormon* than any other book that has ever been written.

THE BEST BIBLE

Now, brethren, I do not want to say anything to hurt anyone's feelings about books that are written. I read the Bible through once, and when I got through I said: "I will never tackle it again in the flesh;" but I have read in it and I am acquainted with it and I have marked it. I would not give my Bible for all the Bibles in the world, because it is the only Bible I can find anything in.

DEBT THE WORST HELL

I believe in all that President Grant said. I preached it years ago, after I went broke, with just as much vehemence as he ever did in his life. I preached until I was almost exhausted. I remember

[287]

a sermon. I think it was a very wonderful discourse, too. I was up in Smithfield at a conference, and I preached to the people on the subject of debt. I had just been through the mill of the gods, and they ground me to powder. I went "over the hill to the poor house," and I think I was able to tell them a pathetic story; they sold me out, just like they would sell cattle; and yet I was in the missionary field at that. I told my story and told it very plaintively; and there was a salesman at this meeting. I saw him the other day at one of our conference meetings. That made me think of it. He was a salesman of the Co-op Wagon and Machine Company. After I preached my discourse I met this man and he said: "Brother Kimball, that is the best sermon I ever heard. I never sold as many implements in my life as I did after you preached that sermon." Think of it, after I had warned the people and forwarned them, that to be in debt was to be in hell—I don't know much about hell, but that is the worst hell I have ever been in—to be in debt.

LORD BLESSES THOSE WHO TRUST IN HIM—WE FORGET THE LORD

I thought I would like to read some scriptures as a closing of my remarks: I am sure I can make it in two minutes. It is something my father read. In reading from his old *Book of Mormon,* that was published or printed in 1830, I found this page almost out, and I wondered what it was. This is what I found. It was just such a condition that we are now in. They had had war, and they had had famine, and then they went to the prophet and appealed to the Lord, so that the famine was withdrawn, and it says: "That ended the eighty and fifth year." In thirteen years that people fell down two or three times, and yet they were God's people.

This is what he said. I want to read it to you and impress you, if I can, with this one thought:

And thus we can behold how false and also the unsteadiness of the hearts of the children of men; yea, we can see the Lord in His great infinite goodness doth bless and prosper those who put their trust in Him. Yea, and we may see at the very time when He doth prosper His people, yea in the increase of their fields, their flocks and their herds, and in gold, and in silver, and in all manner of precious things of every kind and art; sparing their lives, and delivering them out of the hands of their enemies that they should not declare wars against them; yea, and in fine, doing all things for the welfare and happiness of His people; yea, then is the time.

Now, that strikes me as a strange thing. After God had done all that for his children, and it could not be written any better if it were written of this people, how God had blessed them—"then is the time that they do harden their hearts, and do forget the Lord their God and do trample under their feet the Holy One—yea, and this because of their ease, and their exceedingly great prosperity.

"And thus we see that except the Lord doth chasten His people with many afflictions, yea, except He doth visit them with death and with terror and with famine and with all manner of pestilence, they will not remember Him."

OUR HEARTS HARDENED AGAINST GOD

We are just like all other children of God in all other dispensations. Notwithstanding the fact that we are a chosen people for a special purpose, our hearts have been hardened and we have forgotten our God—some of us.

THANKFUL FOR BLESSINGS

Now, brethren and sisters, I am glad; I thank my God that He chastened me. I thank God that I have had the love and affection of my brethren. I thank God that I am alive. I know the Gospel is true. I know it because I learned it through adversity and through suffering and through hardships. I never learned it because I was Heber C. Kimball's son—because I was the son of a prophet. I learned it just as he learned it. I may not have paid as big a price as my father did, but I have paid for pretty nearly everything I have. I have paid well for it, but I am satisfied. I sustain the brethren of the authorities, and I uphold their hands. I never felt better in all my ministry in this Church than I do today. I thank God the sun shines. I thank God the grass is green, and the water runs down hill, as it did not for a long while. The Lord bless you. Amen.

TALK THIRTY-TWO

October, 1922

JEX FAMILY

Before I say anything else, I have something on my mind I want to get rid of. I call attention to this picture—you cannot see it very well at so long a distance. We have on this platform Brother William Jex. He was a great friend of my father's, and if he could not think of anything else to say he began to talk about Heber C. Kimball. This good man is ninety-two years old. He is a patriarch. He lives in Spanish Fork.

I read the notation written under the picture he handed me. He did not imagine I would read it. This picture shows "a part of the family"— there is a multitude of Jexes, this picture being only a part of the family "of William and Eliza Jex, taken at the annual family reunion held January 1, 1914." Thirty-eight members of the family then living were not present—could not get them all in!

"William and Eliza Goodson Jex were married in England, February 22, 1854." That is one year after I was born. I am now going to tell you what damage they have done since. They embarked on a vessel bound for America. "The family now consists of the aged couple, eleven children, 115 grandchildren, 151 great grandchildren, and five of the fifth generation, making a total, on October 1, 1921, of 360—including sixty-four who have become members of the family by marriage. Seventy-four of these have died."

Now comes the climax. "The Jex Family has spent altogether seventy-six years in the foreign missionary service, preaching the gospel, at an expense of seventy thousand dollars of their own means, over and above all their time for which they received no compensation."

I call that faith and works. It puts me in mind of what my father said in talking in early days about this people. He said: "This people will multiply and increase until we will hardly know where to put them." Father told the Gentiles, "You will never be able to kill them off." Brother Jex has taken part in fulfilling this prophecy.

SICKNESS AND FAITH

It is not my purpose to talk very much. I haven't an outdoor voice. I have been trying to be sick for a couple of years, and I have rather fizzled out at it. I feel a good deal like the story I read the other day. "Some fellow was sitting on the pier that reached out into the ocean—and he fell in, and he holloed, 'Help! help! I can't swim.' And an old fellow was sitting on the pier fishing, and he said: 'Neither can I, but I wouldn't brag

[293]

about it.' " I don't want to brag about sickness, because it is a kind of disgrace to get sick in this Church and not have faith to be healed.

I have seen the sick healed under my administration. I have witnessed nearly all kinds of diseases cured. And I will say right here, as far as God is concerned, and Jesus Christ, there is no disease that is incurable if faith is exercised. I know that I have the key, that I hold the priesthood, and there isn't a man in all the world to make me believe that I have not got it.

KEYS OF GOD'S KINGDOM

I feel aroused sometimes and the palms of my hands just itch to take hold of the jawbone of an ass and beat these things into dull men's skulls; I would do it, too, if I only had the jaw-bone. This is what I want to read to you. I want you to think about it. It is nothing new. But I want you to think about it as I have thought about it; for I have read it dozens of times, and that is one big reason I am a member of this Church. If I did not believe what I am going to read, I would quit the Church tomorrow.

These are the Prophet Joseph Smith's own words of instruction to the apostles, at the last meeting held prior to their leaving on missions. You remember when that was, when they went to England and to other places. He said:

Brethren, I have desired to see the temple built. I

[294]

will never live to see it, but you will. I have sealed upon your heads all the keys of the Kingdom of God. I have sealed upon you every key, power, principle, that the God of heaven has revealed to me. [You see we received all the keys.] Now, no matter where I may go or what I may do, the Kingdom rests upon you. [See? He fixed that; he knew something about what was going to happen.]

President Wilford Woodruff, who was one of the most wonderful men I ever knew, was a man who talked to me occasionally; I never arose after a five-minutes' talk that I did not know that he was a Prophet of God. He made these remarks at a Mutual Improvement conference, held June 2, 1889:

Do you wonder why we, as apostles, could not have understood that the Prophet of God was going to be taken from us? Neither could the apostles in the days of Jesus Christ understand what the Savior meant when he told them, "I am going away; if I do not go away, the Comforter will not come."

Joseph Smith made these impressive remarks on the same occasion, "Ye apostles of the Lamb of God, my brethren, upon your shoulders this Kingdom rests; you have got to round up your shoulders and bear off this Kingdom. If you do not do it, you will be damned." [And so will the rest of us if we do not do our duty.]

President Brigham Young said, after the martyrdom of the Prophet, "Thank God, the keys of the Kingdom are here."

President Wilford Woodruff continued:

The keys of the Kingdom will remain with the Church until the coming of the Son of Man, which

[295]

means until the coming of the Lord Jesus Christ in the clouds of heaven to reward every man according to his deeds done in the flesh. There have always been manifested among a certain coterie of men a feeling that Joseph Smith, Brigham Young, and others who have been presidents of the Church were not the right men to lead the Church. [President Woodruff made this broad remark:] I say to all Israel, I say it to the whole world, that the God of Israel, who organized this Church and Kingdom, never ordained any president or presidency to lead the Church astray.

I am glad of that, so that we need not worry about the Church. God knows we have enough other things to worry about. Go home and go to sleep; God will never allow them to lead us astray.

WHY REVELATIONS HAVE CEASED

The question has been asked many times (now I have heard this until I am tired and lame all up the back), "Why it is the apostles who are standing as prophets, seers and revelators do not have revelations?" The answer is given by President Woodruff, and I would like to have this truth soak into you. "I hold in my hand a book of revelations" [meaning the *Doctrine and Covenants*] "which contains enough revelations to lead this Church into the celestial Kingdom of God."

AUDIENCE WENT

I am about through. You are the best outstanding crowd I ever talked to in my life. You know how it is; we get people to talk to inside, and lock them in so they can't get out! I remember being up North. I said, "All you people that want to go, go;" and they nearly all went, and I didn't blame them.

God bless you. Amen.

TALK THIRTY-THREE
April, 1923

BREVITY IN SERMONS

To begin with, if the brethren and sisters desire me to run smoothly and make no breaks, it will be advisable to keep awake until I finish my speech, as it requires exceeding faith to put into practice what you preach, and it calls for much faith to believe what you teach. For me to be my natural self is somewhat dangerous, and to be original would cause the very air to resound with criticism. I fully realize that brevity and "to the point" should be added to the virtues. Horace Greeley used to say that the way to write a good editorial was to write it to the best of your ability, then cut it in two in the middle, and print the last half. I am going to follow this suggestion.

INSPIRATION BY HOLY GHOST

I do not think as a people we have any special use for presidents of stakes or bishops of wards who are not directed by inspiration. Without the guidance of the Holy Spirit we cannot fill our appointment.

SEARCH REVELATIONS

I have been thinking of a subject for a considerable length of time, and I have the idea fixed

[298]

and fastened in my mind. If we as Latter-day Saints will do our own thinking and search the revelations of the Lord, it will help us out of many of our difficulties.

FAITH IN THE SPIRITUAL

What is in the future? How far can we see ahead of us? Some of us cannot see the length of our noses, but the prophets have warned us of the danger that menaces us. We must be prepared and get our feet planted upon the ground, because we don't know (I don't know) what test is ahead of us. The Gospel of Jesus Christ has had to be preached with tears and beseechings, sufferings, adversity, and persecution from one generation to another. No generation accepted it; because their belief in material power was so dense that they lost faith in the spiritual. We have to talk of the temporal. Temporal things have to be attended to, or we all would starve to death. But we must not place the temporal before the spiritual, for if we do, we can look out for disaster and trouble. No men can save the nation or a people when they get the temporal first and forget the spiritual. I went on a mission for two years, and I came home and I loved everybody, but I hadn't been home long before I partook of the environment.

FEAR OF THE FUTURE—NEED TO FIND GOD

No thinking man or woman can be free from deep forebodings, however optimistic we try to

keep ourselves, with this crisis in world history. Fear
has crept into the hearts of men. You talk to them,
and see for yourselves. I think many of the Latter-
day Saints are greatly frightened. You don't know
what is going to happen. Time must be close at
hand when we shall need a living testimony and
knowledge for ourselves that God lives and that
Jesus Christ is the Savior of the world. Have we
found God? Have we found Him strong enough,
so that we are stripped to the skin? Then we cry
out: "I will rejoice in God. I will joy in the God
of salvation." Elias Kimball and I worked for the
Lord, and we gave the very best effort we had while
in the Southern States, and when we came back we
went over the hill to the poor house. We hadn't
a penny left, but we loved God. We had found
Him, and I still rejoice in God.

THE LORD WILL BE KIND

I hope the Lord will be kind to me and not
leave me to forsake Him. I don't think He will,
unless I do wrong, but no one knows how safe he is.
My father said that his election had been made sure,
and that just before his death an angel appeared
to him and told Heber C. Kimball, "Your work is
finished." His work was completed, his election
was made sure. We don't hear much about that
nowadays.

FAITH IN GOD REQUIRES WORK

I pray in your behalf that you will not allow
yourselves to be shaken, but if you desire to have

faith in God and in this Church you have got to work, and you have got to make sacrifice. And the time will come, just as sure as you live and breathe and have a being, when you will not only say that you are willing to place all upon the altar, but you will do it. I am ready now. I haven't got very much, but everything goes. I will stake my all.

The Lord bless you. Amen.

TALK THIRTY-FOUR

April, 1924

GUIDANCE BY HOLY SPIRIT

Every man or woman who is called to a position of this kind has a great desire to be guided and influenced by the Holy Spirit. I have had a great deal of experience during my life in a public way, but never at any time did I feel more uncertain and doubtful as to my success in speaking to the people than I do at the present time. I have had all kinds of experiences in talking to people. When I thought I had the Spirit of the Lord, some of the people did not think so. So that you can never tell; and if you say there is such a man living upon the earth, however inspired he may be or however good a man he may be, who can please and satisfy all people, I question whether that man ever lived. I know mighty well I am not such a man.

AROUSE PEOPLE TO CHURCH WORK

I cannot think of a thing that I ever heard that will be new to you; but if you can be awakened and return to your people and arouse them, then this has been a great conference. I had that feeling while I was away. I have not had as much physical force as I desire. I am a little low on vitality. I run out of gasoline every little while.

AUTHORITIES KIND

The authorities have been very kind to me; they have been most considerate, and I feel very appreciative. I have a letter, that I value more than gold and silver, signed by the Presidency of this Church. They closed their letter to me saying: "You have our love, our confidence, and our blessing." I do not know whether I am appreciative—I think I am. The Presidency never will know how much good that did me. Not that I was in doubt, not that I was in uncertainty about the matter, but I love my people and their leaders.

GOD SAVE THE PEOPLE

I always say, God save the people, for if it were not for people, we would not need this great Church. I do not know what God would do if He had no people. I have said it before, and I say it again. I was with an apostle on a trip in the South, and we found a bishop without any people. He wept, and came to the apostle to know what to do. "Well, you will have to stay here until some people come to you." All the people he had was his wife—and anybody that can preside over his wife, I take my hat off to him.

[303]

THAT STILL, SMALL VOICE

I found God, God answered my prayers, and God softened the hearts of the people, and they fed me and they gave me a place to lay my head. That is the same Spirit, the same guiding Spirit that our elders have, these young "kid-boys" that you are sending out all over the world. They are blessed and set apart, and that Spirit is with them. I remember when I was presiding over the Southern States Mission, that for two years of that time I brought home two emigrations a year. And when I went to the President's office to report, that great Prophet, the President of the Church, Wilford Woodruff, who was interested in me, said: "Brother Kimball, sit down a minute." We only had a few minutes—it didn't take five minutes. He told me more than once: "Now, Brother Kimball, I have had visions, I have had revelations, I have seen angels, but the greatest of all is that still, small voice." Any elder who has gone out and kept the commandments of God knows he has heard that voice behind him saying: "This is the way, walk ye in it, when ye turn to the right and when ye turn to the left."

IN THE KEEPING OF THE FATHER

My brethren and sisters, I am not disposed to occupy any more of your time. I love God's people; I am willing to live and die with God's people, come weal or woe, come life or death. I have a prayer that I offer sometimes when I walk by the wayside, and I say: "I now place myself and all my affairs"—I haven't got any affairs, however—"in the kind care and keeping of the Father, with a loving trust, knowing that all things are working for my best good." Like you, I have committed many blunders; like thousands of people, tragedy has come to our home without any fault of ours; but we love our children, and I am now learning to pray: "O God the eternal Father, I thank thee that the children Thou gavest me are Thy children."

Now the Lord bless you, in the name and through the power of Jesus Christ, Amen.

TALK THIRTY-FIVE
October, 1924

FAITH IN GOD

In the words of an old prophet: "I will say of Jehovah, He is my refuge and my fortress, my God in Whom I trust. I have that feeling, that conviction burning within me. I have faith in God the Eternal Father and in his Son, Jesus Christ. I have been taught these things all my life, from my earliest childhood. And for forty years nearly, including my foreign service, I have been teaching that God is our Father, and that we are the offspring of the living God; and I believe it.

RELIGION WITHIN

I met a Gentile friend—I suppose he is my friend, he has always been friendly—a business man, the other day. He said very pleasantly to me: "Kimball, I do not believe you have got any religion. I do not think you believe what you preach." And I laughed. I learned afterwards that he was a   , so he hasn't got any the best of me. How could he tell from the outside of a man whether he has religion, or faith in God, and in the Gospel of Jesus Christ? That can only be discovered by the life we lead and by the spirit that is within us.

[306]

SUSTAIN PRESIDENT GRANT

As far as the brethren of the authorities are concerned, there has been no president of the Church of Jesus Christ of Latter-day Saints that I have known so thoroughly and so well as President Heber J. Grant. I have traveled with him through the Southern States, all through the South to Mexico. It took us two months before we returned. I have slept with him. We were on very friendly terms in those days. There were not so many stakes, and we became very well acquainted. I have known President Grant and heard about him from his earliest childhood, for my mother was a very dear friend of his mother's and I have been in their home when I was a child. My own father, Heber C. Kimball, took him and stood him on a table and said, "He will be an apostle," and it came true. Yes, I sustain President Grant with all my heart, for I realize in part, at least, what a great responsibility rests upon him.

CONVERT STIMULATES FAITH

I met a horny-handed son of toil the other day near the Church Office Building. He was a Scotchman, and said: "Brother Kimball, will you shake hands with me?"

I said: "Yes, and be ticked to do it."

"Would you like to hear how I came to join the Church?"

[307]

"Yes, I would like to hear it, for I was born in the Church. I never knew anything else."

Then he told me his story. Little did that man know how he stimulated my faith just through that little friendship and testimony.

I HAVE FOUND GOD

Brethren and sisters, I have a conviction burning within me, sometimes, like a living fire. There are a lot of things I do not know, but I know some things. I have paid the price. I have eaten the bread of adversity. I have drunk the water of affliction, and I have found God. I have told you that before. I have found God, and He has answered my prayers. I have heard that still, small voice—we call it a voice—spoken to me not infrequently, and whenever I have followed it, I was right. So that I can say with you that I am blessed in all my ways, because the Father gives to me of His Holy Spirit to guide and direct me in every situation, if I am humble and contrite in spirit and in truth.

THE LORD IS WITH US AGAIN

Brethren, when I think of this gathering (we do not call this a round-up) it reminds me that I attended a round-up on the Fair Grounds, and almost lost my life when that grandstand with three or four thousand people on it burned down in ten minutes. My brother Elias and I happened to be on

[308]

the topmost seat, because it was the cheapest. We were about the first to get out. I said: "Elias, the Lord is with us again. Praised be the name of the Lord." I tried not to be frightened, but you ought to have seen inside of me before I got off that stand.

FAITH-PROMOTING BUILDINGS

The Lord is with us in this gathering of the Saints. If you will stop to think for a moment of this building, it is faith-promoting. I helped to haul sand here, with other Kimball boys, every Saturday, to lay up these rock pillars. I was but a boy. I followed my father around the Temple many times when I was a young boy.

These buildings and grounds are faith-promoting, and it is wonderful to me the things that have been accomplished by this people, as recounted by President Grant. I enter the Temple twice a week, and as I walk around it, I have often wondered if President Young, and others of the pioneers, can picture what has been accomplished. I have been in Central Park, New York, years and years ago. I saw in that park million dollar bridges. I have been in Golden Gate Park, time and time again, in San Francisco. I was in Denver a short time ago. They have twenty-four parks in that one city.

But I want to tell you that to me there is not a place on God's green earth like this place right here. I thank God that the brethren take good

[309]

care of it. No cleaner, sweeter place is to be found anywhere in the world than right here. It is part of the vision that Brigham Young saw.

SWEETEST BREAD IN YOUR LIFE

Think of the Temple! When Brigham Young struck his cane in the ground and said, "Right here we will build a temple to our God;" it was in the time of their poverty when they were so poor that father came along when the men working on the Temple were soaking their bread in the stream of water. Father said: "To you it will be the sweetest bread in all your life."

SALT LAKE TEMPLE

It took forty years to build that Temple. I will never forget when it was dedicated. I was in the Southern States where they were driving us like wild animals, and we took our lives in our hands. I heard our prophet say when the Temple was dedicated, as I was here on a visit: "From this time forth the hearts of the children of men will be softened toward us." I stand before you as a witness of the softening of the hearts of the people in the South.

GOD PROTECTS HIS SERVANTS

See what has been accomplished. At one time, Elder Elias Kimball had 550 elders in the South, and during his presidency he handled 1,750 elders. Only two died out of that great number of elders, exposed as they were. You cannot tell me that God does not answer our prayers. You cannot tell me that He does not protect us when we trust in Him.

LOVING HIS ENEMIES

For the past year I have been working like a Trojan to love my enemies. I am making slow progress, but if I can live a little longer I will make it yet. The Lord bless you, which I pray for in the name of Jesus Christ. Amen.

TALK THIRTY-SIX

April, 1925

WILLING TO SERVE THE LORD

There has never been a time in my life when I felt better spiritually and more willing to do my duty and serve the Lord and labor for His cause and for His interests. I pray God that the time shall never come in my life when I shall fear the face of man. The Lord at one time in the early history of the Church, in a revelation reproved the elders because they would not open their mouths and use the talents which He had given unto them.

NOT ALL ALIKE

I appreciate the fact that we are not all alike. I have not been reared in the same pasture as some men have in this day and generation. Neither do I speak the same language, but I try to make myself understood.

WHY DO I LIVE?

I often ask the question, "Why do I live?" That puts me in mind of a story by Eugene Field, that master of tender verse. He tells the story of a young man, an ambitious poet, who sent him a poem, "Why do I live?" And Field immediately answered, "Because you sent your poem by mail."

THE GREATER PHYSICIAN

During the time of my poor health my family were very much concerned. They wanted me to go through a physical examination. Nothing in the world frightens me like a scientific examination. I went to the clinic of the Stanford University, to a young physician of some considerable renown. I passed through an examination—the X-ray, and all that stuff. This young doctor did not believe in God, man or the devil; I found that out. I told him I was a Mormon.

He said, "You will never get any better."

I said, "O, yes, I will. I have a greater physician than you are."

He said, "Who is he?"

And I said, "The Lord Jesus Christ."

He said, "There's nothing in it."

He was drowned last year and I am still alive."

FAITH IN JOSEPH SMITH

Whenever I am called to speak in the Tabernacle, I always put up the danger signal, "Safety first," because I am always in danger.

Now, brethren and sisters, in all solemnity I want to read to you a little. I am sure I will be safe if I stick to the text. I was acquainted with the Prophet Joseph Smith, only through the testimony of my father. No man in this Church had greater faith, greater respect, and did greater honor to the Prophet of God than Heber C. Kimball. His

[313]

knees never trembled, his hand never shook, he never failed to sustain the Prophet of God.

A CHOSEN PEOPLE

I desire to read to you something, not new, not startling—the idea that we are the chosen people of God. Joseph Smith, the Prophet of the living God, organized the Church of Jesus Christ of Latter-day Saints, and the members became the chosen people of God to perform a great and lasting service for mankind.

To preach the Gospel of Jesus Christ, they were entrusted with a mission which carried with it suffering, sacrifice, sorrow, hatred, and persecution. But the message brings to the human family, if they will have faith in God, repent of their sins, and be baptized by immersion, and have hands laid upon them by the authorized servants of God for the reception of the Holy Ghost—there will come to them joy, happiness, virtue, goodness, and godliness.

To accept this mission is to fill a high place in the world's history. To be a chosen people we have gone forth through trials, tribulations, suffering, sorrow, hate and agony, sacrifice and humiliation, and have humbly and faithfully performed the heavy, responsible tasks laid upon us by Jesus Christ for the good of His Father's children. Surely we ought to be blessed, rewarded and entitled to recognition.

A chosen people should not indulge in the

[314]

thought that God's whole attention is absorbed in watching over and caring for a favored few. Let the righteous of all nations rejoice in God's grace and exult in His justice, which means that the righteous of all other nations have a share in the teachings of the Kingdom of God and His righteousness.

TOO YOUNG TO DIE

I know I have spent a good deal of time, brethren, in trying to live. About Christmas, 1923, I thought I was dying. I had a hemorrhage of the lungs, and I bled quantities of blood. I thought I had scarcely a pint left in me. I sent for my wife and handed her the keys to my safety box and said, "Here is the key to my safety box; there is nothing in it. God bless you." I then sent for a great specialist to examine me and see what was the matter.

He examined me and said, "How old are you?"

I said, "I am seventy years old."

"Well," he said, "I thought you were forty-seven."

I replied, "If that is the way you look at it, I am going to get out of here," and I did.

CHRIST'S TEACHINGS WILL RULE

Christ was the Son of God and His teachings will rule this world. "Rejoice and be exceedingly glad" on this return of the season of promise, this opening of another year.

[315]

God bless you, my brethren and sisters, God bless His Church forever, and His servants, and may God inspire them to be prophets, seers and revelators unto the children of men, I pray in the name of Jesus Christ. Amen.

TALK THIRTY-SEVEN

April, 1926

SPIRIT QUALIFIES FOR SERVICE

I have had some experience, along with my brethren in the Church, and while I may not have accomplished everything that I was appointed to do to the very best advantage, I desire to say to you that I have never been appointed to do a single thing in this Church but that, when I got the spirit of my appointment, I was qualified and fitted to assume that responsibility.

INSPIRATION AND REVELATION

Brethren, I want to read to you. I do not read very often except to myself. When I find a good idea—which is not very often—I write it down. When you get an idea, write it down. That is what the Prophet Joseph tried to teach this people. When the Lord gives you a sudden idea, write it down, and then watch it. If it comes from God, through His Spirit, it is inspiration; and when it comes true, that is revelation. Try to remember that.

SEEK THE LORD EARLY

I am now going to read to you something that I have tried to make work—though I am not making very great progress. I have written it down partly because I have a poor memory, like my father. The Prophet Joseph Smith told father, when he tried to teach him grammar, "Heber, if you don't repeat that, I'll whip you."

Father said, "Well, Brother Joseph, you will have to whip me; I can't repeat it."

Joseph said, "I would just as leave whip a child as you."

The quotations I am about to read are such that I might repeat them a million times, and never live up to them, and I am afraid some of us Latter-day Saints read a good deal, but do not think and put it into our every day life: "He that seeketh the Lord early shall find Him, and shall not be forsaken." No wonder we are trying to teach our children. Some of us did not seek the Lord until we became old. It is a mighty good thing to begin early.

THE LORD SHEPHERD OF MISSIONARIES

"The Lord is my shepherd." Do you believe that? "The Lord is my shepherd; I shall not want." Then why worry your head off for fear you will go to the poor house? But that is where some of you will go if you don't wake up. Because the Lord "tempers the wind to the shorn lamb." Haven't I testified of that? In all my wanderings in the South, God led me to the doors of the honest in heart, and they fed me and gave me a place to lay my head.

[318]

And that is what I am telling our elders, these young boys going on missions. I am trying, when I set them apart, to impress them that the Lord is their shepherd and they shall not want. One good mother stated that her son wrote her and said:

"I have only three dollars, and if you do not send me some money I will be licking the paste off the signboards."

And the mother came to me somewhat disturbed and said: "Brother Kimball, what shall I do?"

I said, "Let him lick paste for a while; he will find the Lord, but he never will with his pockets full of money."

WITHOUT PURSE OR SCRIP

I have repeatedly told the Mormon elders that they never found God yet with their pockets full of money. I do not say that you do not have to have money, but you do not worry much when you know where to get the money, where you are going to sleep, and where you are going to eat. I know mighty well that I would not worry the Lord if I had a five dollar bill in my pocket; I would go and get something to eat and have the agony over. I do not think the Lord respects a Mormon elder who will howl and whine around when he has money in his pocket and is hungry. If he does, he ought to starve; that is my doctrine.

[319]

J. GOLDEN KIMBALL

YE THAT ARE HEAVY LADEN

"Come unto me, all ye that labor and are heavy-laden." God knows that we have thousands in this Church who have labored and are weary. And there are thousands of people in this Church, mothers and old men, the best people God ever created, who never had a banquet or a chicken dinner in their lives unless they cooked it themselves. No wonder they get weary—they are made to feel they are no longer wanted. "Come unto me, all ye that labor and are heavy laden, and I will give you rest." And that is the only place you can get real rest.

FEAR DOES NOT COME FROM GOD

As I tell our missionaries, do not let doubt and fear creep into your hearts, for God never planted in one of His children the spirit of fear; it does not come from God. For when you have faith in God, you have no fear, you have no doubt; you know. But you will have trials and be tested; you will eat the bread of adversity and drink the water of affliction. That is the only thing that will keep you humble. You have to knock some Mormons down every little while to keep them in the Church. It is too bad that we as Latter-day Saints cannot be prospered without some of us getting arrogant and proud and forgetting God.

[320]

YOU CANNOT DECEIVE GOD

Surely God reads our hearts; you cannot deceive God. You can deceive a bishop, sometimes, not all the time; you can deceive a president of a stake, not all the time; you may deceive the apostles of the Lord Jesus Christ, not all the time; but you cannot deceive God any of the time. And don't ever try it.

GOD HEALS THE FAITHFUL

Brethren and sisters, the time is up. I have only gotten started. Why don't you read these things and write them down, like our fathers and mothers did of old, and think about them and make them work? And when you are sick, have faith and be healed. Christ never diagnosed a case in His life; Christ never asked a woman what was the matter; He never asked her what kind of a disease she had.

I know as I know I live and breathe, although I may never feel its power, that authority has been vested in me, as I have seen people healed—not many, it is true—but some were healed as soon as I took my hands off their heads. Yet doctors have said that those diseases were incurable, but people have been healed nevertheless. They tell me that epileptic fits are incurable.

I cannot cite you so many cases, but I can point you to a poor widow, who lived in the sagebrush, in Idaho, that came to me after a conference.

The bishop of the ward and I administered to that good old woman, and she never had a fit after. I can cite you to a poor old widow in the North Country who had a cancer. She had fasted for three days, and came to the same conference, and something said to her, "That is the man." I do not think I amount to much, but we administered to that poor old widow, and God healed her. I have had splendid success with widows; especially when they were in poverty! But I have never had any success with rich people. I do not know why. Maybe it is because they have but little faith.

THINK OF GOD

May the Lord bless you. Think of God. How many of us think of God thirty minutes out of twenty-four hours? There is not one out of five hundred that actually thinks of God and his Son, Jesus Christ, thirty minutes a day. I try to; but the first thing I know, my mind wanders off on something else. My brethren and sisters, God bless you and be with you and help this people, I pray, in the name of Jesus Christ. Amen.

TALK THIRTY-EIGHT

October, 1926

FOLLOWING GREAT SPEAKERS

It has been a number of years since I have followed Elder Roberts in the pulpit. The first time I ever saw President Roberts was in Chattanooga, Tennessee. The first time I ever heard him preach the Gospel was in Burke's Garden. I confess, at that time and for a considerable length of time afterwards, I was always awe-struck, and beaten into silence when asked to follow him in his public addresses. But I am thankful to the Lord that I have gotten over it, that I no longer feel so much that way. It has been a fight all my life to follow men who have great ability and who were greatly blessed as public speakers.

NO MAN TOUCHES ALL MEN'S HEARTS

My lesson came to me in this way: I discovered that no man was ever created that could reach all the people at one time, and I figured that there must be some poor soul with bowed head who was discouraged and disheartened to whom I might, through the blessings of the Lord and under the influence of His Holy Spirit, give a word of cheer. And it has proved to be true, for I think now of several occasions—three distinct places, I remember

[323]

at the present moment—when persons met me on the street disheartened.

They had fallen by the way; they saw no way out of their difficulties, and were in a suicidal condition. For the first one who came to me in that condition I had no answer. I did not know what to do. "Why didn't you go to your bishop? Why did you come to me?"

"Brother Kimball, I heard you preach and I thought there might be a chance."

In those cases I went to the Presidency of the Church, and that is where I learned the great magnanimity and the charitableness and bigness of the Presidency of the Church. In each of these cases I was used as an instrument. They never asked me the names of the young men; they simply wanted me to take up a labor with them, and if they repented I was authorized, not by the bishop nor the president of the stake, in those particular cases, but by the Presidency of the Church, and the young men were baptized. They were confirmed and they were started out to serve God and as far as I know, in each and every case, they made good.

GOD FORGAVE HIM

I remember one young man, highly cultured and educated in the University of Utah. I will never forget that young man, no matter how long I live. It was at the time of the World War, and

[324]

he had been unfortunate. I did not know him—
I never saw him before. He came to me in great
distress. I went to the Presidency, and that young
man repented, and he was baptized and confirmed.
He went into the war, became a lieutenant, and the
last I heard of him—he wrote me several times
—his letter stated: "I know God forgave me, for
I felt the influence of His Holy Spirit in the army,
and it has brought me joy and peace and happiness."

NO MAN KNOWETH HOW MUCH GOOD HE DOES

So that I feel to encourage the Priesthood of
God. We never know how much good we do when
we speak in the name of the Lord. I don't believe,
I can't believe, that I ever converted a man in my
life, but I have taught the truth, I have preached the
Gospel, and my voice has been heard from Canada
to Mexico more times than once. I was in the
General Board of the Young Men's Associations for
thirty years and I have never had greater joy or
greater happiness than in lifting up my voice among
the rising generation. How much good we do, as
I stated before, no man knoweth. I claim that
every man fills his niche when he is called of God
and set apart and ordained to an office. He may not
fill it in the way someone else would fill it, but if
he is a man of courage he will fill it in his own way.
under the influence of the Holy Spirit.

[325]

LIKE MY FATHER

I have no apology to make for my origin. I was told once that my trouble was, I was trying to be like my father. Well, thank God I can try to be like him a little, but I was too young when my father died to remember his mannerisms and his method of speech.

LUXURY A DANGER TO RISING GENERATION

My brethren and sisters, in conclusion I want to lift up a danger signal to the rising generation. In doing it I want to be very careful the way in which I express it, so that I shall attempt to read it, although it is against my grain to do so.

This great country, North and South America, the Prophet Joseph Smith declared, is Zion, the land of the pure in heart. It would seem to me that a great responsibility rests particularly with the young men and women of this generation.

The question naturally arises: What is the trend of the times for modern sons and daughters of Zion? Riches and culture, ease and luxury. Everything is money and money is everything. The golden key unlocks all doors, that is, it prys them open.

Plenty of money entitles you to anything: honor, society, and emoluments. The rising generation who are poor look upon this pleasure-loving people with envy and a yearning for worldly things. And as the spirit of the age in which we live takes

[326]

hold of them, they assert their individual independence and break away from what are called "old-
fogy ideas, old bigotries, old superstitions." They go
recklessly wild, at sixty miles an hour, claiming
what is termed the "new liberty of the twentieth
century," and run daringly into forbidden pastures.
Today all over America we see everywhere among
the rich and poor, the cultured, educated, and ignorant, the indications of the sensual tendencies of
the age, and we forget for the moment the degrada-
tion and destruction to which such a life leads.

SENSUAL PLEASURE

No single instance can be given as evidence that
unlawful sensual pleasure can be indulged in without paying for it a thousand times in pain and re-
morse.

The danger signals are set up at the gate of the
garden of sensual pleasure. The angel stands with
his sword of flame, and no man, woman, youth, or
maiden enters unsmitten of him. "In the path of
sensuality in all its multiplied forms our Heavenly
Father has placed barriers mountain high to stop
us and frighten us back from ruin, disease, and deg-
radation."

As wealth increases in any country and with
any people, the tendency to sensuality (through
the many temptations of ease, idleness, and grati-
fication of one's appetite, the elevation of fashion,
style, and living beyond a certain point of safety

and security) is the cause of the downfall of hundreds of thousands of God's children.

That "money-devil," if not used in doing good, is the lion right across the highway of our future, standing, teasing, menacing—just at the forks of the road, to lead us to ruin and unhappiness. If the roofs could be lifted off the palaces of the rich, what sights might not be seen, what skeletons in the closets, what sorrows, what shams, what sights.—*Watson.*

When we open our eyes to the danger that menaces the rising generation, life would seem to be a very dangerous sea if we take note of the ruined thousands that strew its shores.

DEATH NOT A CALAMITY

We, therefore, cannot look upon death as a great sorrow and calamity when it involves no stain of honor and no loss of character. We wisely conclude the hand of Providence is in it, and good must come out of it, and we are comforted.

When we contemplate and think of our young men and women with their bright hopes of love, of truth and purity, of goodly gifts from God, of mind, of all sweet affections and aspirations, gone down, blotted out and spoiled, we cannot feel otherwise—be as hopeful and cheerful as we may—that life is dangerous unless we are guided and influenced by the Holy Spirit and directed by steady hands, by men and women as teachers of virtue, truthfulness, and happiness, who are not afraid to speak in the name of the Lord.

BY THEIR FRUITS YE SHALL KNOW THEM

The fruit of religion manifests itself in the lives of men. By their fruits ye shall know them. There can be no deception by men who love God and keep His commandments. We are one and all God's children. He created us and He never created a failure, and He created you.

HAPPINESS THE DESIGN OF OUR CREATOR

"Men are that they might have joy." Happiness is the object and design of our creation and will be to the end of our existence if we pursue the path that leads to it. This path is virtue, uprightness, faithfulness, holiness. To keep God's commandments we must know them. To know them we must read the scriptures and repent and be in tune with the Holy Spirit and He will lead us into all truth and show us things to come. I promise you that you shall hear a voice behind you saying, "This is the way, walk ye in it."

TEMPTATIONS

Remember this always: Temptation somewhere in the life of all finds us, as this life is a testing time. Therefore, watch and pray and ask God to leave us not in temptation and deliver us from evil, as temptation is ever lying in wait, and in a thousand forms is temptation repeated. There is divine wisdom in praying always and avoiding the very appearance of evil.

[329]

A HELPING HAND

There is very little use of preaching religion
or morals, or honesty, virtue, and truthfulness to
those whose motives and tendencies all point toward vice and sensuality unless they repent and sin
no more. These wild, reckless, dissipated young
people will not come to us, so we must reach out a
helping hand and go to them.

RESPONSIBILITY OF PARENTS

This great change for the uplift and better-
ment of this great country—Zion, the pure in
heart—rests very largely, almost entirely, with the
home and the parents.

BACK TO CHRIST'S RELIGION

We must, for the safety of the youth of Zion,
come back to Jesus Christ's religion and its spiritual forces. We must teach the gospel of repentance and forgiveness which has made men's and
women's lives happier, tasks lighter, judgment
steadier, as it truly comforts the disconsolate, forgotten sinners, and leads them to a clear life of
virtue, love, and happiness. No child of God can
escape Christ's religion. Intelligence and knowledge of the right kind walk ever close to religion.

ADVICE TO PARENTS

My conclusion is: There is just one great,
big, life-and-death duty of the parents of children,

the church and the state, and that is to keep every boy and girl under proper schooling and give to them "love, pleasure, work, and worship."

You good people and parents living on your farms in the country, I plead with you not to send your children to cities, where the beautiful spirit of things God created perishes. Let them live in the open, in the beautiful valleys, on the mountains, in God's sunshine, near streams, rivers, and trees and let His Spirit teach them of the things of God.

HAVE GIVEN BEST EFFORT

My testimony, brethren and sisters, in all confidence, is that I know this work is true. I have tested it out. I have found God. I am a man of weakness; I am a man full of faults; but God knows I have given Him the best effort there was in me.

GOD LIVES

I know God lives, that Jesus Christ is the Son of God, the Redeemer of the world. And when men have tempted me to deny this—which they have tried to do—I have talked to some of them, learned men, I have talked to doctors, I have talked to young men who have gone out and filled missions, come home and got education, and they have tried to burn all my bridges behind me but, thank God, I had a testimony and I know! I have told them: "In what you offer me there is no happiness."

[331]

J. GOLDEN KIMBALL

JOSEPH A TRUE PROPHET

If any man can prove to me that Joseph Smith is not a prophet of God, he has taken everything; he has burned every bridge behind me. I never saw the Prophet, but I have heard my father talk about him and I have read his revelations and his prophecies, and I know they are true. He is a Prophet of God. I sustain the Church and uphold the hands of the priesthood as best I know how. God bless you. Amen.

TALK THIRTY-NINE
April, 1927

AMBITION TO SERVE GOD

I am very desirous that what I may say to you good people will be under the influence of the Holy Spirit.

I have been in the service for a long time. If I have ever been vain—and no doubt I have been—I think men are really more vain than women, and that is a hard blow!—I have no ambition at the close of my life other than to serve God, keep His commandments, give service, and do my duty.

SPEAKER MUST FEEL HIS MESSAGE

I do not know that I have ever had a greater desire in delivering a message to the people that the Lord will burn into their hearts. After years of experience, I have learned that it is not what you say that counts, it is what you feel. It is not what the speaker delivers, it is what he thinks.

SAINTS MUST DO OWN THINKING

If Latter-day Saints are to fulfill their destiny among the children of men, they must do their own thinking. Men and women and children in this Church, if they keep the commandments of God and are under the influence of the

[333]

Holy Ghost, are entitled to inspiration, to revelation, to dreams, and visions, for their own salvation. But that is as far as you can go. And any person who thinks he is living so close to God that he can direct this Church, unless he repents he will apostatize, as surely as God lives. God never gave us inspiration and revelation to take the place of the Prophet of the living God.

FORWARD VISION

I am a great believer in looking forward, not backward. I am not a believer in looking backward, except for wisdom and for the experience that others have had. With me, it is the future.

A NATIVE SON

I am about to read something to you. You know I am a native; I guess I look like it, too; don't I? I was born in these valleys, up here on the hill, six years after the pioneers arrived. I do not remember much about their hardships and about the famine, but I certainly look like I had passed through the famine! I recall that the first thing these great men did, President Brigham Young and his followers, was to select their inheritances. Heber C. Kimball had the privilege of taking one of these city blocks. And now his posterity are a race of people that we think numbers more than two thousand. He went up on the hill, dug the rocks out, and built a stone wall around the block.

And I was kept inside of it on Sundays. And I hate rock walls yet!

MOST BEAUTIFUL OF CITIES

I will read to you from a talk I made in San Francisco about four years ago. I have never delivered it or read it since. I desire to find out what you think about it. It is about "The Most Beautiful of Cities," and it begins with a quotation.

Kenneth L. Roberts said: "There is frequently a peacefulness and tranquillity about various ancient things like old furniture and old books and old clothes and old cities, provided they were good before they began to grow old, that tend to soothe the minds of those who associate with them."

I read Brisbane's comments as he passed through Salt Lake, and, being a native, I branded him as a poor humorist.

"I am told, in a mild-mannered way," said he, "that Salt Lake City would have had a population of 500,000 people, if 350,000 had not gone to California. They have a process of cleaning out the city of all growlers and kickers. They smoke 'em out and then the atmosphere clears, the sun shines, the grass turns green and the flowers grow, and they honestly can claim Salt Lake to be 'the Most Beautiful of Cities.' "

SALT LAKE CITY

The following excerpts were taken from an article entitled "The West as I saw Her." I read

the article while in California, and if I had not written it down, I never would have had it, because I am
like you people, I only hold a pint and I soon run
out. The article was written by Shaw Desmond,
Irish author and publisher, in the March number
of *Scribner's Magazine*. The article is based on
the writer's experience gathered during three visits
to America in which he spent nearly a year, lectur-
ing in the chief cities and covering some fifty thousand miles:

There is a City of Dreams in America as little
known, so far as I have read her guide-books, as one of
Rider Haggard's Lost Cities of Africa. Nobody that I
have met in America knows anything about this city,
and this especially applies to those who say they have
visited it.

It is easily the most beautiful city I have seen on
the North American continent. I think it must be one
of the most beautiful cities in the world, and the way
to it in mid-winter is hard and cold and cruel; then,
all at once, it burst upon me, "my city beautiful." I
was running into Salt Lake. Once more I, with whom
the Indians had ridden along the invisible trail by the
side of which the iron rails had been laid, seen by the eye
of imagination, was looking at a tented wagon, at the
"prairie-schooner" of the old days, about it a body of
silent men, with mouths of leather and jaws of steel as
they broke through the last pass in the mountains to find
the land of promise laid out before them with the snow-
capped mountains eternally sentinelling, [Do you feel
that? I feel that in every fibre of my being] inside which
they were to build their city, the city to be the most
beautiful of the cities of the continent.

I discovered a quiet respect for the Mormons by

their Gentile friends, a constant and everflowing tribute to Mormon industry, Mormon art, Mormon initiative. The Mormons, I discovered, were not 100 but 110 per cent Americans, obvious by their loyalty to the American flag, proud of their American citizenship, and proving it all by shedding their blood under Uncle Sam in the great war. [By the way, the Kimballs were just as loyal, for Heber C. Kimball had thirty grandsons in the world war. I am happy to say that not one of them was killed—and they did not run, either.]

I hold no brief for the Mormon outlook [says this Irish poet] but in a rather lengthy stay in Salt Lake, during which I was afforded unexampled opportunities of investigation free from "suggestions," I accumulated enough genuine data, checked from Gentile sources, to cause a revelation of the real Mormon, whenever it is given to the world. I made hosts of friends at Salt Lake, where I lectured to all sorts and conditions of men and women, from the Chamber of Commerce to a lecture under the auspices of the University of Utah. I came to the city without expectations, I left it with the picture of its icy snows under the dawn's descending, as I lay in my room with its glass walls, left with the memory for all time of its broad streets, of its giant organ, upon which my Mormon friend permitted me to play, of its white Mormon temple, its lake of the dead and the limitless sage and salt surrounding it. It remains for me a remembrance unforgettable.

Did you ever hear a Mormon talk like that? Did you ever hear a Mormon damn this country? Well, I want to advise them to quit it. Every Mormon, son and daughter, ought to lift up his praise to God that He led those great prophets and their people to a place of safety. Think of it for one minute, my father, among the rest, was driven

[337]

from his home five times!   No wonder they felt
to praise God and dedicate this place to His service.

BONDAGE AND DEBT

A new generation has arisen!   The people
seem so content, so free from all concern; but like
the Jews in the days of Joseph, they can be hurled
from their high position into the bitterness of
slavery.   And we are going into slavery and bondage and debt, as fast as we can go!

DANGER FOR NEW GENERATION

We older men think the story should be told
of our pioneer fathers and mothers and the faith
of our ancestors and we write a book, preach a sermon or two, and think our task is ended.

This new generation that has arisen have discovered over night that a new world has been born
and that the United States of America is about to
assume the responsibility of saving the world, and
they are content and satisfied.

At no time in the history of the Latter-day
Saint people has there been greater danger for the
new generation.   The danger comes from ease, idleness, and luxury, as there never was a time when
the people were spending their means so prodigious-
ly as now and ever reaching out after material
things.

The prodigal dollar seems to be swallowing all
that is great and noble with some of the new and
rising generation.

[338]

FALLING SPIRITUAL EFFORTS

To my mind many of the Mormon people are becoming content and self-satisfied. They show evidence of falling down in their spiritual efforts. I know it takes courage to say it. I know that if we say anything to criticize our people, they are disturbed. Well, they need to be disturbed. What they need is a little dynamite! It seems to me a great deal of that which has been gained by faith, adversity, sacrifice, and years of hard work is being let loose of by the thoughtless and careless.

LIVING ON FAITH OF ANCESTORS

Our fathers and mothers died for the faith and we are living on the faith of our pioneer ancestors. But behold! another generation has arisen, and in the very instant of our self-content the silence is broken by our being hurled from our mighty purpose.

MIGHTY CHURCH LEADERS

Joseph Smith, the mighty prophet, was chosen of God to send forth the message of salvation to the children of men—he was martyred—but that was not the end. It was the beginning of this great work.

President Brigham Young rightfully succeeded him, and his followers with him fled to the Rocky Mountains. Brigham Young led the way for the first trekers of adventuresome spirits in the year 1847, and they were the original builders in what Daniel Webster christened "The Great American Desert."

On entering the Salt Lake Valley, Divine Intelligence at once manifested itself. "This is the place." Why, to some people that has become a chestnut, a hoary chestnut! But it was inspiration from God. "This is the place." There beat in the heart of this great man—he was a master, a Prophet of God—a great load of care, the destiny of his people! How I have suffered for just being the father of a family and feeling responsible for the destiny of my children! And here was a great prophet, with the destiny of a great people.

AN EDEN OUT OF THE DESERT

One has to believe to understand the destiny, object, and purpose of this people. The leaders understood and believed; they knew; God revealed it to them. President Brigham Young and his followers said, "We will make this barren waste bloom and furnish clean, unsullied wealth for thousands of poor people from all over the world, who have been crushed under the juggernaut of our Christian civilization. We are going to plant them under the shadow of the Rocky Mountains. We will create an Eden out of the desert. We will lay out townsites, cities, and build churches and schoolhouses, and raise wheat and vegetables. God's children shall be converted to the Gospel of Jesus Christ and be given land. They shall have a chance for life, liberty, and the pursuit of happiness. They shall know their toil will bring them some returns, so that they can have a home and a hope for the future."

It was a big thought, a great idea, manifested by Divine Intelligence. He was a prophet. He had a vision of the future. These great leaders did not want the land and water for themselves; they wanted men to be God's agents—stewards for God and hold the land in trust as a sacred inheritance. This land was to belong to the lowly of the earth and to be saved for the hewers of stone and the drawers of water.

I think of my father, who had his inheritance, and owned the land where most of the Capitol grounds are and away off to the left. I remember that he took these poor English people that had emigrated from Europe, and took them upon the hill, showed them a lot, and asked them if they would build a home. They said they would; and the lot cost them $2.50. Heber C. Kimball and the brethren never speculated and made money off the people. Any charges to the contrary are false.

These valleys in the mountains were to be made to bloom and blossom for the poor, whose hope is the land that gave them birth and life, the land that would receive them in its bosom when they died and made a safe return to their home.

Just take the time to think of the thousands of acres of lonely, thirsty land waiting for centuries to be reclaimed from the ruins of ages. They saw in vision green fields and farms, just as Joseph Smith prophesied it would be. "It is the place where you'll find all the things your souls are hungering for, where the people will own big farms, with green fields of wheat and grass, with purple blossoms and long rows of fruit trees and vegetables." Is that true? It should be true, and that was the intent and purpose of our leaders. My father pleaded with his family, almost as he would plead for life, to keep their inheritance. I am the only one of them left on the block, and I am trying to sell, too! [Laughter]

"All will be most beautiful, in the Desert!" Through those words I can get a vision. I have a moving-picture mind. It was a vision, a dream come true. Nobody was there to despoil their dream.

A new generation has arisen. Think of your pioneer fathers and mothers who built better than they knew. Think of the men, women, and children toiling in sweat shops, with little food; families without money, without hope and without fuel, facing cold winters in these great cities. Think of these people who have been gathered to a barren empire which our ancestors have transformed into an Eden—a land of liberty, a home for the oppressed of God's children, where they can have life, liberty, and the pursuit of happiness and can worship God according to the dictates of their own conscience. The stranger has found his way amongst us and many of us have "sold our inheritance for a mess of pottage" and are seeking elsewhere for more ease, more idleness, more luxury. In this once lonely, sage-covered, wind-swept valley there should be erected a granite monument and written thereon this epitaph:

"Who seeks for heaven alone to save his soul,
May keep the path, but will not reach the goal,
While he who walks in love may wander far,
Yet God will bring him where the blessed are."
—*Henry Van Dyke.*

WILL DESIRE A HOME IN ZION

* * * On that occasion, looking upon those people in the San Francisco chapel, I prophesied (you know I am a son of a prophet), and our young elder, Joseph E. Larkin, wrote:

A prophecy made by President J. Golden Kimball of the First Council of Seventy, at a meeting held in the San Francisco L. D. S. chapel, March 16, 1924, and is, as near as I remember, as follows:

I prophesy that before many of you go to the other side you will have a burning desire in your hearts to return to the places where the leaders of the Church have counseled the Saints to settle, and you will give anything in the world to have a home there.

Brethren and sisters, I am told that North and South America is Zion, but with all of its beauty and splendor and wonderful opportunities, there is no place in the world as safe for the Latter-day Saints as where God's servants had their inheritance. God bless you. Amen.

[343]

TALK FORTY
April, 1928

LOYALTY AND SALVATION

As far as I am concerned, my brethren and sisters, I feel that it is victory or death. I haven't a vision of any kind whatsoever. I have no ambition to achieve honors, and I have only one viewpoint, and that is salvation. I desire most fervently to walk in the footsteps of my father and to emulate, as far as I am capable, his example, and to be one among the number who are loyal and true and faithful to the Church.

You know I am rather peculiar in my thoughts and imaginations. I get to thinking along certain lines. I pick up ideas here and there. They are not original. I haven't been able to get hold of anything original for a long time.

PASSION FOR CHURCH WORK

All the passion I have had for the past forty years I have put into this work, with all the mistakes and blunders, and my spirit has worn out my body. As I grow older, I become more silent, with a desire to be alone. To me, one glimpse of immortality would mean that death would lose all its fear and would hasten my desire to go home. As someone

[344]

has said: "Why fear death? It is the most beautiful adventure of life."

WHAT LIES BEYOND?

What is the good of all this education and science if it cannot tell us that there is a survival after death? What is the good of it all if it cannot answer a simple question like that? Science seems not to know what lies beyond the "no man's land," so we must turn our faces and our desires to God for an answer.

GREAT MEN SIMPLE

It has been remarked very often that when we meet a really big man, we almost invariably find a simple man, devoid of pride and arrogance. One reason lies in the fact that every man holding a big position knows in his own soul, if he be honest, that there are forces entirely outside of himself that have led him onward to do big things. The man of the world calls it luck, just a series of accidents; but Latter-day Saints feel that great men and good women succeed because the front door of their intelligence is always open to inspiration and because of their dogged determination and effort to carry out what God has inspired them to do.

MIGHTY PIONEERS

When I read of those 143 pioneers who landed in this valley on July 24, 1847, and in one short month accomplished more for the beginning of a great work than other men have accomplished in a lifetime, I marvel at it. I can remember reading a discourse preached by President Brigham Young at the funeral of Jedediah M. Grant, wherein he said: "This man who lies before you accomplished more in ten years than some men accomplish in one hundred."

HEBER C. KIMBALL

Heber Chase Kimball was born in Sheldon, Vermont, June 14, 1801. When he was eleven years old, his parents removed to West Bloomfield, New York, where his father, who was a blacksmith, established a large shop in which Heber was taught blacksmithing. At the age of nineteen, he was thrown upon his own resources, his father having failed in business. Heber was assisted somewhat by his elder brother, Charles, who taught him the potter's trade. Heber suffered severe poverty to the extent of actual hunger at this time, but it was largely brought about by his shyness and timidity. . . .

Referring to the vision of the legion of evil spirits in England, on the opening of the mission, Joseph Smith said, "Brother Heber, at that time you were nigh unto the Lord; there was only a veil between you and Him. The nearer a person approaches to the Lord, the greater power does the devil manifest." . . .

On returning to Winter Quarters, Brigham

Young was chosen and sustained as the President of the Church of Jesus Christ of Latter-day Saints, with Heber C. Kimball as his first counselor, in the fall of 1847, a position my father occupied until his death in June, 1868.

I honor my father for his faith, courage, and integrity to God the Father and to his Son, Jesus Christ. He was one of the first chosen apostles that never desired the Prophet's place—his hands never shook, his knees never trembled and he was true and steadfast to the Church and to the Prophet Joseph Smith. . . .

Brother Brigham, Heber and others were en-route to Kirtland. Heber had chills and fever and was very ill. A doctor said he would give him something to relieve him. The doctor was drunk and gave Heber a tablespoonful of morphine. He reeled and fell to the floor. Some of the brethren wept and said, "We will never see Heber again." Brother Brigham cared for him. Heber said: "Don't be scared. You brethren go ahead, for Brother Brigham and I will reach Kirtland before you will," and they did. . . .

He built homes for his wives and children, two flour mills, a carding machine mill, molasses mills, a linseed oil mill, school buildings, barns, cobble-stone walls. He beautified gardens and farms, laid out his inheritance, and laid out city blocks and named the streets. He located hundreds of people who built homes, and he never speculated.

During the famine of 1856 which was likened unto the famine of Egypt, Heber C. Kimball played a part like unto that of Joseph of old. He had prophesied of the famine. He, by his providence and foresight and anticipation of the famine, had saved his grain, filled his bins and storehouse, and he fed a hungry multitude, kindred, strangers, and all who looked to him for succor. His own family were put upon short rations, though he had thousands of bushels of wheat with bran, shorts, corn, and barley in abundance. Several hundred bushels of wheat were loaned to President Young to help feed the hungry and the poor of Salt Lake City.

Bishop John B. Maiben gives an interesting link in the historic chain at the time of the famine. "Some individuals who had flour sold it at $25 to $30 a 100 pounds. Not so with Heber, for at no time did he charge more than $6 a 100 pounds, then the standard tithing-office price. He distributed in various amounts, from five to fifty pounds to the poor, amounting in all to about thirty thousand pounds. His acts of generosity, mercy, and charity during this time of sore distress are worthy of the man. He kept an open house and fed from twenty-five to one hundred poor people at his tables daily with bread, flour, and other necessities that were worth their weight in gold."

It is related that during the famine, a brother,

THE OLD KIMBALL MANSION

sorely in need of bread, came to President Kimball for counsel as to how to procure it. "Go and marry a wife," was Heber's terse reply after feeding the brother. The man thought Brother Kimball must be out of his mind, but when he thought of his prophetic character, he resolved to obey counsel. He wondered where such a woman was and, thinking of a widow with several children, he got busy and proposed. As widows generally do, she accepted him. In that widow's house was laid up a six-months' store of provisions. She surely grub-staked him. Meeting Brother Kimball soon after, this prosperous man of a family said: "Well, Brother Heber, I followed your advice." "Yes," said the man of God, "and you found bread."

In August, 1853, Heber addressed the Saints in the Salt Lake Tabernacle: "I know you will prosper and live in peace in the mountains of Great Salt Lake and be perfectly independent. You will live in peace and God will be your defense. The Lord can turn the nations, as I can an obedient horse. They are governed and controlled by the Almighty. There are a few other things I wanted to say: Take care of your grain, for it is of more worth to you than gold and silver." This theme he stressed for the next three years, but they heeded him not and they suffered the consequence. He further said later: "I would like to see the people manufacture their own clothing, machinery, knives, forks, and everything else, for the day will come when we will be under the necessity of doing it, for trouble and perplexity, war and famine, bloodshed and fire, thundering and lightning will roll upon the nations of the earth, insomuch that we cannot get to them nor they to us."

Brother Brigham said: "This is the place." Brother Heber said: "Here it is on high. It is the best country I ever saw."

At family prayers, just a little while before his death, he remarked that the Angel Moroni had visited him the night before and had informed him that his work on this earth was finished and he would soon be taken. He died the morning of June 22, 1868.

God bless you one and all. I sustain and uphold the hands of the priesthood, and I desire, as you do, to be saved and exalted in the presence of God, which, if I know anything, I know must be the greatest gift of God to His children. God bless you. Amen.

TALK FORTY-ONE

April, 1929

I often tell a story when called up to speak just as we are about to close the meeting, which happens to me occasionally.

ONLY HELD A PINT

A little fellow was sick and he went to the doctor who was a herbalist. The doctor gave him four herbs and told him to boil them in a quart of water and drink it all. The little fellow said: "I can't. I only hold a pint." I am wondering how much you people hold?

I have enjoyed the conference, although I have not had much peace here for a considerable length of time. The President has been calling people up from all around me.

SINCERITY

I trust, my brethren and sisters, that in the few words I speak I may be able to impress the people of this Church with the fact, as I am quite sure I have done in the past, that I am frank and honest and sincere in my faith as a Latter-day Saint.

FAITH IN GOD

I believe all that has been revealed. I have no doubt whatsoever of the truth of this work. I have

[351]

gone out like others have done, and have found God, and God has answered my prayers. I have heard that still, small voice. I have an assurance, and as much knowledge as has been given to me by the influence of the Holy Spirit, that this is God's work. I pray the Lord to bless the people. I have no grievance. No man can ever be treated better than I have been. If I have been corrected once or twice it has done me more good than anything else that has happened to me. The Lord bless you. Amen.

TALK FORTY-TWO

October, 1929

HOPE FOR SALVATION

I desire to say to you that my life is being crystallized into a very few things that are important to me. The great hope that I have is to be saved in the Kingdom of God. I have a great desire to be true and faithful and devoted in my work, to be honest, frank, and straight-forward with the people. I know of no other way. I can see no other outlook, and I have no other desire than to sustain the Priesthood of God, to uphold those whom we sustain as prophets, seers, and revelators in the Church of Christ. If there is not safety in this, there is no safety for the Latter-day Saint people.

BREVITY IN SERMONS

I have never in all my travels and teachings among the people been told what to say. I realize the importance of this occasion. I understand what time means. At the conference six months ago I was fortunate in being called upon, and I occupied three minutes. To my surprise I was complimented everywhere I went. People say it was the best sermon I ever preached. Of course, had I believed what they said to me I would close now; but I have what I think is a message—at least I desire to call your attention to a certain matter that transpired with me this year.

OREGON TRAIL MEMORIAL

About the fourteenth or fifteenth of August, Dr. George W. Middleton, together with Elder Levi Edgar Young, the doctor's son, and myself (I was an invited guest) went by auto to Casper, Wyoming, 515 miles distant from Salt Lake City. The purpose of the meeting which we there attended was to honor the pioneers. It was held under the auspices of the Oregon Trail Memorial Association.

HONOR THE PIONEERS

It is my purpose to enlarge upon this Oregon Trail subject. Never before, strange to say (and I was born soon after the people arrived in this valley) did I get the spirit of what it all meant. I have never understood, I have never comprehended what it all meant to our fathers and mothers, the pioneers. But I confess to you that I have had that feeling burning within my bosom, that desire to do honor to those great men and great women who made it possible in this day for us to enjoy all the comforts of life.

I quote from Professor Driggs:

We are brought a little closer to the tragic cause of it all when we realize that fully twenty thousand lost

[354]

their lives in an effort to reach the Golden West. They had no means of marking the graves of the dead in those prairie stretches. Only one grave out of all of the twenty thousand, so far as we know, is surely marked. I refer here to the grave of a pioneer mother near Scott's Bluff, Nebraska. When Rebecca Winters passed away one of the company had the forethought to pick up an old wagon tire that lay along the trail. Bending it into an oval he set the tire within the grave. On the top of the tire was chiseled the mother's name and age. A party of surveyors laying out the railroad along the North Platte happened by mere chance to run their line right over the mother's grave. Then the surveyors, with a touch of sympathy that is beautiful to think of, went back for twenty miles and changed the line of survey, that it might miss the mother's grave.

There is a story—it is beautiful—I love to make an effort to tell it. The history of the West sounds like tales from the Arabian Nights; but as far as I know, only parts of it have ever been told.

Dr. Driggs asks: "Will the warp hold? It will hold provided we keep alive the sacred stories of the pioneer builders of this nation in the hearts of American boys and girls."

Coincident with the Mormon Pioneer movement, their prophet prophesied they would go to the Rocky Mountains, and, in a way, they were forced to go west. They started out not for conquest, not intent upon spoil, but to worship God, build up cities, do mighty deeds, and build for greater happiness.

[355]

J. GOLDEN KIMBALL

GREAT SPIRITUAL LEADERS

Had it not been for great spiritual leaders, this barren wilderness could never have been peopled in so short a time; and it would not have gained much momentum had it not been for immigration. It would appear that this people threw themselves almost blindly into what would seem to the natural man impossible. But under the leadership of inspired men they accomplished the unbelievable.

We must not forget to remind the next generations of the glorious strength of faith, hope, courage, and the love of God they possessed.

PIONEERS DISAPPEARING

Try to remember that the pioneer, no matter of what race, is fast disappearing. Often he is a tragic figure. History is leaving him behind. Few of us are so gifted as to be able to attract and to converse intelligently with our own children. A parent must be a genius to tell of the days of their strength, the days of their suffering, sorrows, and defeats, and yet make clear how they won glorious victories.

The next generation cannot feel, neither can they understand, sense, or appreciate what it all means, surrounded as they are with ease, comforts and luxuries. They are unmindful, and it should be burned into their souls and memories to respect the doting pioneer, tottering with old age—to remember their minds are stored with the richest experience and historic lore.

We have no way of testing and proving the next generation, through trials, sacrifices, and suffering; neither can we force these historical truths upon them, and to reason would seem fruitless. It is said: "People shape their lives largely the way we are today living."

I have thought a great deal about our fathers and mothers and their great object, and I have wondered what it was that the Latter-day Saint people had—the desire, the ambition, the faith, and the hope—that enabled them to sacrifice, suffer, and die for the Gospel of Jesus Christ.

RESTORATION OF THE GOSPEL

I am made to understand what their great objective was. Something new had transpired. God the Father and Jesus Christ, the Son, had appeared to that young man Joseph; and also the Everlasting Gospel, a knowledge of the truth as it is in Jesus Christ and the power of God unto salvation, had been revealed. The restoration of the Gospel, the restoring of the priesthood with all its keys and its powers and authorities were conferred upon these men; also the eternity of the marriage covenant, including a plurality of wives. The bringing forth of the *Book of Mormon*, the redemption of Zion, the building up the City of Jerusalem, and the gathering of the Ten Tribes—these were the great

[357]

objectives that were placed before our fathers and mothers.

I often think of my mother. She was a very practical woman, a woman who lived by faith, a woman who had suffered and sacrificed, a woman who had left her whole race of people. She was the only one we know of who has ever been converted from her immediate family. Mother had that great vision of the celestial glory, of becoming a queen. And surely she is a queen, because when I visited her people I brought to her over one hundred names of her ancestors, and we went into the temple at Logan and did the work for that good mother of ours.

That was the idea; that was the great vision that they had of the future. And that was why they were sustained in their suffering, in their sacrifices, in their troubles, and in their tragedies.

HELP FULFIL PROPHECIES

My dear brethren and sisters, what is our objective? That question has been put to me more than once. Our objective is to carry out the will of God and through the direction of His servants, the prophets, to fulfil every prophecy and every revelation that we find written in the *Doctrine and Covenants*. For surely God will not forsake His people if they will repent of their sins. It is needless for me to say more.

SERVANTS OF GOD PROSPERED

For the past week or so I have read the *Book of Mormon* through, and I was surprised how deeply interested I became in the people who inhabited this continent. I discovered that whenever they served God and kept His commandments they prospered in the land; and whenever they failed (and I hope we will never fail) then came their destruction until that people became extinct.

I pray God to bless you. I pray God to be with each and all of us, for I do not believe that a man can remain faithful in this Church and devoted and true to his covenants who fails to keep the commandments and who has not a testimony that Jesus is the Christ. To this end I pray that the blessings of the Lord may rest upon us, in the name of Jesus Christ. Amen.

TALK FORTY-THREE

April, 1930

BURNING DESIRE TO SERVE GOD

I am very grateful to the Lord that I am permitted to be present on this occasion. I feel that I am among my friends, and have always tried to feel that way. I have only one great big desire, and that is to live until I have filled and completed my mission here upon the earth. The revelations tell us that if we desire to serve the Lord we are called to the work. I have a burning desire in my heart to follow in the footsteps of my father, and to be loyal and true and faithful, and to be found among the number that sustain God's work and uphold the hands of His Holy Priesthood.

JOSEPH A GREAT PROPHET

I realize, in part only, the great responsibility that is resting on the Presidency of this Church and the Council of the Twelve and all those who take part in this great work. I believe Joseph Smith is one of the greatest prophets that have ever lived. I believe in his prophecies and revelations. While I may be among the number that would like to rush things on a little to see how they are coming out in Jackson County and all that, I am sure that all will be literally fulfilled in the due time of the Lord.

[360]

PRESIDENT GRANT

Whenever the Lord wants to speak to His people He knows whom to talk to. I have known President Grant during my labors in the First Council. I have slept with him and talked with him, but I haven't slept with him since he has been President of the Church. I know of no better man. I am not one of those who cater to men. I sustain them and uphold them, but I have learned that they are human. I sustain and uphold, with all my heart and soul, President Heber J. Grant as the Prophet of God. It was only two months ago that a young lawyer—I suppose he considers himself one of the brilliant young lawyers—undertook to criticize severely the President of the Church. I was somewhat disturbed. I said, "I am going to take out my watch and give you five minutes to name a better man." I haven't heard from him yet. I want to say to you, in full faith and confidence, no man has ever earned his place as the Prophet of God, through loyalty, faithfulness, devotion and sacrifice, more than President Heber J. Grant.

VITALITY OF THE CHURCH

I have a matter that I would like to read to you. It will take me only a few minutes:

It is a very old, old story; but it never needed re-telling so much as in this present hour: His name was Joseph, and he was carried away from home, and found himself in Egypt, a strange, new land. Because he was

[361]

good looking and intelligent and a hard worker he rose rapidly until he became prime minister. Excepting the king, there was no other man in Egypt more influential or more celebrated. His relatives learned with interest of his rise. They followed into Egypt, and with his help they, too, prospered and were likewise influential. It looked as though they were permanently provided for, as though nothing could happen to dislodge them. But in a single generation—yes, in a little fraction of a generation—the unbelievable occurred. The people who were so contented, so free from all concern, were hurled from their high position into the bitterness of slavery. The thing that had happened to them is recorded in a single sentence: "Joseph died."

That has not been the case with the Church of Jesus Christ of Latter-day Saints. Joseph the Prophet died, but the Church has continued to progress and advance and will until it completes its mission.

God bless you. Amen.

TALK FORTY-FOUR

October, 1930

PROPHECIES OF HEBER C. KIMBALL

I claim not to be a prophet, but I am a son of a prophet, and I expect to give you evidence that shall be left with you—that Heber C. Kimball was a Prophet of God. President Brigham Young on more than one occasion said: "Heber is my prophet, and I love to hear him prophesy."

In May, 1868—that is sixty-two years ago—he said:

After a while the Gentiles will gather in Salt Lake City by the thousands, and this will be among the wicked cities of the world.

He said also:

An army of elders will be sent to the four quarters of the earth to search out the righteous and warn the wicked of coming events.

All kinds of religions will be started and miracles performed that will deceive the very elect, if such a thing were possible.

Persecution comes next, and all Latter-day Saints will be tested to the limit.

Many will apostatize, and others will stand still, not knowing what to do.

Before the Temple reaches the square our brethren will be imprisoned until the penitentiary shall be full, and some of them will be removed to other penitentiaries.

Mothers will weep for their husbands, and children will cry for their fathers. Some will die, and sorrow will fill the hearts of the Latter-day Saints.

When the Temple roof is on, the persecution will lessen, but when the Temple is completed the power of the Evil One will be shut out.

The prayers of the Saints will then be heard. The sick will be taken there and healed.

The Spirit of God will rest upon the people, and work for the dead will be continued night and day.

The judgments of God will be poured out upon the wicked, to the extent that our elders from far and near will be called home; or in other words, the Gospel will be taken from the Gentiles, and later on will be carried to the Jews.

The western boundaries of the State of Missouri will be swept so clean of its inhabitants that as President Young tells us, "when we return to that place there will not be as much as a yellow dog to wag his tail."

Before that day comes, however, the Saints will be put to the test that will try the very best of them.

The pressure will become so great that the righteous among us will cry unto the Lord day and night until deliverance comes.

In 1856—that is seventy-four years ago—a small group of friends convened in the house of the Lord, called the Endowment House. The conversation was about the isolated condition of the Latter-day Saints.

"Yes," said Brother Heber, "we think we are secure here in the chambers of these everlasting hills, where we can close the doors of the canyons against mobs and persecutors, the wicked and the vile, who have always beset us with violence and robbery, but I want to say to you, my brethren, the time is coming when we will be mixed up in these now peaceful valleys to that extent that it will be difficult to tell the face of a saint from the face of an enemy against the people of God.

"Then is the time to look out for the great sieve, for there will be a great sifting time, and many will fall.

"For I say unto you there is a test, a Test, a TEST coming."

He further said:

This Church has before it many close places through which it will have to pass before the work of God is crowned with glory.

The difficulties will be of such a character that the man or woman who does not possess a personal knowledge or witness will fall. If you have not got this testimony, you must live right and call upon the Lord, and cease not until you obtain it.

Remember these sayings: The time will come when no man or woman will be able to endure on borrowed light. Each will have to be guided by the light within himself. If you do not have the knowledge that Jesus is the Christ, how can you stand?

Do you believe it?

President George Q. Cannon said, after Heber C. Kimball's death: "Heber Chase Kimball was one of the greatest men of this age." He continued: "No man, perhaps, Joseph Smith excepted, who has belonged to the Church in this generation, ever possessed the gift of prophecy to a greater degree than he."

On the morning of the 22nd of June, 1868, he died. At the funeral President Brigham Young said: "Heber was a man of as much integrity, I presume, as any man who ever lived on the earth— a man of faith, a man of benevolence, a man of truth."

On the evening of January 12, 1862, the Lord made it known to Heber C. Kimball that he should not be removed from his place as First Counselor while he lived in the flesh.

SPIRIT OF PROPHECY

Now, my brethren and sisters, I am here to testify that the spirit of prophecy is in this Church. Any man who has a testimony that Jesus is the Christ has the spirit of prophecy, and I know that we have living prophets. Whenever the Lord desires, and it is His will to speak through His prophets, I have no fear and no doubt, as far as I am concerned, that they have the courage and the faith to speak the words of God.

I HONOR MY FATHER

Now, brethren, that is how I feel about it. I take pride in being a son of my father, and as long as I live I shall never fail to honor my father and his successors, and try to be as loyal and true and steadfast in the faith as they have been. I am the only one that can destroy my faith in this work. God bless you. Amen.

HEBER C. KIMBALL

TALK FORTY-FIVE
April, 1931

AUTHORITIES INSPIRE CONFIDENCE

I realize the responsibility coming to any person who is called to speak to this people. I have sat on the "anxious bench" now for two days, and I feel this morning that everything I have heard, or read, or know, has oozed out of me. I want you to know that I antedate in age and in service, as one of the First Council of Seventy, all of the Council of the Twelve who sit in front of me. I feel honored and have always felt honored to associate with the General Authorities of the Church. I desire to say to the people, the presidents of Stakes and their counselors, the high councilors, the bishops and their counselors, you have always extended to me the greatest courtesy and respect. And whenever I have attended a conference and returned home I have felt that I amounted to something. But after I wandered around here in Salt Lake I sort of lost that feeling, sometimes, and felt like a stranger among strangers.

ENDOWMENT

I desire to refer back to a time when I was about thirteen years of age, when Heber C. Kimball sent word to me and my brother, Joseph Kimball, who is now in the Church Office Building, to come to his office. When we arrived there, mere boys, he said to us: "If you want your father's blessing you be at the endowment house in the morning and have your endowments."

Of course, we were frightened nearly to death. I do not know how people feel when they are going to be executed, but I suppose that is the sort of feeling I had, not knowing and having no conception of what it all meant. However, we were there and we had our endowments. I did not remember much that transpired, but I was awed, and the impression was burned into my soul of the sacredness of that place, and the sacredness of the covenants which I entered into when almost a child. When I was fifteen years old our father passed away, and we were left, as many children are left, to wander and fight our battles as best we could.

UNDER OBLIGATIONS TO GOD

Now the point I want to reach if I can, if the Lord will give me His Spirit, is just this: Heber C. Kimball made the following statement which deeply impressed me: "I would that all men and women who enter these holy temples could be made to understand that we are placed under obligations to God." Whenever we are permitted to enter the holy temples and perform those ordinances we make covenants with the Father, the Son, and the Holy Ghost.

I cannot conceive of a more sacred covenant made by mortal man. That is the impression I desire to impart to you good people, especially those who hold the holy priesthood. I think it is high time that every man who is so honored of God should understand his office and calling. I understand my calling as one of the First Council, a Seventy in the Church of Jesus Christ.

READ THE BIBLE

It is not my province nor intention to preach. I have something here that I would like to read to you but time will not permit. It is scripture; it is the word of God, and I would advise myself and every other man and woman in this Church to read the Bible. It is not read as much as it should be. The same is true of the *Book of Mormon,* the *Doctrine and Covenants,* and the *Pearl of Great Price.* You will find within the lids of those great books many prophecies and revelations. And if you will go to God and ask Him in humility if these things are true He will give you the testimony, and you will know. God bless you. Amen.

TALK FORTY-SIX

October, 1931

MISSION FUNDS

I feel more like saying, this morning, "Cheer up, the worst is to come." All I know, brethren and sisters, is what I feel, what I sense, what I hear, and what I see. I know of no better way to make this clear to you than to relate an incident that happened in my missionary experience at the time I was appointed to preside over the Southern States Mission.

I succeeded Elder William Spry. There was only a few days notice given me. The brethren failed to inquire regarding my financial condition, my wife and children, my physical condition or whether my teeth were all right, etc. They just appointed me without asking me any questions, and I had faith enough to go. The itinerary was made out by Elder Spry to visit those conferences which occurred only once a year, as the mission covered eleven states.

We had the means to go through that mission only once a year. In fact, when Elder Spry turned the mission over to me he handed me thirty-five dollars. I said: "Is that all you've got?"

"Yes."

"How do you get your money?"

"Why we go to the Lord and ask Him."

"Well," I said, "I don't think He is very liberal." [Laughter]

GAINED THE HOLY SPIRIT

The first conference appointed was in West Virginia. I rode all day and all night on the train and we took no berths in those days. I arrived at Crow's Nest. It is about the only place I remember in the South, because it was so lonely and desolate. The elders who were to meet me had returned because the train was six or seven hours late, so I had to find my way to the conference as best I could. I wasn't very well. I climbed the mountain and stopped with a coal miner. He treated me very kindly. The next morning I started for the conference. I had not then received the spirit of my appointment.

As I approached I told the Lord all about it. I don't think I have been able to pray like that since. When I got through praying, I did not see anything, I failed to hear anything. But there was something came over me, a happiness, a joy, that it isn't possible for mortal man to express. I suppose it was a heavenly feeling. I was actually so overjoyed and so happy that I whistled. I haven't whistled since. The twenty miles that I walked was the happiest time I have ever had. That is how

I felt. I know because I was clothed upon with the Holy Spirit. I have regretted more than I can express that the same sensation has not come to me with the same power since.

NEAR DEBT HELL

I had another experience. It was prior to my going on this mission. We were involved in speculation. If we had had our way we would have owned a large holding in Canada. We got into that mess. After having gone through that experience we were as near hell as a man will ever get if he is honest. An honest man is in hell when he is in debt. I know all about the feeling. I went through the mill of the gods, and it grinds slowly, but it grinds fine. If you have anything left when they get through with you, you have had a happier experience than I have had.

CACHE VALLEY FARM

Well, it was on that occasion that I made a public declaration in the Logan Tabernacle—foolish it may have been. We were able to pay all our personal obligations, although it took everything we had in the world—years of hard work, fifteen years in Bear Lake pioneering—and we exchanged it all for a 320 acre farm in Cache Valley. We had two hundred acres of grain and one hundred tons of hay all ready for harvest, and were sold out at the court house door for thirty-eight hundred dollars, and a thousand-dollar judgment. That farm, some years afterwards, was sold for thirty thousand dollars. I speak of this so that you will understand the dream.

A DREAM COME TRUE

After making my declaration in the Logan Tabernacle, that I would never doff my hat and be servile to any man because of his money, that night I had a dream. I am not a dreamer. I believe in dreams when they come true, and I haven't any use for them until they do. It was very vivid. I haven't forgotten it, and it has been nearly forty years since it occurred. I have repeated it but a few times. The devil appeared to me at the northeast corner of the temple block. I was not very well acquainted with the devil. Brother Maeser used to tell us he was a great general. The man that I saw, and I seemed to know he was Satan, was of great personality and imposing in appearance, in height and bigness; he was dark and swarthy and seemed to be a real man. When he looked at me with those black eyes they pierced me to the soul. I trembled as I did in the woods when I was filled with the Holy Spirit of God. I trembled from head to heels with fear. He repeated what I had said at the Logan Tabernacle. The Spirit of God came on me and thrilled me from crown to toe. I told him I would not bow to man. I then became frightened and ran like a coward. I was arrested and put in jail for four years. I saw myself come out of jail. My clothes were threadbare. I was thinner than I am now, if such a thing can be possible; but I was free. In four years from that time our creditors stripped us to the skin, and that dream came true. I do not want any more dreams of that kind.

NOT SUGAR COATED

I am in sympathy with the people. I know we have all been foolish. I am foolish. I don't think there is a bigger fool than an old fool. A man who has had experience ought to know better. One of my brethren said to me—and he is a man so kind and gentle that I had every reason to believe he would extend to me a little sympathy—I told him of one of my last speculations and he said: "If you are as big a sucker as that you ought to take your medicine." I said: "I am taking it, and it is not sugar-coated either." [Laughter]

EVERYTHING EXCEPT THEIR SUSPENDERS

I met a banker a few weeks ago—we were very friendly. Thank the Lord, I do not owe that bank anything, but I owe another bank. [Laughter] I said: "How are things going?"

"Well, we are taking everything but their suspenders."

I thought afterwards that I should have said to him: If that bank hasn't got any more elasticity than my suspenders, I will throw them in. [Laughter]

[374]

THINGS OF GOD NOT ADVERTISED

My brethren and sisters, in a few words I desire to say to you that I think the things of the world are better advertised than the things of God. When I hear those beautiful voices over the radio, advertising the things of the world, I am wonderstruck. If there is anything under heaven they do not advertise, and give it away at a dollar a week, I do not know what it is. By the time they get through with us—the "Lucky Strike" puts over this wonderful music—no wonder smokers' mouths water after hearing it.

SWIM OR DROWN

When men, boys, and girls form the tobacco habit and have acquired the appetite, I do not believe it is in our power to sympathize with them. It is a foolish thing for them to form a habit of that kind and then try to overcome it of themselves. They cannot do it. God has to help them. They have to go to the Lord. When we see these people I don't feel like it is right when a man is in hell, to stand over him and say; "Well, son, you are in hell. Get out the best you can. Sweat it out; swim or drown." It does not sound Christ-like to me.

SOFTEN OUR HEARTS

I pray God to soften the hearts of the people. They are doing wonderful things and they are go-

[375]

ing to do wonderful things. We have the organization. We have the inspiration. We have the knowledge. We know how to take care of people, if the Lord will soften our hearts and help us to give and keep giving. I pray the Lord, while the people are giving, that he will soften the hearts of bankers. As long as you can pay your interest and pay your taxes you are safe, but I want to tell you if you don't pay them they will foreclose to protect the bank and its depositors. As I was once told: "Business is business, believe it or not." I am thankful to the bottom of my heart that I am getting along as well as I am. At my age, I would be as helpless and dependent as a child if it wasn't for the Church and its protecting care for me.

God bless the Church. God bless His servants and help them to see and understand. Above all, help us, O God, to understand people, that we may be patient, that we may be long-suffering, that we may be gentle. that we may not listen to things that are told us, until they are proven to be true. God bless you. Amen.

TALK FORTY-SEVEN

April, 1932

DESIRE TO SERVE THE LORD

I am very anxious that I be under the influence of the right spirit, the Spirit of the Lord. I have no ambition, no desire but to serve the Lord and to keep His commandments and to fulfil and complete my labors.

MY SERMON WILL REACH MY KIND OF PEOPLE

I have been very much impressed with one thought (and I have had quite a number) and that is: the number of speakers that have spoken during this conference. If they have not reached pretty much all the people then they have not fulfilled what I believe. I believe that in this Church and among the children of men there are people—there may not be very many—who understand me. Perhaps I may be the only one among you who can reach my kind of people. Well, if that is true, why not let me be natural and talk to them? You who do not like my talk can go to sleep if you want to. As long as I can reach a soul when under the influence of the Holy Spirit and plant a seed of truth in his heart, it seems to me it would be a wonderful thing.

[377]

J. GOLDEN KIMBALL

APPRECIATE SHORT SERMONS

I remember that not many conferences ago I was called to the stand just before the conference adjourned. President Grant told me I had seven minutes—I took three—and I think it is the only time that President Grant ever shook hands with me after one of my talks. [Laughter] President Grant did not shake hands with me because of what I said; it was because I left him four minutes, and that is more than any of the other brethren have ever done.

CIRCUMSCRIBING THE HOLY SPIRIT

I have had another idea quite a while, and I think I will express it. You see the great big clock over there. I cannot see the hands—my eyes are not as good as they used to be. Well, with that great big clock before me, and this microphone in front of me, then tell a man to get the Holy Spirit! [Laughter]

Now, what I am trying to get at is this: it takes intelligent people to understand what I am trying to get at. I do not do your thinking for you; you have to do your own thinking. If I give you a little chaff to get you to take a little wheat, my trouble has always been, you choose the chaff and lose the wheat.

MISSION EXPERIENCE

I am going to tell you a story that I have never told before. When I was president of the Southern

States Mission, after a year's time I concluded that I would try to hold a conference in a city. Up to that time we had always kept out of cities. So I arranged with the president of the conference to hold such a meeting and to secure some place where we could hold it. We had no money. The only place they could secure was the court house. I told the elders: "I will do the preaching, and if they kill me you need not bother further." The people were very prejudiced. When the time came, I met these elders, a fine body of men, wonderful, courageous men, men of faith—they had to be in the South.

When we went to the court house * * * all those present were men. There wasn't a woman among them, and we all knew what that meant. When there are no women, there is a great deal of danger. It is dangerous enough when the women are present. At any rate, I made up my mind to deliver my message as fervently and humbly as ever a president of a mission preached. I intended to do all the talking.

I went there determined to preach the Gospel. I had my Bible, and I am well acquainted with my Bible. I cannot find anything in anybody else's Bible. I have owned this Bible for forty years and it is well marked and every subject traced in my own penmanship. I would not take money for this Bible. I went there believing that the Spirit of God was on me as the president of the mission. I was humble as a child.

I got up to preach the Gospel, faith and repentance, etc. All at once something came over me and I opened my mouth and said to that body of men: (the building was crowded, among them were some of the leading men) "Gentlemen, you have not come here to listen to the Gospel of Jesus Christ. I know what you have come for. You have come to find out about the Mountain Meadows Massacre and polygamy; and God, being my helper, I will tell you the truth." And I did. I talked to them for one hour.

When the meeting was out you could hear a pin drop. There was no comment; there was no noise or confusion, and we went to the hotel. We had arranged for lodgings at the cheap hotel. Soon we heard a band playing outside. Elder Willard Bean was the president of the conference. I sent him out to find what it all meant. I thought it meant trouble. So he inquired and they told him: "We're serenading that big long fellow." That is the only brass band I have ever had dispense music after one of my talks.

What I want to ask you, good people, is this: Was I moved upon by the right spirit? The next day when we went into the woods to hold our priesthood meeting, which we always held in the woods—we had no other place—I said to those elders: "Don't one of you dare preach that sermon;

[380]

it will cost you your life." And I have never preached it since.

THE LORD DIRECTS HIS SERVANTS

What I am beating around in the bush to put over is this: Does the Lord God direct his servants? He certainly does. If He doesn't we are a failure and we are no better than others. We do not know just what to say. I don't. I don't know just how to say it, but the Lord being my helper, as long as I live I am going to try to be natural and I am going to try to have my mind open with the hope that God will give me His Holy Spirit when I open my mouth, and use the talent which the Lord has given me.

Now, brethren and sisters, I know what that feeling is. I have not had it very often, but I know that there is such a thing as the "still, small voice." I have heard it.

My time is up. But if you people do not be-believe that I sustain the authorities of this Church and uphold God's work, I do. I don't know how I could prove it to you any better than I have in my own way. God bless you. Amen.

TALK FORTY-EIGHT
October, 1933

ANXIOUS FOR INSPIRATION

I presume that in the past forty-one years I have trained the Latter-day Saints, in this Tabernacle, so they are always somewhat anxious as to what success I will have. During this time I have always been anxious, having only one desire; and that is, to say something, under the inspiration of the Holy Ghost, that would be for my good and for your good. The Lord knows my desires, and I pray will give to me His Holy Spirit.

I shall not attempt to preach a lengthy discourse. I realize that time is quite a factor in a general conference, especially as President Grant is noted for wanting as many of the brethren to speak as possible.

ASSOCIATES IN THE COUNCIL

It might be well to inform you that I was ordained one of the First Council of the Seventy, October 8th, 1892. When I became a member of the council there were such men as Seymour B. Young, Christian D. Fjeldsted, John Morgan, Brigham H. Roberts and George Reynolds, who were among the greatest missionaries of our day. I have associated with them a great many years, and in thinking of them since Brother Roberts passed away, I could not help but feel that they were men of God, that no mistake was made, that they were called by revelation. All of these brethren have gone home. I am the only one living that was associated with them. After the date of my ordination, Rulon S. Wells, Edward Stevenson and Joseph W. McMurrin filled vacancies within about five years.

I think there is no man living in the flesh that knew Elder Roberts any better than I did. There was an affection, a friendship, formed in the missionary field that exceeds any love I have ever known, outside of my own family.

FRIENDSHIP BETWEEN MISSIONARIES

A missionary friend, Charles Welch, called on me yesterday. He is now a patriarch in the Bighorn stake. He was formerly a counselor to the president of the stake. He came to my home yesterday to see me. I traveled with him one year under Elder Roberts' presidency in Virginia. I know of no better man than Brother Charles Welch. He was a young man when I was laboring with him fifty years ago, but he told me yesterday he is now seventy-three years old. Ours is a keen friendship, a brotherhood that will last through life, and will continue in the other world. Why? Because he never forsook me. He was to be trusted. I was sick, and he ministered to me, and was so kind and patient. I had boils—called carbuncles, if you know what a carbuncle is. I don't know what kind of boils Job had, but if he had carbuncles I have full sympathy for him. They started on one of my wrists and they followed me all the way up and down. The last one I had was on my knee. We had reached Burke's Garden at that time, after traveling nearly one thousand miles, without purse and scrip.

I am trying to make clear to you, if I can, the friendship that we Mormon elders have for one another. I may not be gifted in coupling together all of those beautiful sentiments and words, but friendship, of the kind I am talking about, cannot be told in words. Brother Welch said to me: "Golden, I have come six hundred miles to this conference, and one of my big objects is to see you."

PRESIDENT BRIGHAM H. ROBERTS

The first time I ever saw Elder Roberts was either in Cincinnati or St. Louis. He had been chosen as president of the Southern States Mission to succeed John Morgan. I left for Chattanooga, Tennessee, with twenty-seven elders, assigned to the Southern States. There were all kinds of elders in the company; farmers, cowboys, few educated —a pretty hard looking crowd, and I was one of that kind. The elders preached, and talked, and sang; and advertised loudly their calling as preachers. I kept still for once in my life; I hardly opened my mouth. I saw a gentleman get on the train. I can visualize that man now. I didn't know who he was.

He knew we were a band of Mormon elders. The elders soon commenced a discussion and argument with the stranger, and before he got through they were in grave doubt about their message of salvation. He gave them a training that they never forgot. That man proved to be President B. H. Roberts.

SECRETARY TO PRESIDENT ROBERTS

On arriving at Chattanooga, I was appointed to labor in Virginia with Elder Landon Rich. I traveled for one year under his direction. President Roberts called me to the office the second year—1884. I slept with him. I talked with him. He trusted me, and I never betrayed him. He confided in me, the only time in his life, about his own affairs, his family, etc. We occupied one room—used as office and sleeping quarters. We paid twenty-five dollars a month for rent and board. It was hotter than hades most of the time. I was his secretary. He walked the floor and dictated (and I wrote long-hand) volumes and stored away a fund of information.

KANE CREEK MASSACRE

I was with Brother Roberts at the time of the Kane Creek Massacre. I was at Shady Grove and was the first to get the information of the killing of Elders Gibbs, Berry and the Condor boys, and of their burial. I was with Brother Roberts when he went out into a cornfield to disguise as a farm

[385]

laborer. We kneeled down and prayed, and we discussed the matter and were satisfied that we should secure the bodies. I said:

"Brother Roberts, let me go. They know you in that section. You have preached there. They will kill you. Let me go."

He said, "No, I am the president of the mission. The Lord will take care of me."

A GREAT LIGHT HAS GONE OUT OF MY LIFE

Eight members of the First Council have died since I was ordained on October 8, 1892, and there isn't one of that number who was so close to me as Brigham H. Roberts. I never felt more lonely or helpless, in a way, than I do now. Brother Roberts has been my mentor; he has been my teacher; he has been my chronicler. I was relieved of reading the great histories; I didn't have to read a whole library searching for information. What did I have to do? When anything troubled me about the history of the Church or scripture, I went to Brother Roberts. He had the most wonderful mind and memory of any human being I have ever known, right up to the very last. A great light has gone out in my life. I will soon follow.

DAVID AND JONATHAN

I am now what they call the Senior President of the First Council of the Seventy. It is not altogether merit. It is just the regular order of things in the Church, just as it is with the Twelve Apostles. I have had the tenacity to outlive my fellow laborers. I have given forty-one years of my life wholeheartedly for the seventies. The First Council are all presidents equal in authority. As much as I honor and respect Brother Roberts, I have never felt inferior to him in his presence; he has never made me feel that way. He had a greater intellect, greater intelligence, but I have had some gifts of my own, that in a way were equal to his. I have preached by his side many times, and after he got through preaching, I reached those that he missed, so it has been that way during all this time. He often said when in the South, "Our love is akin to that of David and Jonathan." Good bless you. Amen.

List of Subheadings

AS THEY APPEAR IN THE BOOK

[391]

LIST OF SUBHEADINGS

LIST OF SUBHEADINGS

[393]

LIST OF SUBHEADINGS

Index

INDEX

[398]